The End of the American Empire

The End of the American Empire

PATRICK WATTS

Tecolote Publishing

978-1-7384469-0-2 (Print)
978-1-7384469-1-9 (E-book)

First edition February 2024

Published by Tecolote Publishing

This is a work of non-fiction. No names have been changed,
no characters invented, no events fabricated. All information
was accurate at the time of writing but due to the nature
of the subject matter, time marches on.

Events, dear reader . . . events.

Sometimes the truth really is stranger than fiction.

Contents

Preface

The idea for this book was conceived in January 2021, during the final weeks of the Trump administration, as I prepared to complete my MA dissertation in International Relations and Contemporary Warfare. My study into the lasting effects of the Trump presidency on established democratic and international norms seemed to be writing itself. Rioters, spurred on by their commander-in-chief, stormed the Capitol building and American democracy was shown to be vulnerable and not as invincible as we had always believed. This violent attempt to subvert democracy, and the subsequent whitewashing of the events by the Republican members of an increasingly partisan Congress, only served to heighten my belief that we were witnessing the beginning of the end of the American Empire.

The motive for writing this book is not to attack, as a foreign commentator, what is in many respects a great country, with great people. I have driven thousands of miles of US highways, visited blue states and red, city and country, Atlantic and Pacific, and my feelings about America have progressed from trepidation to awe, to affection and finally to concern. It is in this spirit that I have written this book, to highlight the warning signs that appear to me to be simultaneously glaring and terrifying, in the potentially naive hope that this decline can be postponed.

I am also under no illusions as to the many faults and past transgressions of the American Empire during its time in the sun, but I have greater concerns for how the world may look after a democratic decline, with authoritarian regimes rising to challenge the established norms of governance. I also have no partisan motive to attack either the Republicans or the Democrats; I simply wish to observe the factors that are driving the parties further apart, creating a "cold civil war" in which agreement and compromise are treated with contempt. The dearth of credible enemies without has driven many to seek enemies within. As political fault lines widen and intolerant discourse spreads, cordial differences of opinion are replaced by expressions of visceral hatred. Shared history and core American values are increasingly forgotten.

This book is also no lazy critique of President Trump. I view him not as evil or deranged but as both a skilled opportunist and a troll par excellence, able to identify and leverage the grievances of many of his countryfolk, to assist in his primary goal: individual aggrandizement above all else. To simply blame one man, or even one party, for American decline would be both wilfully ignorant and dangerously short-sighted.

The world is always changing, and history has not ended. It is inevitable that America's global dominance, or unipolarity, will give way to multipolarity (if it has not already). What is yet to be decided is the timeline of this change and how the world will look geopolitically after this has come to pass. This book aims to highlight the causal factors, both within the US and internationally, which may provide insight into these two great unknowns.

One final point before we begin: I urge every reader to keep in mind why this book was written. Many of you will disagree with some or indeed all of what I say, but to you I offer the following invitation. Rather than hurl insults, why not use your energy more effectively: let's engage in a meaningful dialogue, conducted in a spirit of mutual respect and concern for a better future.

Introduction

What is the American Empire? The label itself provokes argument and disagreement among scholars, diplomats and policymakers. No longer seen as a source of pride, "empire" is now a dirty word, replete with negative connotations, conjuring up images of subjugation and oppression. Those who possess empires and enjoy the associated benefits are at pains to explain why their critics are wrong, and many Americans are particularly keen to argue that global US dominance is in fact "different", benign and well-intentioned.

In Part One of this book, the first task to address is to explain why – contrary to popular opinion, especially within the US – the label of "empire" can and should be attached to US hegemony and global dominance. It may have been masterfully hidden and packaged as something different, but make no mistake: this is a modern empire in every sense of the word that matters. This is of vital importance, as only once this point has been understood can we view the decline of American geopolitical hegemony through the prism of empire and thereby apply the lessons of the past.

Once the definition of "American Empire" has been accepted, we can examine the decline of previous empires, highlighting patterns and similarities with regard to the American Empire today. Do empires collapse due to overexpansion and military misadventure? Sickness and plague? Environmental factors? Largesse and decadence, as victims of their own success? Do they implode through competing domestic interests and civil war, or are they toppled by rising peer competitors? The second chapter will examine these historical questions to establish precedents that will guide us in our study.

The book will then be separated into two further parts addressing the individual aspects of American Empire that could result in its demise before this century is over. The chapters of Part Two will address the internal pressures that can cause an empire to collapse from within. For this to occur, powerful factors must degrade the social fabric that unites the citizenry in striving for a common cause. Seemingly inconsequential decisions can have significant consequences as existing grievances are exacerbated and discontent catches fire. Inequality of wealth is a key issue in this area and will be addressed thoroughly in chapter 3. The entrenchment of political positions of "faux-left" and "faux-right" will also be examined, as traits from each construct deepen existing divisions. The faux-right pursues a destructive goal of "individual freedom at any cost", while the faux-left uses cultish identity politics and puritanical assaults on free thinking to further label and divide. Civil unrest arising from structural injustices, based on race or gender, is weaponized and exploited by media and politicians from both parties, rather than addressed and alleviated. A nation whose history is inextricably linked to genocide, racism and subjugation therefore cannot confront and heal these wounds, as these painful subjects are instead repurposed as a reflection of partisan loyalty. Meanwhile, religious fundamentalism drives Republican policy to an alarming degree in an educated, secular, Western democracy. Rigid adherence to fringe beliefs, at odds with the majority of the population, guides policymakers and judges to restrict individual freedoms for women seeking abortions from unwanted pregnancies.

While the social fabric is fraying, the US political system is broken. This is the subject of chapter 4. The two parties now exist in a state of permanent disagreement, claiming and blindly defending ideological beachheads at the expense of all else. Compromise and the back-and-forth of opposing ideas are banished to history as relics of a bygone era. There exists instead a new political reality: a cold civil war is being fought within America's oligarchical class. Career politicians flourish in a system seemingly designed for corruption – unlimited congressional and senatorial terms; billions of dollars flowing from special-interest groups; industry, religion and ideology shaping elections and the voting intentions of elected officials. The revolving door between private and public sectors ensures that officials can move seamlessly from one to the other, enriching themselves in the process. The decisions they make in government are likely to be motivated by their future outside of it. Elected officials are able to move in and out of stock-market positions using insider information, all while claiming to protect the sanctity of the "free market". The financial system is so complex that those responsible for the largest crash since the Great Depression are not sent to jail, but instead installed in treasury positions – poaching turned gamekeeping writ large. A system of government designed two centuries ago, whose arcane processes have become unfit for purpose, cannot be replaced without provoking accusations of treason against the wishes of the revered founding fathers. The Supreme Court, supposed to represent the highest independent judiciary, is instead stacked on ideological grounds and its rulings are often out of step with the majority of the citizens who will be governed by its decisions. It is not hyperbole to talk of the potential secession of liberal coastal states, aghast at the erosion of reproductive rights for their citizenry. The Electoral College, widely seen as ceremonial but with huge constitutional power, had its procedures nearly hijacked by a president intent on keeping power.

The use of chicanery and deception to subvert democracy is not new, as seen in the 2000 presidential election and George W. Bush's early declaration of "victory" in Florida. Attempts to legislate are stymied by the filibuster in the Senate; for the outside observer this is the most ludicrous example of a broken political system. Rather than attempt to seek common ground and compromise in the interests of the people, an individual politician will instead effectively end a debate by speaking for many hours on often irrelevant topics. Is it any wonder that trust in politicians and the political system is at an all-time low?

Whereas this distrust would be a problem for a single party, America's oligarchical class can continue to flourish by ensuring that, with a few exceptions, everyone continues to play the game. The 2016 election of Donald Trump, a billionaire playing to perfection the role of aggrieved everyman outsider, was in part a reaction to the reality of an exclusive and elitist political system. The oligarchical class provides pantomime political theatre by highlighting superficial differences to keep the public from examining the reality of the system too closely. The average person is not expected to understand how laws are made. This is perhaps fortunate, as the reality of bills passing to committee, just to be bastardized into a Frankenstein's monster, would be horrifying to any who truly understood the process. With these issues at the heart of US politics, is it surprising that Trump's "Big Lie" of a stolen election is believed by over a third of the population?

We are in dangerous territory, as democracy, like any other human-made construct, only exists for as long as people believe in it and grant it power. If it is shown to be a fugazi, a fraud, it will lose the power to control – and this power will not be easily reclaimed. Without thorough action to tackle every deficiency mentioned above, American democracy, and subsequently the American Empire, is likely to enter a death spiral from which it cannot recover. A nation built so heavily on the idea of freedom, whether or not it has always lived up to this ideal, cannot now endure under any other system of government than a liberal democracy.

It is not simply the political class that is involved in the waging of this "cold civil war". The level of distrust and division in the country would not be possible without the concerted efforts of a partisan media, which will be discussed in chapter 5. Traditionally acting as a check on power, the fourth estate, with few exceptions, has been transformed into a partisan mouthpiece designed to use outrage to attract clicks, likes, views and shares. The packaging of news as info-tainment, available 24/7, can be viewed as the beginning of the end of objective media in the US. There are few media outlets – in print, on the airwaves, or online – that can be seen as truly independent, and this leaves the public to "pick a side" and consume their version of current affairs from a cheerleader similarly aligned. This skewed reporting of events, seen constantly through the partisan prism, reduces discourse to mud-slinging and angry invective.

To compound matters, aggressively partisan opinion pieces are presented as fact, and token representatives from the opposing side are offered up as straw men to be smugly dispatched by the standard-bearers of one's chosen side. To reduce politics to sport is a dangerous game, as once people have been taught to hate their own countrymen and -women, it is difficult to bring them together again when necessary to avoid or respond to crisis. The rise of social media is also significant, further damaging the discourse by disseminating unchecked "facts" without any shred of journalistic integrity or peer review. The weaponizing of "fake news" and deepfake videos will further distort the idea of objective truth and fact, leaving the average citizen confused, misled or simply distrusting of anything and everything that does not fit their existing worldview.

The rising belief in conspiracy theories will also be examined in chapter 5, as this represents both the logical end point of growing distrust and a significant threat to the idea of fact-based discourse. This situation is not helped by the numerous failures of traditional authorities and institutions to investigate the truth and present it to the public. Is it surprising that the 9/11 truth movement exists when certain events during the Gulf of Tonkin incident in 1964 were manufactured to justify escalation of the Vietnam War? Are we shocked that people question the accepted narrative of the Wuhan wet market being the origin of the Covid-19 pandemic when the same journalists regurgitated lies about Iraq's weapons of mass destruction? And do we want to ignore the uncomfortable reality that a lot of impoverished white Americans feel so unvalued and disrespected that they gravitate toward QAnon and other conspiracies denouncing the rich and powerful?

The chapters of Part Three will address the idea that an empire can be toppled under pressure from external forces. The changing nature of warfare will be examined in chapter 6, as the realist doctrine of military "might is right" is challenged by changing attitudes to warfare as well as technological and strategic developments. For previous empires, potential competitors could be attacked preventatively to stymie their rise before they could become a realistic military threat. Attitudes to conflict have now changed after the world wars of the twentieth century; any military action must be packaged not in terms of glory and heroic victory but with PR-friendly motivations, like humanitarian intervention and liberation of oppressed peoples. The coming of the internet and the digital age has removed the state monopoly on information and undermined the state's ability to conduct successful propaganda campaigns. The public is rightly distrustful of its government's motivations for warfare after the truth emerged regarding US involvement in Vietnam and Iraq.

Fake news and misinformation have now been weaponized by domestic and international forces to further entrench these feelings of distrust and reduce any support for military actions that lead to bloodshed. What good, US strategists may wonder, are the most sophisticated and expensive aircraft carriers, battlegroups and military hardware the world has ever known, if you are unable to use these resources against your potential enemies? In the same context, wars for conquest and control of territory now seem outdated, the actions in Iraq and Afghanistan exposed as at best pyrrhic victories and at worst humiliating failures.

The changing nature of warfare also presents further limitations, as traditional military might is undermined by new technologies. Interconnected societies are at risk of attack from cyber actors, both state and private, who require only a laptop and an internet connection to wreak havoc. A renewed military space race now exists, with both China and Russia possessing the ability to destroy orbital satellites from the ground, adding an unpredictable theatre to future war planning. Exotic technologies that are being developed apace further threaten the traditional military paradigm, with areas as outlandish as genetic modification and AI moving from science fiction to potential science fact.

Chapter 7 will look at the forces at play on the global stage, as the international system reacts to the unmasking of America's "Hollywood myth" of being motivated by purely benign intentions. The carefully crafted façade of the American Empire has been exposed, revealing motives that are too often cynical and self-serving. If the cruel and indiscriminate massacres in Vietnam and Laos began this unmasking process, then misadventure in Iraq – driven principally by a lust for oil rather than the urge to spread liberty – has compounded the loss of the moral high ground enjoyed after the world wars of the twentieth century. Support for unpopular partners like Israel and Saudi Arabia, and tolerance of their cruel policies toward the Palestinians and Yemeni rebels respectively, further exacerbate the problem. Globalization itself, the engine of American Empire that shaped the world for decades after the Second World War, is under attack from all sides. Nations are increasingly retreating from multinationalism to protectionism, while the actions of President Trump did more to damage the US-led, rules-based order than any adversary has accomplished.

Within this new reality, the rise of China continues at pace; this single-party state is able to plan for generations, not election cycles. Patience has historically not been an issue for China, but impending demographic collapse caused by an aging population and years of depressed birth rates may well shake things up. Chinese motivations and actions will be examined in both chapters 6 and 7 in an effort to understand the threat posed to the American Empire by its Asian rival.

Chapter 8 will focus on environmental threats to the American Empire, some specific to the US and some affecting the entire world. While climate change is quite rightly the most discussed concern in this regard, it is by no means the only environmental threat. Numerous issues require attention if the US is to ensure that its future citizens will be able to breathe clean air, grow sufficient food and respond to viral outbreaks or the spread of antibiotic-resistant pathogens.

Finally, I will aim to peer into the future and look at what could come next. This is never an exact science given that there are so many factors at play, but the conclusions in this book are meant more as guidelines to possible outcomes than predictions made with psychic certainty. Will US democracy survive in its current form if Donald Trump or a fellow election denier wins the presidential election in November 2024? If the Republicans lose, will they simply complain of a "Bigger Lie", and how would the nation's military, judicial and legislative institutions respond? Thinking globally, how will the US behave when confronted with its diminishing hegemony? A slow retreat into isolationism or a catastrophic confrontation with China, either pre-emptively or in reaction to any of the numerous flashpoints currently simmering? Will it be an invasion of Taiwan, actions in the South China Sea or an issue unknown at this point in time that lights the fuse for military confrontation?

The decline of American influence, and the end of the American Empire, is inevitable, like that of all empires before it. But the crucial questions are about the timing, the suffering that might be involved or avoided, and how the world will look in the aftermath.

PART ONE

Empire

1

The History of the American Empire

What is empire in the modern world? Historically, the typical definition of an empire – a group of states or territories controlled by a single leader or government – would have sufficed, as great powers proudly defined their strength by the amount of territory they held, the number of citizens under their control and the reach of their unchallenged influence. Within the confines of this definition, it can easily be argued, as many have, that there is no such thing as an American Empire, since wars of conquest are no longer fought, and the traditional criteria have come to be regarded not as a source of pride but as a source of shame.

Instead of "empire", terms such as "hegemony" or "hyperpower" have been deployed, and these definitions are certainly accurate when describing the US dominance of the geopolitical system post-1991, after the collapse of another empire, the Soviet Union. I do not believe, however, that these terms go far enough; the term "empire" requires updating to reflect the realities of the modern world. This is not simply an argument for semantic change and the updating of terminology; no, the refusal to view US hegemony through the prism of empire blinds us to valuable lessons, parallels and comparisons throughout history. To borrow an oft-misquoted aphorism from George Santayana: "Those who cannot remember the past are condemned to repeat it."[1]

So what defines a modern empire? As modern sensibilities have evolved, the likelihood of any state launching expansive, aggressive wars of conquest, with the goal of expanding their borders and establishing dominion over other citizens, seems to have diminished. To be sure, this is not to say that there will be no further attempts to redraw state boundaries for strategic gain. These will most likely be justified by claiming them to be modest restorations of historical boundaries, or the protection of oppressed populations. The Russian invasion of Ukraine, beginning in 2014 with the annexation of the Crimean peninsula, is the most recent example of this scenario.

These arguments can be made by leaders striving for legitimacy, but the strategic objectives of most military actions are clear and obvious. As NATO expands eastward and formerly Soviet states look westward, the importance of the Crimean peninsula and Sevastopol, historic home of the Russian navy and Russia's main access point to the Black Sea and wider global waters, is paramount. If Putin had stopped in 2014, he might have got away with it, notwithstanding the imposition of sanctions, but his miscalculation was that the West would continue to look the other way as he attempted to take the entire country in 2022.

China has used similar arguments to justify expansionist actions as the "reunification" of Chinese peoples, starting with Hong Kong, originally guaranteed to remain self-governed but now a Chinese vassal. Meanwhile, Xi Jinping has attempted to justify island-building in disputed areas of the South China Sea by asserting that this is a strategic necessity to prevent foreign forces from establishing a forward theatre of operations within striking distance of the mainland. He now aims to pre-emptively legitimize future actions against Taiwan, which is strategically important for the same geographical reason, but also due to its importance for the manufacturing of semiconductors – the vital component inside virtually all modern technology.

Strategic goals will still be sought, militarily or through more indirect means, as nation states battle for advantage over their neighbours and competitors, but conquest simply for the sake of territory is a relic of the past. Interconnectivity of trade and communications driven by globalization, and new methods of hybrid warfare, only strengthen this conclusion. Why spend vast amounts of resources to physically conquer a people and occupy their land when you can instead control the levers of power through coercion and influence, or obtain your strategic goals in a more covert, more socially acceptable fashion? Bearing all this in mind, let us examine the history of the American Empire of the twentieth and early twenty-first centuries.

The Forging of an Empire

The origin story of the American Empire could be started at numerous points during the last three hundred years. Breaking away from the British crown and declaring independence in 1776? The end of the Civil War and the advent of a unified nation state in 1865? The end of a succession of major territorial expansions in 1867?[2] An isolationist US entering and then emerging victorious from the First World War in 1918? These could all be seen as a reasonable starting point. I would argue, however, that the real beginning of the American Empire can be traced to the end of the Second World War, and more specifically to the Bretton Woods Conference held in New Hampshire in July 1944.

Clearly approaching victory against the Axis powers, the Allies sought to remake the world as they saw fit. The US was able to steer proceedings when reshaping the global order, as it was the pre-eminent superpower within the Allies. This would be made all the clearer in 1945 when the US dropped its atomic bombs on Hiroshima and Nagasaki. Rather than focusing simply on territory and spheres of influence as per previous summits, the goal at Bretton Woods was a remaking of the global financial system itself, root and branch, with the US at the centre. Established in 1944, and then ratified in 1945, were two pillars of US influence: the International Monetary Fund (IMF) and the World Bank (originally labelled the International Bank for Reconstruction and Development). As first among equals within these institutions, the US established the dollar as the reserve currency of the globe, claiming responsibility for keeping the price of gold fixed, and adjusting the supply of dollars to maintain confidence in future gold convertibility. In essence, the US was pledging to operate a global gold standard.

Although the gold standard would be abandoned in the 1970s, the dollar has maintained its position as reserve currency for the world. This is of vital importance as not only does it reduce the cost of domestic borrowing, but it also reinforces the perception that the US remains the dominant force in global trade. By applying the "seigniorage" concept, which can be described as an asymmetric financial system, the US has been able to use the international community to subsidize US multinationals and raise domestic standards of living.[3] In the empires of antiquity, a state would fund its expansion and maintenance by more overt methods of wealth extraction, including pillaging, confiscation and taxation. In its heyday, the British Empire relied on the economic advantages of being the dominant global trading power, extracting millions of pounds of value from nations around the world. These were different times, but the goal has always been the same – controlling the supply of money and using dominance to extract wealth from weaker nations.

It has been argued that the American Empire is different from those that came before, as the other nations involved in their transactions have also benefited. While many countries have indeed benefited from US-led globalization, this argument seems strikingly similar to those that justified the actions of empires that have come before; British railways in Africa and canals in India spring to mind. The point of this comparison is simple. Regardless of the supposed benefits to all involved, it is via domination of the global economy – for over half a century – that the US has been able to flourish economically in an uneven system it both created and controls. This is certainly more indirect than previous iterations of imperial taxation or wealth extraction, but the resulting economic wealth has propelled the American Empire to global dominance like major empires before it.

To put this into perspective, the American Empire has generated staggering GDP figures from 1960 to 2020, maintaining its position as the most productive global economy every single year.[4] This dominance is unlikely to last forever: political instability, rising inflation, immense national debt, and competition from both traditional currencies (primarily the euro and the yen) and the emerging cryptocurrency market, are all headwinds that threaten the exorbitant privilege that the US has enjoyed since 1944.

A key feature of empire is the ability to ensure commercial dominance. In antiquity this would take the form of your traders and merchants enjoying unencumbered access when selling their goods to foreign buyers, and the empire would benefit from the associated taxes levied on these sales. As the world became smaller due to technological innovation, opportunities to exploit these markets grew larger, as did the entities responsible. In 2000 BCE, it was individual merchants who plied their trade through the Spice Routes; but by the nineteenth century and the zenith of the British Empire, huge companies had been established to fulfil this role. The British East India Company was such an entity, enjoying a near monopoly – awarded by the crown – to exploit commercial opportunities across the empire.

The American Empire has built on this idea, with US companies and brand names conquering the markets of the world. Since the 1990s, it has been possible in most countries, on every inhabited continent, to fly on board a Boeing-made plane, enjoy a McDonald's cheeseburger and wash it down with a refreshing Coca-Cola. These brands became synonymous with American progress and were able to dominate local competition. Today, some of the brands may have changed, but this level of dominance has not: a glance at the world's ten most valuable brands reveals that US companies occupy the very top spots.[5] The political economist Tanner Mirrlees defines this process in his 2016 book *Hearts and Mines: The US Empire's Culture Industry*:

> In the post-WWII period, the U.S. Empire did not pursue the direct domination of territories, economies, and polities like bygone colonial Empires, but rather, sought to build, integrate and police a world

system of integrated states that shared its model: the capitalist mode of production, the liberal democratic state form, and the consumerist "way of life."[6]

Commercial dominance has not been enabled simply by US control of the global money supply and the sheer size of its economy. The successful cultural exportation of the idea of the "American Dream" has also meant that other nations, rather than resist this dominance, have actively welcomed it. As the historian Victoria de Grazia explains in her 2005 book *Irresistible Empire*, this American "Market Empire" allowed the US to take its place as global superpower by commercial rather than solely military means.[7] This commercial dominance, paired with military superiority, is actually a common feature of empire. The ancient Greeks and Romans were able to influence others to adopt their culture through the methods available at the time, including the exporting of their religions, plays, songs and fashions, to name just a few examples. More recently, the British Empire harnessed the technology of the wireless radio to beam propaganda globally via its BBC Empire Service. The advent of the television age, although occurring during the decline of the British Empire, provided millions of eager eyeballs for British productions. Shows like *The Crown* and *Downton Abbey* continue to ensure that British traditions and institutions maintain relevancy, and shape perceptions of British power globally, years after the end of the Empire.

The American Empire has taken this model and dialled it up to 11. With Hollywood acting as the epicentre of global film and television production, millions of people worldwide have consumed a carefully crafted and cultivated myth regarding the "American Dream". To put this into perspective, every single one of the world's largest ten studios is American. The importance of this dominance is fully appreciated throughout the ruling elite of the American Empire, as the US has always taken steps, both clandestine and overt, to ensure that the American Dream is presented and championed on screens all over the world. It's no secret that CIA officers have advised and exerted influence on Hollywood film studios for decades.[8] More recently, disclosures from WikiLeaks have shed light on the other methods used to further what the academic Paul Moody describes as "contemporary American cultural imperialism".[9]

Commercial dominance has played a vital role in creating the American Empire, but this has also been paired with a staggering military superiority. In 1889 the British Empire adopted a "two-power standard" which ensured dominance of the seas by insisting that the Royal Navy would always be equal to or larger than the fleets of the next two greatest powers combined. The American Empire has followed in the footsteps of its transatlantic cousin, but gone far further, annually spending more on defence than the next nine countries combined.[10] To adapt Theodore Roosevelt's famous quip, this spending has ensured that the US continues to carry the biggest stick.[11]

Military Dominance

The backbone of any empire is unrivalled military dominance, and the American Empire has used many different methods to achieve this goal. The simplest is the sheer volume of dollar bills expended on this endeavour. Since the end of the Second World War, the US has dedicated around 2 per cent more of its GDP to military spending than the global average of the developed world, at times reaching as high as 9 per cent at the height of the Cold War.[12] The Soviet Union attempted to triumph over the American Empire by outspending the US militarily, but unlike their adversary they did not possess an economy capable of supporting these vast expenditures. After the collapse of the Soviet Union, instead of retrenching to focus on financing domestic initiatives, the US has continued to allocate huge sums to preserve its military dominance. America spends in the region of $800 billion on defence annually, more than three times the $230 billion spent by its nearest rival China.[13]

In purely numerical terms, there are areas where the US military may seem inferior at first glance, but it still has the advantage in terms of cutting-edge technology, potential offensive payload and its network of alliances. In a doomsday scenario, Russia has an estimated stockpile of 4,477 nuclear warheads against 3,708 for the US, but the French and UK arsenals take the NATO figure to a total of 4,178.[14] If this comparison ever becomes relevant, then the entire world will be utterly devastated by nuclear winter, as scientists estimate that only 100 warheads would be required for this grim reality to occur.[15]

In terms of active-duty soldiers, the US ranks third globally, with around 1.4 million troops, against the 1 million of Russia and 2.2 million of China. But once again, when NATO is assessed as a whole, America and its allies have over 3 million troops.[16] There are countries with greater numbers of reservists; but as shown by the dismal performance of Russian reservists in the Russia–Ukraine War, there is no substitute for well-trained professional servicepeople. This conflict also exposed the fallacy that numerical advantages in hardware such as tanks would equate to military superiority. Russia invaded Ukraine with a far greater number of tanks, artillery, trucks and fighting vehicles, but poor training, motivation and leadership soon resulted in hundreds of these being captured and repurposed by the Ukrainian army.[17]

If we turn to maritime matters, the Chinese navy is the largest in the world: its fleet boasts more than 770 warships (including around eighty submarines), whereas the US only possesses 490 warships (including around seventy submarines).[18] Of these, the Chinese have 355 front-line warships compared with only 305 for the US. But this does not reflect the full story, as the naval historian Jerry Hendrix explains: "The real number in the competition is the number of missile tubes." David Axe, writing in *Forbes*, has further deciphered the numbers, showing how the US is able to sail into battle with over 10,000 offensive missiles, more than double those available to the Chinese. He correctly points out that the Chinese navy benefits from operating only in the Pacific, while the US fleet also has to maintain a presence in the Atlantic. But the US benefits from having dependable allies with substantial navies of their own, regularly conducting joint exercises and combining to form one massive fleet.[19] The Chinese do not have this advantage.

The US also has a clear edge over their rivals in terms of the size and capabilities of their aircraft carrier fleet. The US has 11 aircraft carriers in active service, against China's two.[20] The US carriers also represent the cutting edge in terms of military technology, although the Chinese Type-003 (which is being fitted out in the form of China's third carrier, *Fujian*) is far closer to the US *Nimitz*- and *Ford*-class carriers than previous Chinese efforts.[21] Overall, the US carriers allow the American Empire to project power anywhere around the globe, supported by nuclear-powered and nuclear-armed submarines, which can remain at sea for up to three months before needing to surface and resupply.

In the skies, the US fleet of 20 B-2 stealth bombers ensures it remains the only nation, apart from Israel, with long-range bombers that are able to operate undetected by enemy radar, and the new B-21 stealth bomber will further enhance this capability. In total, the US has over 13 times more stealth aircraft than China (540 versus 41, including prototypes), and is continuing to widen this gap by spending hundreds of billions of dollars on this technology.[22] The level of deployment of the new F-35 stealth-fighter program is currently being reassessed as the total cost could be as much as $1.7 trillion, but it does not change the reality of the chasm in capabilities between the US and any other nation.[23]

The development and extensive deployment of remotely piloted autonomous drones also gives the US president the ability to assassinate any person on the planet, without risking the life of a single US serviceman. Comparisons are difficult in this area as drone warfare is evolving to include smaller "kamikaze" drones, most recently deployed in the Russia–Ukraine War. Best estimates of the number of offensive, non-kamikaze battlefield drones still give the US a clear advantage: around 330 compared with China's 150.[24] This power over the most fundamental of human rights – the right to life – would be the envy of any emperor from previous ages.

Although the days of conventional territorial conquest are likely to be in the past, the American Empire still realizes the importance of maintaining military outposts all over the globe. In the ancient world, Alexander the Great was able to establish his dominance by building new cities all over his empire, which extended from Greece as far as India. At the height of the Roman Empire, successive emperors could project Roman power through garrisons stationed at imperial outposts as far from the capital as the Farasan Islands, 4,000 miles away in what is now part of Saudi Arabia. Later, the British ensured that any efforts to subvert their control could be crushed militarily by installing colonial outposts as far from London as South Africa, India and Australia, with an unassailable navy able to provide both reinforcements and supplies anywhere around the globe. The American Empire is no different in this regard. Of the thousands of military bases it maintains, around 750 are in at least 80 countries outside the United States.[25]

These imperial outposts are regarded as sovereign US territory, despite being situated thousands of miles away from the homeland, with US law superseding any local or national laws of the host nation. These sites are the deliberate, unquestionable emblems of American Empire, furthering US strategic goals and clearly manned by American personnel.

There also exists a covert web of international black sites situated in allied countries with "morally flexible" (read "illegal") approaches to human rights. These black sites are operated in tandem by CIA personnel and members of the host nation's security apparatus, detaining and interrogating (read torturing) citizens from any nation on the planet, away from the purview of due legal process, human rights or human decency. In sum, these outposts, both official and covert, and the US carrier and drone fleets, allow the American Empire to project military power on every single continent, and to direct it against any nation or individual on the planet – a feat unmatched in human history.

International and Institutional Dominance

Military dominance and power projection are the tools at hand to demonstrate "hard power", but, as well as the commercial power already described above, the American Empire is able to exert dominance through its influence within multinational institutions. As global hegemon and de facto leader of the Western world, the US is able to leverage this status through the multinational institutions it leads, most clearly illustrated by its influence within NATO. A product of the Cold War, the North Atlantic Treaty Organization was originally created to counter the spreading influence of the Soviet Union, by creating a condition of collective security for like-minded western European countries that could not defend themselves in the event of Soviet aggression. Article 5 of the North Atlantic Treaty of 1949 clarified that an attack on one member was deemed to be an attack on all, and would be treated as such, with the US acting as the de facto military guarantor of this policy.

After the fall of the Soviet Union in 1991, NATO's raison d'être seemed to disappear overnight, but NATO did not. Instead of celebrating mission accomplished and disbanding, the organization evolved into a military alliance of ideologically aligned liberal democracies, projecting military power under the auspices of peacekeeping and humanitarian intervention. Seemingly propelled and intoxicated by globalization and the apparently inevitable victory of liberal democracy as the supreme political ideology – which Francis Fukuyama memorably described as "the end of history" – NATO grew both in membership and in scope. Despite warnings of an inevitable future backlash from a humiliated Russia, former Warsaw Pact nations were incorporated into the NATO alliance, and US military personnel, missiles and hardware were installed within striking distance of Moscow. By expanding in this manner rather than disbanding, the opportunity to welcome a seemingly democratizing Russia into the global community was lost, and the West was confronted instead by a renewed Russian nationalism bolstered by understandable fears of encroachment by the US-led NATO alliance.

It is no wonder that the kleptocratic Putin regime has been able to leverage these fears to ensure his rule remains effectively unchallenged. NATO is currently experiencing a second evolution, with humanitarian interventions falling out of favour with Western policymakers, and the United Nations now taking the lead in peacekeeping operations. Despite repeated criticisms from the leaders of NATO's own member states in recent times, including threats to withdraw from the alliance by President Trump, Secretary General Jens Stoltenberg aimed to avoid obsolescence by expanding NATO's remit as a guarantor of liberal democracy. He had a new target in mind: China. This pivot was swiftly redirected back to the original Russian enemy after Putin's invasion of Ukraine, but it is likely to occur again in future. Herein lies the truth of an organization that exists primarily as an extension of the American Empire. As made clear above, the US does not really require military assistance from NATO members. In the event of a direct attack (however unlikely that might seem), the US can respond with such devastating power that the aggressor would be reduced to rubble and ashes. The primary function of NATO is therefore to provide political cover to ensure the actions of the American Empire are seen to be supported by a network of liberal-democratic allies.

The only time in NATO history that Article 5 has been used was in response to the terrorist attacks of 11 September 2001. The US did not require any military assistance to track down the perpetrators; it simply wanted the political cover to launch a regime-change war in Afghanistan, and it therefore sought to involve its allies in the conflict. Utilizing foreign troops to achieve imperial goals is nothing new. For Rome, alliances were forged with many different peoples to assist in projecting power, pacifying indigenous populations, or conquering common enemies. As a result, mercenaries came to represent a sizeable portion of the Roman army. Further back in time, the army of Alexander the Great also consisted of mercenaries from many different states, and from many newly conquered territories. And more recently, the British had numerous regiments of non-British nationals serving in its army's ranks, with the fearsome Gurkhas being the most well-known and well-regarded example. Times change and political realities change with them. While previous empires enlisted foreign nationals – as imperial army recruits and as mercenaries – for more straightforward reasons of manpower and headcount, the American Empire enlists the aid of foreign soldiers to provide legitimacy. This is not to denigrate the efforts made by those NATO soldiers who put their lives on the line in the name of protecting democracy, but it is important to provide a clear and honest assessment of the situation. This is how a modern empire must operate, within the confines of acceptable societal and political realities.

It is not simply NATO that the American Empire has successfully leveraged to provide a screen of legitimacy to justify its actions. The UN has also served this role on many occasions, when it suits the strategic interests of the US. The manner in which the UN has been disregarded, enfeebled and ignored also highlights the uneven nature of the relationship and the hard reality of empire. Basking in the glow of Cold War victory, the US, backed by a UN resolution and a multi-national coalition, drove Saddam Hussein's army from Kuwait back to Baghdad in 1991. The fact that the Americans were unable to "finish the job" and enact Iraqi regime change would become a constant lament of key political figures in the US. With international support – and therefore legitimacy – only extending to reversing the invasion of Kuwait, the true strategic goals of the US remained unmet.

Just over a decade later, the US decided to act to remove Saddam Hussein from power. Given that the justifications for military action were spurious, trumped up or patently false, the UN refused to pass a resolution for military action in 2003. Instead of taking heed, the US simply declared that "diplomacy has failed", ignoring the UN in order to gather its allies into a "coalition of the willing". The illegal war that followed would end in a failed state, the rise of ISIS, and 200,000 documented civilian casualties.[26] A more realistic estimate puts this figure closer to 500,000.[27] Over 4,500 US soldiers also lost their lives during the conflict and many veterans have killed themselves in the years after returning home.[28]

It is not simply in military conflicts that the US is willing to show disdain for the global community. The US remains the only country not to ratify the UN Convention on the Rights of the Child. It also has failed to ratify the Convention on the Elimination of All Forms of Discrimination against Women, the Convention on the Rights of Persons with Disabilities and the American Convention on Human Rights.[29] In 2002, the Bush administration decided that the Geneva conventions did not apply to American enemies, a view rejected in 2006 by the Supreme Court.[30] The US also refuses to support efforts to investigate crimes committed against the Palestinian people by the state of Israel. The willingness to utilize international institutions when necessary – both to hold other nations to account for misdeeds and to support US military actions – and then subsequently ignore them when it is not expedient, illustrates the power of a modern empire.

America's ability to conduct diplomacy from a position of power allows outsized influence and leverage, as the US can apply pressure on allied nations to ensure that strategic goals are met. This influence takes many forms. Organizing support for punitive actions like sanctions is a direct method for attacking a rival's economic infrastructure and requires collective action for it to be successful. Organizing the detention of foreign nationals by allied countries is another example;

the arrest of Huawei executive Meng Wanzhou in Canada in 2018, following a US extradition request, illustrates this point clearly.[31] Coercing weaker states to lend their votes to further US strategic interests at the UN is also a successful strategy that is regularly deployed.

The US is also able to ignore the requests or wishes of allies as it sees fit, treating them with the same disdain as a Roman emperor would when dealing with his vassal states. The US reserves the right to operate a strict no-extradition policy, ensuring that any citizen on US soil remains within the US legal system unless the relevant authorities decide otherwise. After the killing of British citizen Harry Dunn on UK soil, the result of dangerous driving by a US national, extradition was repeatedly refused.[32] The opposite is expected from allies, and any attempts to ignore US extradition requests are met with concerted pressure and accusations of insufficient loyalty. The pressure placed on the UK government to force the extradition of Julian Assange is a case in point.

Similarly, the treatment of allied nations by the Trump administration after intentionally collapsing the Iran nuclear deal shows this contempt once again. After the signatories refused to be complicit in the US torpedoing of the deal, widely regarded as a move purely motivated by Trump's desire to undo any Obama-era policies, the US prevented any foreign companies from trading with Iran under threat of sanction. These are not isolated incidents and examples; they are indicative of the manner in which an empire treats not just its adversaries but also its allies.

At its core, the power of empire is to decide what is legal or illegal, allowable or punishable, and to enforce these parameters and punishments throughout its dominion. In antiquity, this would be expressed via imperial decree and mercilessly enforced at the point of a spear or the tip of a sword. In the modern world, the American Empire does not have to resort to spear or sword or missile, as the written word will often suffice. International law governs the actions of nations and is maintained by a shared belief in the values it attempts to enshrine and the rights it attempts to guarantee. The US, as the standard-bearer for liberal democracy and as the "shining city on the hill", has been instrumental in writing many of these laws and ensuring adherence to them. These efforts are, however, undermined by actions which consistently subvert international law when it suits US policy objectives. The spectre of communist Russia was used to justify illegal actions throughout the Cold War, and the "war on terror" after 9/11 performed the same function in the 2000s. The American people must understand what has been done in their name over the years, and must question what continues to be done, if their empire is to move forward in a manner more aligned to the lofty goals and hopeful rhetoric they have been brought up to believe. The following summaries address some of the more difficult or painful episodes in America's past, beginning with three of the most significant. Honestly acknowledging these historical truths is important if the US is to make wise decisions about its future.

Three Key Episodes

Slavery (c.1526–c.1866)

An estimated 12.5 million men, women and children were trafficked from Africa to the Americas as slaves. Of these, 10.7 million survived the passage, and more than 90 per cent were sent to South America and the Caribbean, including 4.86 million to Brazil alone. Of the 10.7 million survivors, the estimated number of African slaves arriving in North America during the slave trade was 450,000.[33]

Although slavery is far older than the American Empire, and also not confined to the Western hemisphere, this does not diminish the legacy of suffering and oppression, the effects of which are still felt across the US today. We will examine these matters further in later chapters.

Native Americans (1776 onwards)
When the American Revolution began, Native Americans had to choose whether to choose sides or stay neutral. In the years after independence, as the US began to take shape, there was much bloodshed and slaughter and the forcible relocation of the Native American tribes that had previously inhabited the North American continent. Quality of life on the reservations to which they were moved still trails that in the rest of the country, and a 2021 CDC study indicated that Native Americans had an average life expectancy of 71 years. This is compared to 82 years for Hispanic people, 78.8 years for white people, and 74.8 years for black people.[34]

The atomic bombings of Japan (6–9 August 1945)
The atomic bombings of Hiroshima and Nagasaki remain the only occasions when nuclear weapons have been used in conflict to this day. Civilian populations were deliberately targeted, resulting in hundreds of thousands of deaths and radiation-related illnesses. Debate continues to this day as to the legal and ethical justification for the attacks, which would certainly be considered illegal today.[35] However, the bombings can be said to have saved many lives thereafter, namely by forcing the Japanese to surrender and creating an ongoing taboo against the use of such weapons. A 2017 UN treaty declared nuclear weapons illegal, but this is largely symbolic as the nuclear-armed powers have not ratified it.[36]

Now let's turn to US actions and influence around the globe in the twentieth and twenty-first centuries.

South-East Asia

The Gulf of Tonkin incident (August 1964)
Two confrontations between US and North Vietnamese naval forces – the latter of which almost certainly never happened – were used to justify US escalation of the conflict in Vietnam. The Vietnam War

would lead to the deaths of more than a million civilians and soldiers on all sides, including around 58,000 US servicemen.[37]

The Mỹ Lai massacre (16 March 1968)
The mass murder of some five hundred Vietnamese civilians, primarily women, children and old men, was covered up at first, until the truth emerged.

US bombing of Laos (1964–73)
Over 2 million tonnes of cluster bombs were covertly dropped on Laos, which was a neutral country, in an effort to disrupt communist supply lines into Vietnam. This amounted to more bombs than were dropped during the entirety of the Second World War, making Laos the most heavily bombed nation on earth.[38]

US bombing of Cambodia (1969–73)
Estimates vary, but several hundred thousand people were killed as US bombers attempted to cut North Vietnamese Army and Viet Cong supply lines.

Support for Pol Pot and the Khmer Rouge (1980–86)
Khmer Rouge forces in exile benefited from millions of dollars of US financial aid from 1980 to 1986, as well as opportunistic political support at the UN.[39] An estimated 1.2–2.8 million Cambodians had died during Pol Pot's genocidal reign between 1975 and 1979.[40]

Latin America

Guatemala (1954)
After the popular overthrow of US-backed dictator Jorge Ubico in 1944, the CIA launched Operation PBSUCCESS by bombing Guatemala City in 1954. Thirty years of brutal repression from US-backed military dictators followed and an estimated 200,000 people died as a result.

Haiti (1959)

The US supported François Duvalier and his son Jean-Claude from 1959 to 1986, during which time hundreds of victims died at the hands of security services – and torture, disappearances and political killings were commonplace.

Brazil (1964)

Popular president João Goulart attempted to reform tax laws and redistribute land to benefit the Brazilian people. US ambassador Lincoln Gordon organized support for a military coup to oust Goulart, recommending in a top-secret cable that the US arrange "a clandestine delivery of arms" as well as oil and gas shipments, supplemented by possible CIA covert operations.

Uruguay (1969–74)

US efforts directed by Dan Mitrione gave training and weaponry for local police to torture political opposition. Juan María Bordaberry led a CIA-backed coup in 1973 and remained in power until 1976. Hundreds of people were murdered, tortured, imprisoned and disappeared during his presidency.

Bolivia (1967–77)

Guerrilla leader Che Guevara was assassinated in 1967 in a CIA-backed mission after he led a popular revolt against the Bolivian regime. General Juan José Torres, a reformer, came to power in 1970 but was overthrown less than a year later in a bloody military coup led by Colonel Hugo Banzer Suárez, who ruled brutally for a further seven years with CIA backing.

Chile (1973)

CIA actions to destabilize the Chilean government of President Salvador Allende paved the way for a coup led by General Augusto Pinochet on 11 September 1973. Pinochet ruled Chile for 17 years, forcing over 200,000 Chileans into exile. His regime's victims of repression and torture number around 40,000, including some 3,000 murders.

Argentina (1976)

Argentina was the operations centre for the CIA's entire Latin American strategy, known as Operation Condor. With US support, the ruling juntas brutalized the citizenry through the killing of over 30,000 people. Some 500 babies born during detention were taken from their parents by the regime.

El Salvador (1980s)

During the bloody civil war of the 1980s, the US provided billions of dollars in economic and military support for the oligarchs and generals who had ruled for decades, ensuring a peasant population remained impoverished and illiterate during this time. Some 75,000 Salvadoreans were killed, mainly by the military and its death squads, supplied with US counterinsurgency training.

Panama (1979–89)

President George H. W. Bush launched an invasion of Panama to unseat dictator Manuel Noriega and ensure US interests were protected, after sanctions and a failed coup had been unsuccessful. The same Manuel Noriega who had collaborated with the CIA in assisting the Contra rebels in Nicaragua was rebranded as a ruthless, drug-trafficking criminal. This was not inaccurate but the US had known about these activities as early as 1972.

The Middle East

Iranian coup (1953)

The CIA played a central role, via Operation Ajax, in the coup that toppled the democratically elected government of Prime Minister Mohammad Mosaddegh, restoring the monarchy of the Shah. The attempt to preserve Western dominance of the Iranian oil industry would then lead to a nationalist uprising against the repressive regime of the Shah, culminating in the 1979 Iranian Revolution. The resulting religious theocracy has ruled Iran ever since, brutally enforcing Sharia law, restricting women's rights and crushing political opposition.[41]

Iran–Contra Affair (1980–87)

With the full knowledge of President Reagan, the US sold weapons to Iran for it to use in the ongoing Iran–Iraq war – in contravention of a US trade embargo. The arms sales would also enable the release of seven Americans held by the Iranian-backed militant group Hezbollah in Lebanon, despite Reagan promising voters he would never negotiate with terrorists. To further complicate matters, the funds from the arms sale were secretly funnelled to Nicaraguan right-wing groups, known as the Contras, to buy weaponry to continue the fighting against the socialist Sandinistas. The Contras were described by Reagan as "the moral equivalent of the founding fathers", despite being blacklisted for support by Congress because the majority of their funding originated from the cocaine trade.

Iraq (1980s)

The US provided Saddam Hussein with billions of dollars in loans to buy weapons for his war against Iran, including controversial cluster bombs. Deals to provide biological agents, including anthrax, were facilitated by future Defense Secretary Donald Rumsfeld. This occurred even though it was known that Iraq was using chemical weapons in the conflict. The Iraqis also used intelligence provided by the US to launch chemical-weapon attacks using mustard gas and sarin in 1988. It is ironic that the same chemical and biological weapons program that Rumsfeld had helped to build would be cited as a major justification for the 2003 US invasion of Iraq.

Iraq War (2003–11)

Falsified claims of a nuclear weapons program and the harbouring of Al-Qaeda terrorists were used by the US to justify an illegal invasion, without UN support. Civilian casualties have been estimated at 500,000, no nuclear weapons were found, and the resulting failed state and power vacuum led to the rise of ISIS.

Abu Ghraib prison, Iraq (October–December 2003)

US service personnel subjected Iraqi prisoners of war to torture, which Major General Antonio M. Taguba described as "sadistic, blatant and wanton criminal abuses". Ritual humiliation and intimidation included threatening male detainees with rape, sodomizing a detainee with a chemical light, forced masturbation and using dogs to frighten and even attack prisoners.[42]

Guantanamo Bay (2002 onwards)

Established in 2002 at an American military base in Cuba, this detention camp became the epicentre of the torture program that was rebranded "enhanced interrogation" by the Bush administration. American law and international law regarding treatment of prisoners was ignored, with nearly 800 prisoners held here, mostly without charge. Many prisoners were innocent of any crime except being in Afghanistan at the time of the US invasion. The legacy of Guantanamo is described by Amnesty International as one of "flagrant human rights abuses, racism and Islamophobia and impunity for torture". The camp still holds prisoners without charge today, despite promises by multiple presidents to close it down.[43]

Extraordinary rendition (2002 onwards)

During the war on terror, the US frequently kidnapped potential suspects, trafficking them to CIA black sites in friendly countries to be tortured. Hundreds of people were victims of extraordinary rendition and denied the right to a fair trial. Assistance in these activities was provided by the secret police in states such as Egypt, Yemen, Syria and Uzbekistan. This practice is in direct contravention of the US Senate-ratified UN Convention Against Torture, and a 1998 federal statute.[44] In purely practical terms, it has been proven that torture rarely provides reliable, actionable intelligence.

Yemen (2015 onwards)

In 2015, President Obama provided assistance to the Saudi-led military assault in Yemen in a civil war between a corrupt authoritarian government and opposing Houthi rebels. The opposition contains many disparate groups, including Islamic militants guilty of their own human rights abuses, but the Yemeni citizenry remain caught between the two sides. Between March 2015 and July 2021, the Saudis conducted at least 23,000 raids, killing or injuring some 18,500 civilians. This is in addition to enforcing a blockade that has weaponized starvation, creating a failed state. US assistance has continued ever since 2015, despite Joe Biden promising to end support during his presidential campaign in 2020.

Israel and Palestine (1948 onwards)
US economic, military and political support for Israel has hindered efforts to find a workable two-state solution. Illegal land seizures and continued occupation by Israel have been described as "apartheid" by UN rights experts and Amnesty International, and these activities continue to this day. The knowledge of unwavering US support lessens Israeli motivation to achieve a workable solution. It is also an open secret that Israel possesses nuclear weapons – a fact which the US tolerates while it strenuously opposes the attempts of any other Middle Eastern state to acquire this capability.

Following the brutal attack on Israel by Hamas in October 2023, and Israel's actions in defence of itself, the prospects for long-term peace and a two-state solution seem particularly bleak. The potential for the conflict to involve or antagonize other Middle Eastern powers presents a major threat to the stability of the region and the American Empire.

Worldwide drone warfare program (2002 onwards)
This program started during the Bush administration but expanded massively under the Obama and Trump administrations. As a result, the US has executed thousands of people without trial. US leaders possess the ability to kill whomever they wish, almost wherever they wish, without risking the lives of their military personnel. This program of secretive targeted assassination is orchestrated via a "kill list", often signed off by the president personally.[45]

Conclusion

A realistic, clear-eyed assessment of the American Empire is required. If you write the laws and punish those who contravene them, while contravening them yourself, you are not a hegemon – you are an empire. Reading through this litany of transgressions, it would be reasonable to wonder why anyone would support the continuation of the American Empire, but my answer is simple. We must take the world as we find it, while also attempting to change it for the better.

Acknowledging the mistakes of the past is the most effective way to avoid repeating them. This lesson was illustrated by President Obama's visit to Laos in 2016, where, although short of making an apology, he spoke of the "moral obligation" of the US to help the country heal, and also to educate American citizens as to what had occurred there. The American Empire is in its relative infancy, and over time it is maturing to understand the responsibility that comes with unmatched power. It would be pure naivety to believe that any previous iteration of empire would have acted with a greater level of benignity. Would Genghis Khan or Alexander the Great have exercised restraint when presented with such an awesome power disparity? More importantly, would any modern rival? If Hitler's Third Reich had possessed the atomic advantage, would the world be a better, fairer, freer place? If the Soviet Union had won the Cold War, would the global community be rejoicing under Moscow's thumb?

This brings us to the heart of the matter: if the American Empire does indeed collapse, the most likely replacement is not the democracies of western Europe, but something far more authoritarian in nature. A Chinese-led global order is not a desirable future for anyone used to living in a liberal democracy. This is the most modern surveillance state in history, with an unchallenged ability and motivation to deploy every aspect of it to control its citizenry. The US is indeed imperfect, but its people, if not all of its politicians, believe in ideals of liberty and justice, whether or not these have truly been achieved in the past or will be attained in the future.

Now established beyond reasonable doubt, the label of empire, as applied to the United States, is accurate. The next task is to consider why this is important, and what lessons can be learned from history, by journeying back through time to examine the decline of previous empires.

2

The End of Empires

Nearly four and a half millennia ago a man of humble background, whom we now know by the name Sargon of Akkad, united a series of independent states in the region around the dual rivers of the Tigris and the Euphrates. He thereby created the first empire in recorded human history. At its height, Sargon's empire encompassed parts of what is now Iraq, western Iran, Turkey and Syria. Where Sargon led, many have followed – arguably almost a hundred entities since that time can claim the title of empire.

The relative impact and influence of empires can be measured using many different means, with population, area, duration and economic dominance all serving as useful criteria. But we don't need to decide which empires wielded the most influence, comparatively, as this provides little insight. Instead, we will look at the *manner* in which they fell, in order to discern patterns and similarities that will be useful in our consideration of the American Empire and the probable nature of its demise.

Bringing into focus a range of empires that have long since disappeared, this chapter is intended to provide some context to assist us in our search for modern parallels. Any attempt to describe a hundred empires in these pages would be akin to Gandalf's warning to the Balrog in the mines of Moria: "You shall not pass!" Rather than test the reader's patience, I have offered instead a brief summary of a selection of the largest or most significant empires in history, providing for each one some possible parallels with events and developments occurring within the American Empire today.[1]

The Achaemenid Empire

Period	550–330 BCE
Region	Western Asia
Extent	2.1 million square miles
Population	17–35 million

The Achaemenid Empire, also known as the First Persian Empire, was founded by Cyrus II, and under Darius I and Xerxes I it controlled territory as far west as Macedonia and Libya and as far east as the Hyphasis River in northern India. It extended to the Caucasus Mountains and Aral Sea in the north and to the Persian Gulf and Arabian Desert in the south. A total population of up to 35 million[2] may not seem as substantial as some other empires, but at the time it represented perhaps 12 per cent of the people on earth. For comparison, the British Empire is the largest modern empire and controlled around 23 per cent of the global population at its height.[3]

Unlike many other emperors, Cyrus and his successors were mindful of the benefits to imperial cohesion that could be gained by tolerant and practical methods of incorporating conquered peoples. This included religious and cultural tolerance as well as installing conquered kings within the imperial government, thus legitimizing Persian rule and ensuring loyalty.

The fall of the empire can be traced back to the Ionian Revolt of Greek regions in Asia Minor in 499–493 BCE. Although that was unsuccessful at the time, it led to Persian invasions of Greece by Darius and his son Xerxes. The latter will be familiar to film fans, as he was the villain of *300*, sending wave upon wave of soldiers against Greek forces led by the Spartans at the Battle of Thermopylae in 480 BCE. Success for Persia at Thermopylae was followed, however, by naval disaster against the Athenians at Salamis and a combined Greek army at Plataea. This ultimately brought an end to the Persian invasion of Greece.

The Delian League, formed to take the fight to the Persians, morphed thereafter into what can be described as the Athenian Empire. It successfully freed the cities of Ionia from Persian domination before hostilities in the Greco-Persian Wars drew to a temporary halt. The Greeks would resume the conflict and end the Achaemenid Empire, later in the fourth century BCE, under the leadership of the Macedonian king Alexander the Great. During his brief reign, he routed the Persians in several battles, reached the Hindu Kush in what is now Afghanistan, and ushered in a 300-year period of Hellenistic influence.

Contributory factor in collapse	Modern parallel in the US
Military mistakes and failures at Salamis and Plataea despite greater strength	Military mistakes and failures in Iraq and Afghanistan despite greater strength
Military defeat by rising power led by Alexander the Great	Rise of China militarily, although direct Chinese attack is unlikely at present

The Macedonian Empire of Alexander the Great

Period	336–323 BCE
Region	Greece, Egypt, Asia
Extent	2 million square miles
Population	20 million[4]

This was one of the largest – and also one of the most short-lived – empires in history. As seen in many other cases, its disintegration can be traced to the death of its leader and the subsequent battles for succession. It was initially Alexander's father, Philip II, who was responsible for extending the imperial might of Macedonia, located in the northern part of Greece, and he was preparing to launch a campaign against the Persians when he was assassinated in 336 BCE. It was his son Alexander who took up the mantle and embarked on his audacious and extensive invasion of Asia during his 13-year reign, earning himself the epithet of "the Great" and a place in the history books.

The reach of Alexander's empire was truly staggering, ranging as it did across areas of Greece, northern Africa, the Middle East and on into India. During his campaign Alexander created some twenty new cities, many bearing his name, to act as imperial outposts to control subject populations and spread knowledge, culture and trade. This expansion into so many differing territories and cultures led to issues of assimilation – attempts to hybridize Greek institutions with foreign cultures caused a loss of identity and resentment among the Macedonians. Rather than embracing the positive impact of diversity within the empire, many Macedonians lamented the dilution of their culture and traditions. This was felt most keenly within Alexander's army as soldiers were recruited from conquered populations, leading to resentment within the ranks. It was, however, the death of Alexander in 323 BCE that ultimately shattered his empire, with no successor nominated before he died. As with many empires that followed, the subsequent battles over succession legitimacy would lead to decades of internal war and the disintegration of the empire into four weakened yet somewhat stable entities.

Contributory factor in collapse	Modern parallel in the US
Legitimacy of succession disputed	Legitimacy of elections disputed (Russiagate and Trump's "Big Lie")
Perceived loss of shared identity as empire expands causes resentment among the Macedonians	Perceived loss of shared identity, as ethnic majority share of the population declines, leading to rise of "white replacement" theory

Contributory factor in collapse	Modern parallel in the US
Internal civil war leading to disintegration of the empire into weaker entities	Potential secession of states from the union, peacefully or violently, with worrying levels of support for a "national divorce"

The Han Empire

Period	202 BCE to 220 CE
Region	East Asia
Extent	2.5 million square miles
Population	60 million[5]

Born into a peasant family, Liu Bang led a successful revolt against the Qin dynasty and went on to become the first emperor of the Han dynasty in 202 BCE. Apart from a brief interruption (the Xin dynasty of 9–23 CE), the Han Empire lasted until 220 CE when Xian ceded the throne to Cao Pi, who established the state of Wei as China entered the Three Kingdoms period.

The Han dynasty is not just famous for its duration or reach, but also for its many notable achievements. These included the development of a meritocratic structure for government and civil service, the invention of paper, and the use of water clocks, sundials and woven silk. These contributions shaped Chinese culture to such an extent that the word "Han" became the Chinese word to denote someone who is ethnically Chinese.

The empire would suffer many environmental problems, including cattle plagues, locusts, droughts, floods and earthquakes, which all took a cumulative toll. Tensions with tribal groups on the borders of Han territory were a constant problem, and a superiority complex led to a failure to assimilate these non-Han peoples. Internal politicking also caused unrest and instability as factions vied for control, including the court eunuchs whose scheming would place an 11-year-old Emperor Ling on the throne in 168 CE. Numerous outbreaks of a lethal plague during the 170s and 180s, coupled with heavy taxation, led to a series of peasant rebellions as people blamed the emperor for not being able to find a cure. The troubles began with the Yellow Turban Rebellion, which, although quashed, led to further peasant rebellions.

The empire's lack of external enemies has been cited as a contributory factor in its collapse, as battle-hardened generals turned their attention inwards in the absence of external threats. After the death of Emperor Ling in 189 CE without an heir, bitter palace infighting ensued in a violent battle of succession. The resulting instability led to a power vacuum which was filled by competing warlords, and the empire eventually split into three regions, resulting in the Wei dynasty and the states of Shu Han and Wu.

Contributory factor in collapse	Modern parallel in the US
Environmental factors: plague, droughts, floods, earthquakes	Increasing frequency of extreme weather events; potential threat of major earthquake or supervolcanic eruption (Yellowstone Caldera)
Internal politicking and bitter battles for legitimate succession	Legitimacy of elections disputed (Russiagate and Trump's "Big Lie"); increasing loyalty to party over country
Assimilation problems	Rising Hispanic population in southern states could encourage the spread of secessionist or identity-based ideology, weakening social cohesion
Internal revolts by exploited peasantry	Rising inequality and anger at 2008 and 2021 corporate bailouts could lead to increased protesting, rioting or violent uprisings

Contributory factor in collapse	Modern parallel in the US
Weak and unpopular leaders	Unpopular and flawed candidates put forward by both major parties

The Roman Empire

Period	27 BCE to 476 CE
Region	Europe
Extent	1.9 million square miles
Population	50–80 million[6]

Famous for roads, gladiators and sanitation – among many other things – the Roman Empire dominated western Europe, stretching from Britain to Egypt, and lasted for over 400 years. Many reasons have been given for the eventual collapse of the Roman Empire: the German historian Alexander Demandt, for instance, provided a staggering 210.[7] The most routinely cited reasons are the negative impacts of overexpansion; excessive centralization; a descent of the ruling class into decadence and corruption; excessive taxation; inflation; and external attacks.

These factors are all certainly responsible for a downfall that would have been unimaginable when the empire was at the peak of its power. Overexpansion played its part, requiring unpopular levels of taxation to finance wars of conquest, but it was the slowing of imperial expansion, and the steady supply of slave labour it provided, that led to labour shortages, drops in commercial production, and slowdown in trade. The resulting price inflation was exacerbated by corruption within the ruling classes and a loss of popular confidence in all levels of leadership. This political corruption was evident in overtaxation and kleptocracy, as infighting and politicking led to a series of weak emperors, with more than twenty holding the post during a period of

50 years in the third century CE. The Praetorian Guard, originally an imperial bulwark, became increasingly responsible for this political instability, wielding an inordinate amount of power in deciding which imperial candidates to promote and which to eliminate. The civil war resulting from the death of Serverus Alexander in 235 CE is the starkest example of when the legitimacy of succession is disputed and political infighting erupts.

There were also external threats from groups like the Goths and Vandals, as well as popular rebellions, all of which weakened the once formidable Roman military. The faltering legions struggled to recruit soldiers and turned increasingly to mercenaries who had little allegiance to the empire and were happy to turn against their employer when it suited them. Religion also had a part to play in the imperial decline, as the decision to embrace Christianity inadvertently reduced the power of the emperor among the people by removing the demigod status conferred by Roman religion. If emperors were merely men, and men are fallible, then their actions and errors could be questioned in a manner that was previously impossible. As with the Mongol Empire later, the sheer size of the empire necessitated a distribution of power and authority to ensure effective governance, and the split between the eastern and western parts of the Roman Empire led to each half drifting from the other and failing to act in unison toward a common goal. Finally, by the year 450, endemic and epidemic disease had ravaged the empire, and by 476 the last Roman emperor in the West, Romulus Augustus, was deposed.

Contributory factor in collapse	Modern parallel in the US
Overexpansion	The US maintains a colossal military infrastructure, including military bases around the globe, at vast cost
Excessive centralization	Federal government overreach and ruling by decree via presidential executive order

Contributory factor in collapse	Modern parallel in the US
Corrupt ruling class	The American oligarchy is an unaccountable elite ruling class, apparently indifferent to rising inequality
Excessive taxation and inflation	The 2022–23 inflation spike is a potential precursor of worse to come
Endemic and epidemic disease	Upheaval of the recent Covid pandemic and the threat of a more deadly virus next time; growing problem of antibiotic resistance; costs and consequences of unhealthy lifestyles and the obesity crisis
External attacks	Possible challenge from China

The Byzantine Empire

Period	395–1453
Region	Europe
Extent	1.3 million square miles
Population	26 million people[8]

The Eastern half of the Roman Empire managed to survive for 1,000 years after its Western counterpart disintegrated into various feudal kingdoms; the Ottomans finally overran what we call the Byzantine Empire in 1453. The seat of the empire was located between the Black Sea and the Mediterranean, perfectly situated between Europe and Asia Minor, and began life as Byzantium. In 330 CE it was renamed Constantinople by Emperor Constantine I with the intention of creating a new Rome. The city's location, which had been so beneficial in the early years of empire, led to unforeseen problems, including attacks from both east and west, and religious and ethnic hostility within.

As with many empires, military conquest brought not just glory but also problems of assimilation, organization and unmanageable pressure on the administrative structures required to rule effectively. By the time the Ottomans laid siege once more to Constantinople in 1453, the city had diminished from a population of over 400,000 in the twelfth century to less than 50,000, but its walls had still never been breached in over 1,000 years and were still considered the most formidable in Europe. The Ottomans were not fighting with the same tools deployed over the past 1,000 years, however, and the cannon bombardment, led by the super-sized Dardanelles Gun, signalled the end of the Byzantine era and the beginning of the Ottoman. The city became known as Istanbul. As the fall of the Ottoman Empire several centuries later would illustrate, technological superiority is an ever-changing landscape and does not endure forever.

Contributory factor in collapse	Modern parallel in the US
Attacked by multiple enemies	There is currently little chance of a state or alliance of states directly attacking the US
Overexpansion and inability to control the empire	The ability to project power globally requires vast funding for the Pacific and Atlantic fleets and for military bases around the world, which could become unsustainable
Religious and ethnic hostility exacerbates assimilation problems	Rising Hispanic population in southern states could encourage the spread of secessionist or identity-based ideology, weakening social cohesion
Military technological advantages of the Ottomans	Potential for new technologies to be used in warfare by competitors (AI, quantum computing, bioweapons, etc.)

The Ottoman Empire

Period	1299–1922
Region	Western Asia, southern Europe and northern Africa
Extent	Over 2 million square miles
Population	Over 25 million people[9]

One of the longest-lasting empires under discussion, spanning a staggering six centuries, the Ottoman Empire encompassed territory from the Danube to the Nile, including areas of Asia Minor, south-eastern Europe, the Middle East and northern Africa. The military might required to control such a large area was sustained by lucrative commercial revenues across the various imperial territories. As is to be expected for an empire that lasted 600 years, there are many factors that contributed to its decline and ultimate collapse – the First World War simply provided the final swing of the axe.

The gradual decline of the Ottoman Empire earned it the unfortunate but accurate moniker of "the sick man of Europe", evoking the fading of an agrarian society into obscurity and irrelevance as rivals industrialized and modernized beyond its borders. This failure to modernize was starkly illustrated when war broke out in 1914: after choosing to side with the Central Powers, the Ottoman Empire was unable to produce the heavy weaponry, munitions, iron and steel required to sustain a twentieth-century war effort. This was compounded by a failure to modernize educationally and the absence of a robust professional class, caused by a staggering 90 per cent illiteracy rate.

Even before the outbreak of the First World War and the Wilsonian push toward self-determination for nation states, the Ottomans were challenged by independence movements in Bulgaria and by the Balkan Wars of 1912–13, leading to huge losses of territory and signalling that the empire's end was very much nigh. The sheer size of the empire and the multitude of different ethnicities and languages, not to mention the economic and geographical variations, hampered any possibility that the empire might evolve into a multi-ethnic, multi-federal, modern democratic state. A shared "Ottoman" identity was simply impossible in these circumstances.

In the end, a destructive rivalry with the neighbouring Russian Empire (which supported the independence claims of Balkan nationalists), the strategic error in siding with Germany in the First World War, and direct attacks by the British and the French in the Middle East and northern Africa, all contributed to the ultimate military demise of the once great Ottoman Empire.

Contributory factor in collapse	Modern parallel in the US
Gradual decline after centuries of dominance	Potential slow decline if the US is able to avoid collapse in short/mid term
Poor education and mass illiteracy	Falling educational attainment and weakness in relation to global peers
Failure to evolve from agrarian to industrialized economy	Risk of being beaten by China in an AI and high-tech arms race that will revolutionize economic systems and military technology
Unable to establish shared Ottoman identity	Inability to reconcile changing racial and social make-up of country; rise of "white replacement" theory
Military defeat due to inability to produce weaponry and obtain raw materials to sustain a modern war effort	Possibility of exhausting or dangerously depleting military and other supplies in support of allied nations fighting proxy wars

Contributory factor in collapse	Modern parallel in the US
Nationalism and ethnic independence movements, supported by Russia	Rising Hispanic population in southern states could encourage the spread of secessionist or identity-based ideology, weakening social cohesion

The Umayyad Caliphate

Period	661–750
Region	Northern Africa, Middle East, Asia
Extent	Over 4 million square miles
Population	30–62 million people[10]

The Umayyad dynasty was the first major Muslim dynasty, coming to power in 661 after the death of Ali, the Prophet Muhammad's son-in-law. Mu'awiyah was its first caliph, who moved the capital of the empire to Damascus and extended it outwards using the Syrian army, spreading Islam and the Arabic language over a huge area. This army permitted Mu'awiyah to exert a level of control over tribal rivalries and conquered provinces which had not previously been seen. The peak period for the dynasty was under Abd al-Malik, who ruled between 685 and 705, with his empire extending from Spain to central Asia and India via northern Africa.

The decline and eventual collapse of the empire began with military defeat by the Byzantine emperor Leo III in 717, as the empire became overextended and unable to defend its borders or prevent insurrections. The problems continued with a financial crisis during the three-year reign of Umar II (717–720) in spite of his commendable attempt to create a more even society for all Muslims, regardless of ethnicity. These issues reduced the ability of the empire to maintain control, and dormant feuds resurfaced between southern (Kalb) and northern (Qays) Arab tribes, further reducing the empire's military power. These feuds erupted into major revolts in Syria, Iraq and Khorasan, and the empire finally fell after a rebellion by the Abbasids in 750.

Contributory factor in collapse	Modern parallel in the US
Overexpansion and inability to maintain control over the empire	The ability to project power globally requires vast funding for the Pacific and Atlantic fleets and for military bases around the world, which could become unsustainable
Internal feuds led to revolt and rebellion	Breakdown of civil discourse and distrust in the independence and integrity of institutions could lead to further violence, insurrection or even civil war
Financial crisis	Rising inequality and anger at 2008 and 2021 corporate bailouts could lead to increased protesting, rioting or violent uprisings

The Mongol Empire

Period	1206–1368
Region	Asia
Extent	9.3 million square miles
Population	Over 100 million people[11]

The inspiration for Khal Drogo and his Dothraki horsemen in *Game of Thrones*, Genghis Khan established and expanded the Mongol Empire in the early thirteenth century. After his death in 1227, it grew to cover some 24 million square kilometres, a staggering one fifth of the earth's land surface area – the largest contiguous empire in history.[12] Fierce warriors spread outwards from the Mongol homeland under the leadership of the Great Khan, and in the Pax Mongolica that followed in the wake of conquest and bloodshed, technology, ideology and commodities were transported along vast trade routes that spanned the Asian continent.

The collapse of this empire provides a fascinating case study, as many familiar factors were involved. The death in 1227 of such a dominant leader in Genghis Khan was the primary reason for imperial disintegration, but the seeds were actually sown by him before his death. The sheer size of the empire, and the limitations of communication and technology of the time, rendered it ungovernable by one person, so Genghis Khan had divided the empire among his sons while he was still alive. This would eventually result in the empire being split into four main "khanates": the Golden Horde in Eastern Europe, the Chagatai Khanate in Central Asia, the Ilkhanate in Southwest Asia and the Yuan dynasty in East Asia. This division diminished shared identity and adherence to common objectives: a gradual decline became inevitable. Arguments over succession and legitimacy raged as tribal loyalty replaced imperial loyalty, leading to fragmentation and frequent conflict between the khanates. The adoption of cultural practices of conquered peoples within some khanates and not in others exacerbated this problem.

The Mongols built their empire upon the nomadic values of pastoral traditionalists but, in the attempt to govern their conquered peoples effectively, these values were replaced in some places by the sedentary practices of the newly conquered. Vast conquest requires massive military spending, and unpopular taxes were introduced by the Great Khan Möngke to finance military adventures. Although the subsequent riots and rebellions were quashed before his death in 1259, the taxation created lasting bitterness within the population. Möngke, although no Genghis, was another popular leader and his death unleashed a four-year civil war within the Chagatai Khanate between his two younger brothers. Environmental factors also weakened the empire: as in much of Europe at the time, the Black Death ravaged the population, killing vast numbers.

Similarly, the military campaigns waged by the Yuan dynasty, led by Kublai Khan, weakened this khanate both economically and militarily. Some, such as the invasions of Japan and Java, were abject failures, but even "successful" campaigns against Burma and the island of Sakhalin were hollow victories providing little benefit compared to the costs incurred. Local Han Chinese, feeling no affinity to the Mongol invaders, overthrew them and launched the Ming dynasty in 1368.

The Golden Horde struggled after the death of the respected leader Öz Beg in 1341, and the subsequent murder of his successor hastened the decline by increasing division and disunity. As with the Chagatai Khanate, the Black Death ripped through the population, while successful invasions of its territory drained the khanate of its skilled craftsmen, who were forcefully deported, stripping the technological edge that was vital to its supremacy.

The Ilkhanate, centred in what is modern-day Iran, ruled the region between 1256 and 1335. It suffered attacks from former allies the Golden Horde and the Chagatai Khanate while also experiencing rebellion and revolt within its borders. Religious differences further fragmented any shared identity, with years of religious tolerance evaporating as various rulers converted to conflicting Sunni and Shia practices, while also persecuting Christians, Jews and Buddhists. Again, the Black Death decimated the population but also destroyed the trading routes that the Ilkhanate relied upon, and with it the wealth that resulted from being the prominent trading hub in the region. After the death of Abu Sa'id Bahadur Khan in 1335, the Ilkhanate disintegrated and was eventually swallowed up by the Golden Horde in 1357.

Contributory factor in collapse	Modern parallel in the US
Tribal loyalty replaces imperial loyalty	Increasing loyalty to party over country
Legitimacy of succession disputed	Legitimacy of elections disputed (Russiagate and Trump's "Big Lie")
Unsustainable military spending	Soaring Pentagon budgets
Loss of shared identity as the empire expands	Inability to reconcile changing racial and social make-up of the country
The Black Death	Upheaval of the recent Covid pandemic and the threat of a more deadly virus next time

The Aztec Empire

Period	1428–1521
Region	Central America
Extent	Over 77,000 square miles[13]
Population	Over 5 million people[14]

In the course of the fifteenth century, the Aztecs built up a large tribute-based empire in what is now Mexico. The city of Tenochtitlán became the dominant city-state in a triple alliance, holding sway over subject populations that were forced to supply their imperial overlords with food, gold and human sacrifices.

The Spanish under Hernán Cortés arrived in the early sixteenth century, bringing with them old plagues and modern weapons. Millions of indigenous people died from smallpox and other diseases to which they had no prior immunity. The Spanish conquistadores used their military superiority, cunning and tactical alliances with local enemies of the Aztecs to bring about the collapse of the empire by 1521.

The Aztec appetite for sacrificial victims was clearly detrimental to imperial cohesion, leading to rebellions among conquered peoples and, more fatally, resulting in their collaboration with Cortés. This was a vital component in his military success over the Aztecs, but the role played by microscopic invaders was equally crucial.

Contributory factor in collapse	Modern parallel in the US
Inflicting customs of human sacrifice on conquered peoples weakens imperial cohesion, leads to rebellion and encourages them to form alliances with conquistadores	Rising Hispanic population in southern states could encourage the spread of secessionist or identity-based ideology, weakening social cohesion
Pathogens carried by conquistadores	Potential for a new pandemic with a higher mortality rate than Covid-19; distrust in authority leading to domestic opposition to vaccination and lockdown measures
Military and technological advantages of conquistadores	Potential for new technologies to be used in warfare by competitors (AI, quantum computing, bioweapons, etc.)

The Inca Empire

Period	1438–1533
Region	South America
Extent	770,000 square miles
Population	9–12 million people

The Incas, who created the largest empire in the pre-Columbian Americas,[15] also fell victim to invading Spanish conquistadores, but the decline was already under way prior to their arrival. Conflict over succession and legitimacy caused lasting damage to internal stability, with civil war breaking out in 1529. Supporters of the illegitimate but capable Atahualpa, in the northern administrative area of Quito, clashed with the forces of the legitimate heir, Huáscar, who held the southern capital of Cuzco. Atahualpa was victorious after three bloody years of internecine fighting, but he was soon captured by the invading Spanish under Francisco Pizarro. Their technological advantages were simply the final nail in the coffin, after the damage done by imported European diseases such as smallpox, influenza, typhus, diphtheria, chickenpox and measles. Millions died, decimating the population, reducing agricultural output and impairing the ability to communicate over wide areas of the empire – a task traditionally carried out by human runners relaying messages from ear to ear.

Contributory factor in collapse	Modern parallel in the US
Legitimacy of succession leading to civil wars and internal instability	Legitimacy of elections disputed (Russiagate and Trump's "Big Lie")
Pathogens carried by conquistadores	Potential for a new pandemic with a higher mortality rate than Covid-19; distrust in authority leading to domestic opposition to vaccination and lockdown measures
Military and technological advantages of conquistadores	Potential for new technologies to be used in warfare by competitors (AI, quantum computing, bioweapons, etc.)

The Spanish Empire

Period	1492–1976
Region	Global
Extent	5.3 million square miles
Population	27 million people[16]

Following the marriage of Isabella of Castile and Ferdinand of Aragon in 1469, Spain emerged from disunity and division to become the strongest state in Europe in the sixteenth and early seventeenth centuries. The Spanish Empire was predominantly located in Central and South America, but it also had smaller outposts in parts of Europe, Africa and the Pacific.

After the Spaniards conquered far-flung lands through a combination of guns, germs and steel, it became increasingly difficult to maintain these colonial outposts so far from the homeland. The waging of endless European wars led to high taxation and ravaged the Spanish economy and the flow of precious metals from South American mines into Europe caused inflation to surge. A European plague in the late sixteenth century also worsened the economic situation, which was followed by a shift in European commerce from the Mediterranean to the Atlantic. The Napoleonic wars on the Iberian peninsula led to the isolation of colonial territories from the mother country. Nationalist movements and ultimately independence revolutions resulted. Lacking the manpower and resources to cross the Atlantic and suppress decolonization attempts – attempts which were supported by the nascent British Empire – the Spanish Empire collapsed under the weight of its overexpansion. The British would be the beneficiaries of this collapse, with access to South American markets helping to create suitable economic conditions.

Contributory factor in collapse	Modern parallel in the US
Overexpansion and inability to control areas far from the empire's centre	The ability to project power globally requires vast funding for the Pacific and Atlantic fleets and for military bases around the world, which could become unsustainable

Contributory factor in collapse	Modern parallel in the US
Endless wars	Constant warfare in the 2000s was a drain on resources, but the public mood has shifted away from military intervention, though this could change in future
Shift in epicentre of European commerce from Mediterranean to Atlantic	Rise of developing world as possible economic alternative to the American system. Expansion of the BRICS bloc and further moves away from the dollar's hegemony as the currency of global trade
Inflation and high taxes	The 2022–23 inflation spike is a potential precursor of worse to come
Plague in Europe	Potential for a new pandemic with a higher mortality rate than Covid-19; distrust in authority leading to domestic opposition to vaccination and lockdown measures

The Russian Empire

Period	1721–1917
Region	Europe, Asia
Extent	8.8 million square miles
Population	125.6 million[17]

Long before Vladimir Putin, Russia's rulers also lived in a similarly lavish style, far removed from the grim realities endured by their subjects. Sharing the same autocratic tendencies, the Romanovs were brought down by revolution, provoked by immense suffering, popular uprisings and the regime's incompetent or merciless responses to them.

Military defeat in the Russo-Japanese War of 1904–5 was followed by disorder throughout the empire, especially violent in non-Russian regions. All strata of society united in their request for change, but peaceful protests were met with bullets, most notoriously on Bloody Sunday in St Petersburg in 1905. This kind of cruelty seemed to puncture the air of permanence surrounding tsardom, enabling the legitimacy of the regime and the status quo to be questioned and challenged.

The First World War greatly exacerbated the empire's existing troubles. Strikes and military mutinies ensued. Nicholas II was forced to abdicate in early 1917, the Provisional Government inherited the chaos, and Lenin soon returned from abroad, demanding an end to both the war and the resulting food shortages. In October of that year, with the political, military and economic crises still unresolved, the Bolsheviks staged a coup d'état. Russia descended into civil war, Lenin held onto power, and the Romanovs were executed. The Russian Empire became the Union of Soviet Socialist Republics.

Contributory factor in collapse	Modern parallel in the US
Governing system loses legitimacy after attacking peaceful protests	Trump's efforts to mobilize National Guard against BLM protesters
Governing system loses veneer of seeming permanent and unchangeable	Attacks on democracy and the electoral system lead to questioning of the utility and legitimacy of the system itself
Inequality and civil unrest lead to revolution	Inequality and civil unrest have the potential to lead to revolution
Failure to adapt to changing methods of warfare	Potential for new technologies to be used in warfare by competitors (AI, quantum computing, bioweapons, etc.)

The Austro-Hungarian Empire

Period	1867–1918
Region	Europe
Extent	240,000 square miles
Population	51.4 million[18]

A sprawling central European empire ruled by the Habsburg dynasty, Austria-Hungary came into existence after a dual monarchy was established in 1867. Franz Joseph reigned as Emperor of Austria and King of Hungary all the way through to his death in November 1916, when he was succeeded – for less than two years – by his grand-nephew Charles.

The end of the Austro-Hungarian Empire had several similarities to the decline of the Ottoman Empire, in both circumstantial and temporal terms: the Habsburgs were the victims of military failures in the First World War, nationalist claims of self-determination from a multi-ethnic population, and economic crises. The Russian Revolution in 1917 also showed a possible alternative to the status quo, and inevitable national strikes and military mutinies applied further pressure. Environmental factors also contributed, with a devastating crop failure leading to widespread famine in 1918. The failure to uphold the ruler's end of the bargain – provision of food and security – brought down the empire at the close of the First World War.

Contributory factor in collapse	Modern parallel in the US
Environmental: devastating crop failure	Extreme weather and soil degradation might impact ability to reliably produce food
Civil unrest, mutiny and national strikes	Civil unrest, driven by inequality, might escalate

Contributory factor in collapse	Modern parallel in the US
Nationalism and ethnic independence movements, buoyed by revolution in Russia, reject the status quo	Breakdown of civil discourse and distrust in the independence and integrity of institutions could lead to further violence, insurrection or even civil war

The Japanese Empire

Period	1868–1947
Region	Asia
Extent	2.9 million square miles
Population	Over 150 million[19]

After the Meiji Restoration, the Japanese imperial system ruled without question over a population of homogenous Japanese whose compliance owed much to the demigod status of the emperor. With comparatively little territory to govern at first, and given there were no issues of multiple ethnicities within the population on the Japanese home islands, the empire could well have endured if it had not been for significant imperial expansion in Asia and strategic military mistakes.

By siding with Nazi Germany in the Second World War and by taking the disastrous decision to bomb Pearl Harbor, the Japanese sowed the seeds of their own downfall, bringing a reluctant and isolationist great-power adversary into the conflict. A profound misidentification of both the resolve and capabilities of their ideological enemy ultimately led to the demise of this empire.

Believing that the "soft" democracies of the West would not have an appetite for war, the Japanese did not expect the US response. Like the Ottomans, the Japanese at this time lacked the technological prowess of their enemy, devastatingly illustrated by the nuclear attacks on Hiroshima and Nagasaki. Although these dual blows were the final act in the destruction of the empire, this simply hastened the timetable set by the Allied naval blockade, which caused widespread shortages of both food and military equipment. Imperial control and propaganda had so shielded the Japanese population from military realities and impending disaster that the nation's defeat, when it finally occurred, came as a devastating shock for most ordinary people.

Contributory factor in collapse	Modern parallel in the US
Military mistakes: siding with Nazi Germany, bombing Pearl Harbor	Military mistakes in Iraq and Afghanistan not insurmountable, but the effect of a future China conflict is unpredictable
Blindsided by development in warfare – atomic bombs on Nagasaki and Hiroshima	Potential for new technologies to be used in warfare by competitors (AI, quantum computing, bioweapons, etc.)
Geography: island status leads to susceptibility to blockade and resultant shortages of food and military equipment	Chinese control of US debt and manufacturing can be exploited in a future war
Propaganda failure – reality of military failure shocks population	Embedded journalists in Iraq and Afghanistan present sanitized version of conflicts; analogous shock at rise of ISIS and the chaos of withdrawal from Afghanistan
Misunderstanding of the enemy's ideology – perception of Western democracies as weak or decadent	US may not fully understand or appreciate the Chinese policy of strategic patience or what might cause China to abandon it

The British Empire

Period	Sixteenth to twentieth centuries
Region	Global
Extent	Over 13 million square miles
Population	Over 400 million[20]

The British Empire had its origins in the establishing of overseas colonies in the sixteenth century, but its rise did not accelerate until the eighteenth century. The opportunities afforded by naval dominance and control of trading outposts in that era enabled the British to create the largest empire the world had ever seen. Encompassing around 25 per cent of the global land surface, 23 per cent of the world's population[21] and over 400 million people at its peak in the early twentieth century, it was known as the empire "on which the sun never sets".

It remains a contentious topic in the UK to this day, as revisionist views clash with traditional patriotic jingoism. Critics highlight the negative aspects of British imperialism, including massacres, slavery and theft of both natural resources and indigenous artefacts, all justified at the time by a deeply held and widely preached belief in the supposed supremacy of white people and Christian values. What had begun as an essentially commercial enterprise, with the privately owned East India Company given monopoly status by the British crown, morphed into an ideological and truly imperial endeavour. Company rule ended after the Indian Rebellion of 1857, the British government took over, and by 1876 Queen Victoria was styling herself Empress of India.

The twentieth century saw the empire reach its geographical and demographic zenith, but the economic impact of fighting two world wars, the changing of attitudes regarding imperialism and the rise of the American Empire all contributed to its eventual disintegration. Although the UK was among the victors of the First World War, global favour was thereafter shifting away from empire to independence, propelled by American president Woodrow Wilson and his blueprint for self-determination. The decision to intervene in support of the Allies during this conflict was the moment that the US abandoned a policy of isolationism for a more global role, ultimately supplanting the empire of its linguistic cousin across the Atlantic. Then, when the Second World War ravaged Britain's empire and economy, the US did not intervene directly until the attack on Pearl Harbor. America's Lend-Lease program also ended up saddling the British with high levels of debt that would not be fully paid off until more than fifty years later.

Although once again among the victors at the end of the war, the British found their empire quickly unravelling as the domestic economy struggled to support the vast sums required to maintain the UK's global possessions. Independence movements flourished after the non-violent campaign of civil disobedience led by Gandhi in India, and decolonization occurred in all corners of the empire in due course. As will be seen in chapter 5, colonial control of the media had been weakened by this point, and anticolonial movements were increasingly able to spread their messages and swell their ranks.

There is no clear-cut end date for the British Empire, but the London Declaration of 1949 regarding the Commonwealth of Nations – and India's continued membership after its independence – is a symbolic moment. Today, King Charles III still acts as the official head of state in Commonwealth countries such as Australia and Canada, and the likeness of the late Queen Elizabeth II will continue to adorn banknotes and coins in 35 countries for a while longer.[22] The British government also still controls overseas territories in places like Gibraltar and the Falklands, not to mention a number of tax-haven dependencies such as the British Virgin Islands. It is perhaps this enduring presence around the world that has prolonged a sense of imperial importance for the British but, if any point can be said to have signalled the end of their truly global power and influence, it is the national embarrassment caused by the Suez Crisis in 1956, when the US left little doubt as to which Anglo-Saxon nation was now in the imperial driving seat.

Contributory factor in collapse	Modern parallel in the US
Resources drained by world wars	The ability to project power globally requires vast funding for the Pacific and Atlantic fleets and for military bases around the world, which could become unsustainable
Changing attitudes to empire and conquest	The US is limited by modern attitudes to conquest, invasion and regime change; domestic and international opinion would not back the launching of a pre-emptive war against imperial rivals such as China
Changing attitude to warfare; Suez Crisis	The global unpopularity of US military intervention in Iraq and Afghanistan limits its options and influence in future
Superseded by the US	Difficult to predict – the Eurozone could potentially rise to take the US's place, but it is currently too disjointed
Loss of dominance of the media and inability to suppress anticolonial messages	Whistleblowing exposes US war crimes in various conflicts; rise of alternative news and fake news challenges dominant or self-serving narratives or myths

Conclusion

As this brief tour of history illustrates, the same causes of imperial collapse occur time and time again. A disintegration in the perceived legitimacy of the ruling structures and the rulers themselves often occurs, especially at times of succession when the legitimacy of that succession is under scrutiny. Differing factions competing for power and influence exacerbate this issue, often leading to revolution, civil war and ultimately the empire's collapse.

A weakening of collective identity can also have a serious impact. This is frequently caused by problems of assimilation that lead to a perceived diminishing of an "original" culture, or the damage is done by rulers moving away from previously shared values. Economic crises are often a key contributory factor to imperial collapse, with excessive taxation, inflation and inequality regularly increasing social tension and stoking popular anger and resentment. These economic crises are often caused by neglect and mismanagement by the ruling class, while military overexpansion and overspending regularly plays a key role. A failure to adapt to new technologies of warfare can have devastating and unforeseen consequences, as can individual military errors. Unpredictable factors such as disease and changes to environmental conditions can also wreak havoc on a seemingly stable and unassailable empire.

As we have seen, it is very rare that a single cause will be responsible for the fall of an empire, and most often a combination of factors will be responsible. These factors can be from within or without, damaging the legitimacy, social cohesion, military strength and overall power of an empire before it collapses or fades into obsolescence. It is only by recognizing these factors and identifying their modern parallels that the American Empire can address these issues and course-correct before it shares the same fate. In Part Two, beginning with an assessment of the social fabric, we will examine the internal domestic challenges and crises that endanger the continuation of the American Empire in its current form.

PART TWO

Internal Threats

3

Society: Decay from Within

Society could be described as a large group of people living together in an organized way, making decisions about how to do things and sharing the work that needs to be done. But does this description sound like an accurate representation of the US currently? Are people actually living together in an organized way, making decisions about how to do things? Is it not the case that people are at loggerheads, manipulated into partisan feuds based on nonsensical, reductionist, tribalist arguments? Are all members of society really sharing the work that needs to be done?

Staggering levels of inequality in the US would suggest not. This inequality is underpinned by the greed of America's oligarchical class, exemplified by government bailouts not being used to rebuild household finances or help struggling workers; instead, the money is used to fund share-buyback schemes and increase dividend distribution to shareholders. As the 1 per cent get richer, the remaining 99 per cent are getting poorer. Social security and the welfare state has become a tribal issue, and the problems associated with structural inequality are dismissed as being due to "laziness" and a refusal to work. Some blamed an apparent labour shortage on the coronavirus pandemic and its effect on the working motivations of the population, but the truth is more depressing: there is no shortage of workers, simply a shortage of jobs that pay living wages.

By almost every possible metric, the US is going backwards domestically and has become the only state in the G20 to have a declining life expectancy in many areas of the country. This chapter will examine the causes, effects and dangers of this societal decay, before the next chapter examines the role of politics in creating and maintaining these problems.

Life Expectancy

Life expectancy, the simplest of statistics when examining and assessing the wellbeing of a modern state and its citizens, is also the starkest measure of an empire in decline. Major wars aside, the average life expectancy of a citizen in a modern developed nation normally follows a rising trajectory. Healthcare improves, wages increase, and more people are lifted out of poverty and into a thriving middle class. They spend their money on products and services, they grow the economy, and they feel like they are *living*, not simply existing. In the US, however, this upward trend has hit the buffers and started to reverse, with life expectancy declining in many states.[1] The reasons for this are myriad, including Covid, suicide, homicide, obesity and the opioid epidemic.

This declining life expectancy falls most heavily on the poorest in the country, with a substantial and widening gap between those in the top 5 per cent and those in the bottom 5 per cent in terms of household income. By 2014 the differing life expectancy for members of these groups at age 40 was a staggering 10 years – 89.4 and 79.7 years respectively.[2] There is often a racial or ethnic dimension to this, with the non-white population impacted far more than their white counterparts.

The effect of Covid on life expectancy was significant: the largest decline since the Second World War was witnessed in 2020, and it was 8.5 times greater than the equivalent decline in similar peer countries.[3] The poorest are always hit the hardest by such plagues; they have less access to healthcare and are more likely to be working in conditions conducive to viral spread rather than safely working from home. Given the seductive societal myths embodied in such concepts as "American exceptionalism" and "bootstrap success", those who fall through the cracks in ever larger numbers are not sufficiently helped, but instead are written off as "not industrious enough" or "baskets of deplorables" by a sneering ruling class. This is intrinsically linked to a weaponization of the term "socialism". It is deliberately conflated with communism by those who do not wish for a more equitable society, and this pernicious effort endures because of the deeply rooted Cold War mentality within the national psyche. It is no surprise that generations who were born after the Cold War ended can see through this ruse and earnestly strive for a fairer, more equal society. This provides some comfort that change is possible, because if inequality continues to increase, the gap between rich and poor in life expectancy will continue to widen – and more citizens, especially non-white citizens, will be adversely affected.

Annual deaths from homicide, suicide, substance abuse and obesity add up to a sobering 450,000 Americans per year. This *annual figure* is half of the estimated 1 million deaths from Covid during the pandemic, another damning statistic that is world-leading in the worst sense.[4] This is to say nothing about the societal damage caused by every one of these deaths, as the lives ruined and trauma suffered does not simply end with the deceased. The ill effects spread through a society like ripples in a pond. With all these modern plagues attacking the American Empire from within, there may end up being little need for an external antagonist to strike; America's enemies can simply wait and watch. As with many empires before it, the greatest enemy of the American Empire is likely to be itself.

Homicide, Suicide and Firearm Ownership

The US is ranked 77th globally in the number of deaths by homicide, which may not sound too bad at all. The issue arises when we scan the countries above the US and notice the absence of any developed Western democracies. At 4.96 homicides per 100,000 people, the US rate is four times that of the UK or France, both at only 1.2 in 148th and 150th spot respectively.[5] There may be many reasons behind this fact, but it is no coincidence that neither the UK nor France allows their citizens easy access to firearms. It is far more likely that a disagreement, altercation or domestic argument will lead to a fatality in a country awash with firearms. While the argument is often made that it is not the gun but the person who wields it that is to blame, the person in question is far more deadly when they are armed with a pistol rather than a kitchen knife.

The US has the second highest number of gun-related deaths globally (some 37,000 in 2019), not that far behind Brazil (over 49,000), and firearms are the means used in around 75 per cent of all homicides.[6] If we factor in total population, the US falls just outside the 20 most violent countries, with 10.89 firearm-related deaths per 100,000 people, but this is nothing to celebrate. Most of western Europe has a rate below three deaths per 100,000 (the UK's is 0.24).[7] America's *annual* death toll from firearms is more than ten times the number of victims of the 9/11 terrorist attacks, and over five times the number of US servicepeople killed in Iraq and Afghanistan.[8] This is completely unsurprising in a nation that has the highest level of gun ownership in the world, and *more guns than people* – the rate of civilian ownership is around 120 guns per 100 people.[9]

Hidden deeper in the data is another bleak statistic: 60 per cent of deaths from firearms are suicides, and firearms are the method used for around half of all suicides nationally.[10] Just as widespread access to firearms increases the likelihood that they will be used fatally against other people, there is also a far higher chance that a suicide attempt involving a firearm, as opposed to another method, will result in death: around 85 per cent of such attempts do so, whereas less than 3 per cent of drug overdoses – the most widespread attempted method – are fatal.[11] It is this finality and grim efficiency that exacts such a devastating human toll; once the trigger is pulled, there is little chance of survival, assistance or change of heart.

Why is this state of affairs permitted to continue? The usual culprits of money and influence are involved, mixing with identity politics and a cultish adherence to individual freedom above all else. This creates a toxic situation in which even questioning the wisdom of the status quo is deemed "anti-American". We will examine the last two points in detail later, but now we can simply follow the money and note that over $12 million is spent annually in lobbying by the firearms industry, a figure more than five times the $2.3 million or so spent by those aiming to influence policy toward gun control.[12] If the statistics for homicides and suicides were not sufficiently bleak reading, there also exists a parallel epidemic ripping through all levels of American society – deaths caused not by bullets, but by pills or powders.

Substance Abuse and the Opioid Epidemic

The US has the most medicated citizenry on earth; it's estimated that 66 per cent of adults take prescription drugs regularly, compared with around 26 per cent in the UK. As this figure continues to rise, so does the number of people misusing prescription drugs – there has been an increase of 250 per cent over 20 years.[13] The epidemic of substance abuse has crept up on the American Empire and is now so widespread that it cannot be simply ignored as a crisis that affects only those on the margins of society. The relationship between physician and pharmaceutical company has regularly compromised the relationship between physician and patient, with none more culpable than Purdue Pharma and their opioid OxyContin. The company and the drug represent ground zero for the opioid epidemic, illustrating in microcosm the problems eating away at the core of the American Empire.

First, the numbers. Since 1999, almost 1 million people in the US have died from drug overdoses, and opioids are a factor in seven out of ten of overdose deaths.[14] In 2021, there were over 106,000 deaths from drug overdoses in the US, which was up from nearly 92,000 the previous year – and of these deaths, opioids were involved in around

80,000, with fentanyl being the primary weapon of choice. Stimulants such as cocaine, one of the biggest targets in the traditional "war on drugs", were involved in the death of around 32,000 people in 2021. Fewer than 5,000 people died from a heroin overdose without other opioids present.[15]

How does Purdue fit into this? Between 1996 (when OxyContin first came on the market) and 2002 the company spent hundreds of millions of dollars to promote and distribute the drug, utilizing every single area of the supply and distribution chain to devastating effect. Doctors were wined and dined and bombarded with promotional material, using dubious claims to downplay the addictive nature of Purdue's "miracle drug". At best, this led to honest doctors and pharmacists being unwitting accomplices; at worst, it created cottage industries of "pill mills" – illicit operations whereby medical professionals sold millions of tablets to those their oaths had sworn them to protect.[16]

Purdue not only looked the other way; they actively sought to increase the quantities sold. Seventy-five per cent of their total advertising spend in this period was after the year 2000, the year that Purdue told Congress they first became aware of the growing number of cases of OxyContin abuse and resultant deaths. During this time, they pulled every available lever within the medical industry to ensure sales of $2.8 billion by the middle of 2001.

Where Purdue led, others followed, as their competitors were also named as defendants in the subsequent 1,500-plus lawsuits. By the time the fraud was discovered and prosecuted, the damage was done and millions of victims had now become addicts. These victims, now unable to access opioids via prescription, had little choice but to turn to more dangerous replacements. Fentanyl and similar substances, dispensed not by doctors but by dealers, criminalized Purdue's victims in the thousands. For their part, Purdue was fined $600 million in 2007, a figure that may seem large but that represents less than 25 per cent of their revenue from four years of OxyContin sales alone.

Surely the executives responsible for this fraud are in jail? Not so –
fines of $34 million and zero jail time were deemed sufficient in 2007
for knowingly contributing to an opioid crisis that federal officials
calculate to have cost $500 billion in 2015 alone.[17] In 2019, Purdue
finally was forced to file for bankruptcy, and its owners, the Sackler
family, reached a settlement in 2022 that will force them to pay billions
towards claims by states, hospitals and individuals.

Without further examination, this may seem like justice served.
However, this is not how things are done in the oligarchy of the
American Empire. The Sackler family, after all, is a generous benefactor,
funding all manner of institutions – their collective wealth was estimated at around $11 billion in 2021.[18] Richard Sackler, who was
president and chairman of Purdue before its collapse, is also not behind
bars. Moreover, he and his family are safe in the knowledge that the
settlement all but guarantees there will be no further repercussions or
public disclosures of their role in the OxyContin affair. It ensures them
protection from any further lawsuits resulting from the opioid epidemic,
and it assures them that the family itself is largely absolved of responsibility.[19] There is still hope for a reckoning, as the settlement was
overturned in December 2021 by a federal judge, but in 2022 an
improved offer was agreed – on the basis of future immunity.[20]
Whatever the final outcome, a society that allows one family to cause
so much damage, and still emerge with billions of dollars, is not a
society that is functioning correctly.

Food Insecurity and Nutrition

The American Empire has prospered through its cultivation of the
American Dream, a powerful creation myth that endows every
citizen with an inalienable right to pursue happiness and all the
trappings that this brings. Coupled to a model of unchained capitalism that requires ever-increasing levels of consumption to
maintain corporate profits, at the expense of consumer protection,

the American Dream has become a nightmare for many. Lobbying groups for "Big Food" (unhealthy food and beverage companies) ensure compliance from elected officials through campaign donations to the value of tens of millions of dollars per year, critical to their continued relevance and electoral success.[21] The methods used by the industry to ensure their influence do not simply involve co-opting legislators, as they also:

- Finance shadow advocacy groups and industry-friendly scientists to sow confusion and hide negative data, in much the same manner as Big Tobacco years ago.
- Litigate against attempts to regulate the food industry, under the guise of "free speech".
- Block litigation efforts against the industry.
- Use the guise of "self-regulation" to avoid external independent oversight.[22]

As one expert described, "They lobby about anything that's going to affect their business, no matter how remote ... I can't think of a single area of food or nutrition policy that isn't subjected to lobbying."[23]

American citizens are bombarded from cradle to grave with advertisements that have one goal: consumption. Portion sizes are often grossly excessive and unhealthy. Obesity and the resultant type 2 diabetes can be viewed in the same way as another disease caused by overconsumption. Unlike gout, though, obesity is not simply "the disease of kings", as mass-marketed unhealthy food and drink are available to all and they are priced so cheaply that, for many working families short of time and money, this is the simplest and most obvious option. It all leads to an estimated 280,000 deaths per year and shows no signs of abating.[24]

Even school lunches are not immune, as private companies with a single-minded focus on profit are allowed to control the nutritional intake of the nation's younger generation. This early adoption of unhealthy eating and drinking habits has led to record levels of diabetes, with around 10 per cent of the adult population suffering from the disease – the most in the developed world. In sheer numbers, the US has almost 30 million cases, which is around two thirds of the 46 million cases seen elsewhere in the developed world.[25] This is unsurprising with a population where more than 40 per cent of all adults are clinically obese, a figure that has increased by over 25 per cent since 2008.[26] The number one cause of death in the American Empire is heart disease, and the main causes of this are intrinsically linked to the unhealthy diets and lifestyles emblematic of overconsumption.[27]

This is one end of the spectrum, while on the other end an estimated 34 million people, 9 million of whom are children, are worrying where their next meal will come from and are deemed by the US Department of Agriculture (USDA) to be food-insecure.[28] Once again, non-white members of the citizenry are more likely to be adversely affected. Moderate or severe food insecurity affects 8.2 per cent of the US population, which does not compare favourably with most of its western European peers (for example, the figure for both the UK and Germany is 3.5 per cent).[29]

For a country whose average income per year is the seventh highest in the world, and the highest among any country with over 10 million citizens, America's level of food insecurity reflects a growing gap between rich and poor.[30] The most basic needs that a state must satisfy are those for food, shelter and security. America's astronomical spending on servicing the latter need – supported by both major political parties – has been a direct factor in the dire state of the other two. As we have seen, this would not be the first empire to crumble due to food shortages and the unrest that typically follows. The national baby-formula shortage of 2022 serves as a powerful, highly emotive warning sign of what could go wrong and how next time could be much worse.[31] As if this situation wasn't critical enough, the restrictions of a healthcare system driven by the goal of shareholder profit, rather than patient welfare, only exacerbate the problem.

Healthcare

Unlike most modern industrialized states, the US operates a for-profit system of healthcare, and the dual oligopolies of insurance and drug companies work through the elected puppets they have funded to ensure the status quo endures. This state of affairs makes for grim reading. American citizens pay more per person toward healthcare than any other developed nation, and more than double the OECD average. This would not be an issue if the healthcare provided was world-beating and available to all, but in every measurable metric the US is found wanting.[32]

The US has a low number of hospital beds per person, with only 2.8 per 1,000 people – a fact brutally exposed during the Covid-19 pandemic. This figure is in stark contrast to those for Germany (7.8), Korea (12.7) and Japan (12.6).[33] Access to medicine is also more difficult for US citizens due to the staggering costs, a direct result of the toxic influence of the pharmaceutical industry. Belief in the "free market" means that the pharmaceutical oligopoly is able to set their own prices, with no centralized body able to negotiate preferable terms for the American people. The resulting prices are typically more than double those in other OECD countries.

In addition to this, attempts to replicate expensive treatments with generic alternatives are strangled by litigation to maintain this oligopoly. A lack of transparency in the industry and mass direct-to-consumer marketing further exacerbate the problem.[34] There are stark examples of terrible price comparisons: a 10 ml bottle of life-saving insulin might cost around $20 in Canada but more than 20 times that in the US. These kinds of disparity mean that many people have to illegally import prescription drugs from other developed countries, criminalizing them through their actions, and also exposing them to the dangers of buying through unofficial channels. In popular culture, the circumstances of this tragic farce are depicted perfectly by Matthew

McConaughey and Jared Leto in the 2013 film *Dallas Buyers Club*. The cost discrepancy of a selection of the most expensive drugs in the US compared to the equivalent price agreed and negotiated by the NHS via their price regulator (NICE) illustrates this point clearly.[35]

The differences in cost are truly breathtaking and all the more damning when we consider that for some people this provides no alternative but illegal importation. If this route is not chosen, they can either choose financial ruin, by paying what is charged in the US, or they can die. The pharmaceutical industry, or "Big Pharma", would have us believe that these prices are justified based on free-market arguments of supply and demand. This simply cannot be legitimate when the demand is generated by a person's decision to live or die. The drug companies also stress both the value of maintaining the integrity of intellectual property and the associated costs of research into new treatments which may never become profitable. There is logic in these arguments, but the question of fairness becomes unavoidable when we look behind the curtain at the extravagant levels of CEO remuneration in the industry.[36]

It is not just CEOs who enjoy these grotesque profits: the potential for shareholder returns ensures the status quo continues. In 2018, the average dividend yields in Big Pharma were 2.4 per cent per annum, coupled with a strong potential for growth in share price.[37]

The Covid pandemic, although dampening returns initially, has proven incredibly lucrative for many of the biggest names in Big Pharma due to the immense profits generated from Covid vaccines. AstraZeneca, a British firm, is seemingly less beholden to lobbying efforts and is therefore able to prioritize public health, with the associated bonus of enhanced reputational standing compared to the vaccine manufacturers in the US. AstraZeneca rightly earned praise for agreeing to sell their vaccine at cost price, but they have since confirmed the end of this practice and a plan to "transition to modest profitability" as the virus becomes endemic.[38] Both Moderna and Pfizer in the US, and

BioNtech in Germany, decided that although public health was important, there was also money to be made. The three firms charged an
estimated $41 billion for their vaccines above the cost to develop and
manufacture them, with Moderna and BioNtech reaching profit
margins of 69 per cent.[39] The shareholders were clearly pleased, as
Moderna's board agreed a golden parachute deal for their CEO,
Stéphane Bancel, to the value of almost $1 billion.[40]

Due to the unprecedented nature of the threat and the danger to global
public health, the three firms also benefited from over $100 billion in
public funding to assist in the development of a vaccine. Moderna
and Pfizer also benefited from the intricacies of the US taxation system,
paying very little in taxes on these profits, with only 7 per cent and
15 per cent paid respectively, well below the statutory level of 21 per
cent. Accusations of "war profiteering" have been levelled and seem
entirely justified.[41] As Oxfam America's private-sector engagement
manager Robbie Silverman succinctly stated in 2021:

> Big Pharma's business model – receive billions in public invest-
> ments, charge exorbitant prices for life-saving medicines, pay little
> tax – is gold dust for wealthy investors and corporate executives but
> devastating for global public health ... Instead of partnering with
> governments and other qualified manufacturers to make sure that
> we have enough vaccine doses for everyone, these pharmaceutical
> companies prioritize their own profits by enforcing their monopolies
> and selling to the highest bidder. Enough is enough – we must start
> putting people before profits.[42]

The problem for Mr Silverman, and the rest of the world, is that
people will never be put before profits while the system continues to
operate in the interests of the powerful. Politicians will continue to
take campaign donations to ensure re-election. Shareholders will
continue to profit and ensure that the status quo endures, because it
makes them money. These shareholders include dozens of members of
the US Congress who continued trading in Covid-related stocks

throughout the pandemic.[43] This is all perfectly legal, so why would they not?

Average American citizens are also making similar investments; the US economy rests on such behaviour and this is where things become more complex. Pension funds, and the institutional investors acting on their behalf, are mandated to generate the best possible returns for their members – US seniors and future pension recipients – and Big Pharma is a vital part of this strategy. One estimate from Slavek Roller puts the contribution of public investment into biomedical research and development at over 30 per cent. We might well ask what happens when members of pension funds are essentially captive beneficiaries of these programs, and also shareholders. As Roller puts it:

Adding investments by governmentally-mandated retirement schemes, central and promotional banks, and sovereign wealth funds to tax-derived governmental financing shows that the majority of biomedical R&D funding is public in origin. Despite this, even in the high-income countries patients can be denied access to effective treatments due to their high cost. Since these costs are set by the drug development firms that are owned in substantial part by the retirement accounts of said patients, the complex financial architecture of biomedical R&D may be inconsistent with the objectives of the ultimate beneficiaries.[44]

If Big Pharma is chiefly responsible for many of the problems within the US medical sector, Big Healthcare comes a close second. Too many in the US do not approve of healthcare as a fundamental human right, decrying European countries who provide this to their citizens as "socialists". The very principle is anathema to the American myth of rugged individualism above all else. Instead of state-run and state-provided healthcare, the US has once again allowed the "free market" and private enterprise to create a system that prioritizes profit over patients, leaving many citizens without any access to medical treatment. Americans have the worst of both worlds, as they receive less care and have worse health outcomes than their peers in comparable OECD countries, yet spending per citizen in the US ($10,637 in 2018) is roughly double the average amount spent in peer nations ($5,527 per person).[45] Why is this, and where is the money going?

We have already analysed the impact of pharmaceutical costs, but there are other factors that produce this depressing state of affairs. Inpatient and outpatient care represents the biggest category of health spending in both the US and comparable countries, but Americans spend far more in this category – it accounts for 76 per cent of the difference between the US and its peers. These costs include payments to hospitals, clinics and physicians for services and fees such as primary care or specialist visits, surgical care, and facility and professional fees. These costs are on average $3,906 more than in their OECD counterparts ($2,718), with US citizens averaging $6,624 per person in this area. This is despite US hospital stays being shorter on average, and the number of visits fewer, than in OECD counterparts.[46]

Another category, healthcare administration, is responsible for 14 per cent of the discrepancy in per-citizen spending, costing Americans far more at $937 per person compared to only $201 in comparable countries. Where is this additional $736 going? Forty-seven per cent of these administrative costs are due to government programs like Medicaid and Medicare, but the remaining 53 per cent are costs levied by private healthcare companies. Long-term care costs are the only metric where US citizens pay less than their counterparts, but this saving is nowhere near sufficient to affect the overall difference.[47]

Once again, by following the money we can see the reasons behind these discrepancies in costs. If we begin with the CEOs of healthcare providers, we see a familiar picture. As with their counterparts in Big Pharma, the pandemic was kind to those at the top of Big Healthcare. The median compensation for 178 CEOs in healthcare provision in 2020 was over $9 million, up from 2018 and 2019 figures, with 30 making more than $30 million each. The highest earner, Joe Kiani of medical device firm Masimo, made a staggering $210 million in a single year, with the Masimo stock price jumping by almost 70 per cent after a 22 per cent increase in sales. These increased sales were due to the "unprecedented demand" for monitoring devices to treat Covid-19 patients. Two further executives received over $100 million in compensation for 2020, including Leonard Schleifer of Regeneron Pharmaceuticals, a company that manufactures a treatment for Covid-19.[48] Is it a hallmark of a well-run system, intended for the benefit of all, that the total CEO compensation in 2019, even though less than 2020, was four times greater than the total available to the Centers for Disease Control and Prevention to study and prepare for all "emerging and zoonotic infectious diseases" in the year before the pandemic arrived?[49] Compare these figures to the £300,000 earnings of their equivalents in the UK – although it does not have a perfect system by any stretch – and ask which model is more equitable.[50]

What is the upshot of these huge profits and the staggering executive compensation in Big Healthcare? Soaring individual premiums. Annual increases of up to 30 per cent are commonplace, and this has a direct and indirect impact on widening inequality. First, let's consider the direct. As costs soar, so must the requisite insurance premiums, forcing many Americans into a situation where they simply cannot afford to insure themselves. In 2021, an estimated 27.5 million non-elderly people in the US were uninsured.[51] Now the indirect: for the 156 million or so Americans whose employer provides their healthcare insurance, the situation is also precarious for two reasons.[52] Firstly, especially in smaller businesses, higher premiums result in squeezed profit margins, and this leads to reductions in salaries and bonuses at a non-executive level.[53] Secondly, US employees are subject to among the loosest employment protections in any developed country, allowing employers to fire people far more easily, and thereby remove their access to healthcare. This constant job insecurity is all the more potent when your continued access to healthcare is also at threat. Employment is treated at a federal level as "at will" and can be terminated at any time for a lawful reason, and there is no federal or state provision that dictates that notice must be given. Compare this with the UK; for over forty years, workers have benefited from statutory minimum levels of notice (one week per year of employment, up to a maximum of 12 years' service) and more recently guaranteed redundancy payments and statutory protections against unfair dismissal.[54] Lest we forget, unlike their American counterparts, UK workers also have free access to the NHS, so their ability to access healthcare is not dependent on the security of their jobs.

We have examined the huge disparities between medical costs in the US compared with other developed countries, but there is a further comparison to be made and that is within the US itself – between costs levied to insurance-funded healthcare and those costs paid for by the state through Medicare. It is estimated that while the Medicare program pays around 1.5 times as much as the OECD equivalent, privately funded healthcare (individual or group) costs around 4.5 times as much.[55] There are different reasons for this disparity, and once again the free market of unchained capitalism seems to be the main issue.

Like the NHS in the UK, the Medicare program has the ability to set prices collectively on what it will pay based on hospital costs, whereas private companies have to negotiate on an individual basis with hospitals and doctors. Lack of competition caused by geographical healthcare monopolies also exacerbates the problem, as insurance companies have no alternative but to accept the terms offered as they have to offer access for their policy holders. This is if the insurance companies even deem it in their interest to strive for the lowest costs possible; as is especially the case with many larger company plans, insurance companies earn a percentage of the total bill, and it is therefore in their interests for the prices to be as high as possible.[56]

The impact of the so-called free market does not stop there: without centrally agreed remuneration levels for healthcare professionals, specialists are paid an average of $316,000 per annum, more than twice as much as their counterparts in comparable countries.[57] Hospital oligopolies also add further costs by levying administration fees and moving testing procedures from outside the hospital to inside, while also inserting anti-competition provisions into their contracts. By the time these practices are declared illegal, the guilty party has often already become an indispensable member of the Big Healthcare oligopoly.[58] This is not to say that the alternative is without flaws, but applying free-market principles to talented healthcare specialists seems to be misguided, considering the end goal of patient welfare and a healthy citizenry. We might ask again how a system so riddled with flaws, disparities and conflicts of interest is permitted to continue. The answer has to do with the same factors that maintain the status quo of Big Pharma: the vast sums spent on lobbying by Big Healthcare ensure compliance.

Between 1999 and 2018, Big Pharma and the medical products industry spent $4.7 billion, at an average of $233 million per year, on lobbying the US federal government, including $414 million on contributions to presidential and congressional electoral candidates, national party committees, and outside spending groups; they also spent $877 million on contributions to state candidates and committees.[59] To put these figures in perspective, five of the largest eight lobbying sectors over the period were healthcare-related. Big Pharma and the medical products industry lead the way with a total of 7.3 per cent of all lobbying spend, equating to $4.7 billion. The insurance industry is a close second with 5 per cent of total spend, equating to $3.2 billion. Within this lobby, the top spenders are healthcare insurance providers, with Blue Cross, Blue Shield, AHIP, Cigna Group and Aflac representing four of the five highest-spending groups annually.[60]

Within the other areas of Big Healthcare, lobbying by hospitals and nursing homes equated to $1.9 billion, healthcare professionals $1.7 billion, health services and health maintenance organizations $1.3 billion, and miscellaneous health organizations were responsible for an additional $139 million. As the health policy expert Oliver Wouters illustrates, these dollars are directed precisely at the lawmakers who are supposed to be responsible for maintaining the integrity of the US medical system: "Of the 20 senators and 20 representatives who received the most contributions, 39 belonged to committees with jurisdiction over health-related legislative matters, 24 of them in senior positions."[61]

As with every other aspect of the American oligarchy, these contributions are not directed to one party in particular. The Democrats and the Republicans each receive tens of millions of dollars every year.[62] Contributions to individual politicians and their campaigns often top $1 million per year, with 18 of the top 20 recipients receiving more than this from the industry in 2022. Of this top 20, 13 were Democrats and seven Republicans.[63]

Finally, as we saw with stock ownership in Big Pharma, we can also follow the money when it comes to Big Healthcare. While it remains illegal for members of Congress to knowingly conduct insider trading, it is perfectly legal for them to hold shares and therefore have a financial interest in Big Healthcare. In 2013, over $64 million was held by members of Congress in healthcare-related stocks, with a median average holding of $65,000 in 2014.[64] Covered within this total holding are all areas of Big Healthcare that we have discussed.

While there is no major difference in the level of holdings between those members of Congress who have influence on committees and subcommittees and those who do not, the fact that those with such influence are permitted to benefit financially from the success of healthcare firms is a recipe for conflict of interest at best, corruption at worst. To establish again why the status quo endures, we can look not only to lobbying, campaign contributions and congressional stock ownership, but also to the huge positions held by pension funds (the largest pooled public investment groups in the US). As with Big Pharma, US healthcare stocks are consistent top performers and represent a major industry holding within pension portfolios. One such firm,

United Healthcare Group Incorporated, has seen five-year total returns of 224 per cent up to 2022, far in excess of the S&P index, which returned 84 per cent in the same period.[65]

To not hold these stocks would be seen as dereliction of duty by the pension-fund managers who must strive for performance for their policy holders at all costs. The extent to which this ensures that the status quo endures can be seen by the investigation into pension-fund holdings in Blackstone and KRR, two private equity firms accused of direct responsibility for driving up healthcare costs in 2019. The pension funds in question, among the largest in North America, refused to comment on this conflict of interest, while Jack Hoadley, a health policy analyst at Georgetown University, commented at the time: "State legislatures are making decisions on protecting consumers from surprise medical bills. Yet certain state pension funds invest in firms employing doctors who benefit from surprise bills."[66]

This tangled web of money, politics and influence is responsible for the dire state of the healthcare system in the American Empire. But with so many invested stakeholders – ranging from powerful elites to powerless citizens – there are few signs of reform on the horizon.

Infant Mortality

Infant mortality, another useful gauge of societal health (or sickness), is also higher in the US than in most other developed countries, with the US recording similar levels to Serbia and Malaysia.[67] A staggering 50 per cent of pregnancies are unplanned in the US, and some of these involve women who do not realize they are pregnant in time to receive proper prenatal care, resulting in more premature births and postnatal difficulties. The cultural, religious and societal issues surrounding abortion further exacerbate the problem; women become less likely, or even unable, to receive assistance with their unplanned pregnancies, thus carrying more babies to term.

For the most part, the number of children dying in the US before one month of age is at a similar level to other developed countries, but it is after this point that socio-economic factors influence the figures and the gap widens. Unsurprisingly, children of wealthier and better-educated Americans have a similar chance of survival as their equivalents in developed European countries. It is within the less educated and less wealthy populations, however, that the figures change, with children born in these circumstances having less chance of survival than those born into similarly disadvantaged groups in equivalent developed European nations.

A large cause of these deaths is sudden infant death syndrome (SIDS), which is more prevalent among ethnic minorities. This is unsurprising as ethnic minorities are more likely to fall within the less educated and less wealthy sections of society than their white counterparts. Many of the factors that are believed to contribute to the incidence of SIDS can be linked to economic constraints endured by less wealthy families, such as the need for bed sharing and the inability to access costly home nurse visits.

Another major factor is the absence in the US of any paid maternity and paternity leave, a unique position within OECD countries. Sixty per cent of employed mothers are able to take 12 weeks of unpaid maternity leave, but for the remaining 40 per cent who are ineligible and for many of the 60 per cent for whom it is not a realistic economic proposition, this is not possible. In the UK, by comparison, mothers are given a mandatory two weeks of paid maternity leave, with a possible total of 52 weeks (six of which are on 90 per cent of full pay, the following 33 are also on 90 per cent or a maximum of £172.48 per week (whichever is lower), and the remaining 13 are unpaid).[68] In other European nations the gap is even wider, with Swedish mothers receiving ten weeks of fully paid leave and 480 days of shared parental leave after this point. In Estonia, mothers can take fully paid leave for the first 18 months of their child's life.[69] If mothers cannot afford home visits from nurses and are afforded no time away from work to help with the first important stages of their child's life, it is no wonder that the US figures for child mortality after one month are higher than their OECD peers. For many Americans whose wealth ensures they will not suffer these hardships, abortion rights are a bête noire to be attacked and rolled back at all costs for cultural, religious or opportunistic political reasons. The second a baby is born, however, their pro-life support comes to an end.

The notion that all children are born equal, with the same chance of success, is a fallacy. Too many infants are born with the odds stacked against them. Addressing and exposing this injustice is no simple task, as it is deeply rooted in and perpetuated by the toxic lie that individual agency is responsible for all success. This uniquely American mantra is hard-wired into the national psyche: "I never had any help growing up and I did just fine – people just don't want to work hard enough." Admitting that a privileged position at birth provides an advantage does not have to be viewed as a denial of the hard work that followed; it is simply a recognition that not all are born with the same opportunity for success.

All in all, these issues surrounding pregnancy, birth and infancy in the US are highly significant in the present day, and they have the potential to contribute to the decline of the American Empire in the decades to come. Children are the future of the nation, and if parents cannot care for their children in their formative years, these future American adults will have an impeded start to life. This will hinder their chances for educational and professional success in the long term. In neglecting its youngest and most vulnerable members in the here and now, the US may be sowing the seeds of its own demise.

Literacy and Education

The American Empire is suffering from a decline in the simplest of requirements for a modern society: the ability to read. While Ivy League universities continue to provide an educated elite with the tools needed to succeed, this represents less than 1 per cent of the population. Declining educational standards are the primary culprit for this deterioration in literacy across the US; rather than addressing the root causes, there is a partisan focus on the banning of certain books, rather than the encouragement of reading in general. As standards decline in schools, many parents are unable to pick up the slack at home as a lack of jobs paying a living wage requires both parents to work long hours, often in multiple jobs, simply to put food on the table and a roof over their heads.

The decline in child literacy leads to a decline in adult literacy, resulting in further problems for individuals and society as a whole. A decline in educational standards coupled with a scarcity of skilled jobs leads to unemployment and all the negative consequences that follow from it. The overall result is a population that is losing its ability to digest information, and to separate fact from fiction. Let us examine the data to identify the key issues and explore ways to improve the situation.

To produce an educated workforce, high standards of education are required from the earliest years through to university. Unfortunately, instead of leading the world in educational attainment, US schoolchildren are no better than average. Figures from 2015 (the latest available at the time of writing) show that US high-school students aged 15 ranked 38th out of 71 countries in mathematics, and 24th in science. When compared solely with their 34 OECD peers, the US ranked 30th in mathematics and 19th in science.[70]

Younger American students fare better but are still not what could be described as world-beating, placing 11th out of 48 in mathematics, and 8th out of 48 in science for 9--10-year-old children; the picture is similar for those aged 13–14. Figures for children in both these age groups in 2015 also showed the first decline in mathematics proficiency since 1990.[71]

Why is it that the global superpower is falling so far behind in this area? Many of the reasons stem from a single truth: chronic under-funding. For many schools, funding levels are lower than before 2008 and the financial crisis, leading to overcrowding, fewer programs, fewer teachers, and ultimately more school closures. Declining salaries for teachers also reduce the attractiveness of the profession and the quality of applicants. American poverty, as mentioned previously, requires many parents to work multiple jobs and reduces the time available to assist with learning in the home.[72] Marc Tucker, an education expert, believes that while there is nothing inherently preventing the American education system from mirroring those of the top-performing countries, short-termism caused by swings from Republican to Democrat and vice versa, is preventing a coherent, apolitical, long-term strategy from coalescing. Systems that complement each other at every level of education are required, and progress is not achieved overnight – more likely over one or two decades. Tucker believes that efforts by the Biden administration will provide the funds and time for such systems to be developed.[73] Is this likely to be exposed as wishful thinking, or naivety, if a Republican-controlled Congress and White House are both a reality by January 2025?

There has also been an explosion in the number of children who are home-schooled, estimated at more than eight million in 2021.[74] While home-schooling is not inherently detrimental, it clearly has to be done correctly to ensure a wide breadth of knowledge and skills are passed to the next generation. In certain countries, such as Germany, the risk of "closed-off parallel societies" is deemed too high and the practice of home-schooling is illegal.[75] In the UK, where home-schooling is allowed, far fewer children are educated in this way; a rise of 34 per cent in 2020–21 due to the Covid pandemic still only resulted in a total of some 115,000 home-schooled children.[76] It is difficult to identify whether the huge numbers of home-schooled children in the US are due to the comparatively poor levels of education on offer from the public system, or to efforts by parents to control what their children do and do not learn. Either way, the results of this phenomenon will be difficult to discern for a number of years, by which point, for many children who do not receive a well-rounded education, it may be too late. As with so many issues within the American Empire, admitting there is a problem is the first step to overcoming it; but for a nation built upon the myth of American exceptionalism, attempts to encourage honest self-examination are too often met with indignation and ignorance.

Undereducated children tend to become undereducated adults, and while 12 per cent of US adults achieve literacy scores at the highest levels (i.e. 4 or 5 on a scale of 1–5), which is about average for the OECD, the proportion of US adults who possess poor levels of literacy is far higher than the OECD average. One in six adults does not possess level 2 literacy skills, compared to one in twenty for Japan. For numeracy the same is true, as only 8 per cent of US adults (compared with the OECD average of 13 per cent) score the highest levels of 4 and 5, and nearly one in three scores below level 2.[77]

The US does have the fifth highest number of people who have attained higher education, and this figure is above the OECD average.[78] However, other nations are closing the gap, and only 30 per cent of Americans are now achieving a higher level of education than their parents. This figure indicates a decline in the trajectory of upward mobility and, if it continues in this manner, it is likely to lead to societal stagnation and decline.

One of the major factors in limiting or slowing access to the upper levels of education is the extortionate cost of tertiary education in the US – an individual student's debt can run into hundreds of thousands of dollars. The average cost for an undergraduate education in the US is over $100,000, including forgone earnings – twice the OECD average. Within this figure the direct costs (like tuition fees) are by far the highest within the OECD, at $61,000, over five times as much as the OECD average of $11,000.[79] This issue has been recognized by a small number of US policymakers, with Bernie Sanders campaigning for an end to student debt and cancellation of all outstanding debt.[80] Unfortunately, at a cost of over a trillion dollars, this seems unlikely to be achieved any time soon, and President Biden's plans to offer some modest debt relief have encountered difficulties in the courts. There are also many vested interests to contend with, as profit is derived not only for the federal government, but also for investors and their advisers, via the trading of packaged student debt in the form of asset-backed securities.[81] This practice of hamstringing the nation's future adult population for the benefit of the current adult population is short-sighted and emblematic of the troubling issues at the heart of the American Empire.

Climate Change, Renewable Energy and Energy Security

One metric used by the UN as a measure of progress is the extent to which a nation is transitioning away from fossil fuels, which are destructive to the environment, and toward renewable energy sources. The reason for this is simple: this transition is required to avoid an existential threat to human life on planet earth. One instructive measure is the percentage of primary energy which a nation creates using renewable sources, and in this regard the US (around 10 per cent) lags behind both the rest of the world (over 13 per cent) and the OECD (over 15 per cent).[82]

More worrying than the above statistics is the fact that this matter, like many issues within the American Empire, is perverted by partisan politics, special interests, money and misinformation. We should also consider the extent to which established, verifiable climate science is accepted by the American people. According to a wide-ranging analysis by the Pew Research Center, belief in the extent to which human activity is responsible for climate change is split down predictably partisan lines. Eighty-four per cent of liberal Democrats surveyed believe human activity "contributes a great deal to climate change", with 96 per cent agreeing that human activity "contributes at least

91

some amount to climate change". This compares to only 14 per cent of conservative Republicans who agree that human activity contributes "a great deal" to climate change, though 53 per cent believe it plays at least some role. Most strikingly, 45 per cent say humans play "not too much" or no role at all in climate change.[83] Herein lies the issue: in most developed countries the science has been accepted and progress can be made on an apolitical, bipartisan basis, but not in the American Empire. We will examine the reasons behind this shortly, and they will not be surprising.

Published annually since 2005, the Climate Change Performance Index (CCPI) is another excellent resource on this topic, characterized by the team behind it as "an independent monitoring tool for tracking countries' climate protection performance. It increases transparency in national and international climate policy and enables comparison of individual countries' climate protection efforts and progress."[84] The US is ranked in 52nd place globally,[85] up from 61st in 2021 but still far behind most developed countries.

The CCPI's report on the US gives the nation a very low (i.e. very bad) rating on its greenhouse gas emissions. Its climate policy under Joe Biden has been rated "medium".[86] Republican opposition in Congress has been a significant obstacle to progress, but the Biden administration was also unable to pass significant climate-related legislation, the Build Back Better Act, due in large part to the intransigence of Joe Manchin, a senator from coal-reliant West Virginia. His opposition, while couched in terms of protecting local jobs, may have something to do with his ties to the coal industry. Once again, following the money leads us right back to the American oligarchy.

The influence of the US fossil fuels lobby is staggering: the oil and gas industry spends more than $120 million per year to control, delay or block policy dedicated to combating climate change.[87] In the same manner as Big Pharma and Big Healthcare, the Big Oil lobby has ensured compliance from tame politicians through generous campaign funding. This is best illustrated by examining the reaction to the Biden administration's decision to try to tame climate change by pausing new oil and gas leases in 2021, which was quickly denounced by 29 lawmakers. The reason for this? They had received contributions totalling $13.4 million from oil and gas interests and $23.6 million from energy and natural resources interests.[88] These lawmakers routinely regurgitate industry-commissioned research and label any legislative efforts in this area as leftist or economic suicide, with no mention of their ties to the industry.

Senator Joe Manchin is a case in point. Manchin wielded an unusual level of power within the Democratic Party and Congress during Biden's first two years in office, due to the 50-50 split in the Senate. For Democratic bills to proceed, all Democrat votes are required, allowing Manchin to delay, torpedo or gut legislation. Unfortunately for those aiming to tame global warming, Manchin's priorities seem to be strongly shaped by his deep financial ties to fossil fuels. For example, as governor of West Virginia in 2009, Manchin supported a bill that would reclassify coal waste, a highly polluting form of energy, as "renewable" and therefore able to be used in meeting clean energy targets. If we seek an explanation for such behaviour, we might note that Manchin's family-owned business, Enersystems, was perfectly positioned to take advantage of the change and profit handsomely from the sale of this coal waste. There can be no conflict of interest, of course, as it is Manchin's son, Joe Manchin IV, not Manchin himself, who runs the family business, which is held in a blind trust (a completely legal arrangement).[89] Does anyone really believe that a man who has received over $5 million in under ten years, and annual dividends of around $500,000 from his coal company, can be remotely impartial? These financial rewards represent around 70 per cent of his total dividend income and 30 per cent of his net wealth.[90]

Manchin is not alone in this regard, and the tendrils of influence are cultivated via the usual suspects of stock ownership, executive positions and nepotistic appointments within the industry for the progeny of lawmakers. A 2021 analysis showed that at least 100 lawmakers have financial interests in the fossil fuel industry, with a slight majority of Republicans over Democrats. Broadly speaking, though, this is a bipartisan problem. The largest holdings belonged to Republican lawmakers, a great number of whom also happened to sit on committees that decide upon legislation to regulate the industry.[91] The primary problem with this perverse situation is that no rules are being broken and these activities are deemed to be legal. Ethics seem nowhere to be found.

It is not simply in Congress that these efforts to stymie progress are being made; there are also problems within the judicial branch of government. The conservative majority on the Supreme Court has resulted in rulings in 2022 and 2023 that limit the ability of the Environmental Protection Agency to regulate power-plant emissions and protect wetlands.[92] As we shall examine later, the conservative majority on the Supreme Court, a purportedly apolitical arm of government, is producing many other controversial rulings that not only go against the will of the majority of the American people, but risk damaging the cohesion of the nation itself.

While the speed of transition to renewable energy, and the acceptance of climate science as fact, is undoubtedly a valuable metric – as it is vital for the long-term survival of the US and the planet – we must also consider short-term domestic energy security. The ability to provide for one's own energy requirements is of paramount importance, as shown clearly by the weaponizing of energy supply by Russia in the aftermath of the Ukraine invasion in 2022. Nations that had not fully considered this fact, such as Germany, are quickly realizing why it is of such geopolitical significance and vital for their continued security and prosperity. In this regard, recent focus on shale gas extraction as well as Trump administration policies led to the US becoming not only the master of its own energy destiny for the first time but also a net energy exporter in 2020.[93]

The US is certainly taking concrete steps to ensure energy security, and it will not find itself in a similar position to many European countries that have struggled to extricate themselves from their dependence on Russian oil and gas. This energy independence will help to prop up the American Empire for a while longer but, if efforts are not made to tackle climate change and the conflicts of interest inherent within American policymaking at every level, the empire may not be habitable for all of its citizens before too long.

Infrastructure

An empire of any size, let alone one that spans an entire continent, requires constant investment and improvements to its basic infrastructure. The Romans built and maintained vast road networks to allow for the flow of goods and soldiers, and the British did the same using canals and railways. Alexander the Great created outposts that grew into cities to secure power over his dominion, a tactic followed by the Romans with their imperial outposts and the British with their colonial garrison towns. As noted in chapter 1, the American Empire has copied this blueprint, maintaining a vast global network of military bases which, combined with its fleet of aircraft carriers, allow it to project power worldwide.

While this global military infrastructure is without equal, what of the domestic infrastructure required to ensure stability and prosperity on the home front? As with the Romans, are the vast sums spent maintaining a global empire starving the US of the funds needed to maintain the homeland? There are many ways to analyse a nation's economy and how it spends its money. Let us begin with the basics. The gross domestic product (GDP) of a nation measures the monetary value of goods and services produced per person within a population. Nations with huge populations, such as China, will therefore struggle to perform well according to this metric, and smaller nations like Luxembourg, Ireland, Singapore, Norway and Switzerland will be deemed highly successful. In pure GDP terms, the US is able to produce a competitive amount of output per capita (over $75,000), surpassing the OECD average of around $54,000 and trailing only the aforementioned states.[94]

With this ability to generate huge amounts of economic output, the US should have no issue investing the monies required to ensure its domestic infrastructure is second to none. If we analyse the total infrastructure spend, we get this impression. The US spent approximately $4.9 trillion in 2021. This figure, although lagging far behind China's $11.5 trillion – which reflects that country's investment in transitioning from a largely rural to a heavily urbanized economy – is similar to the total spent by all nations within the EU, a continental collection of states with double the population of the US.[95]

But this is not the full picture. By focusing on the individual sectors where investment is made, we gain a better understanding of what is going on. This investment is measured as gross fixed capital formation (GFCF), namely the acquisition of *produced* assets (not simply acquired assets like land or natural resources) minus disposals. Under the 1993 System of National Accounts (SNA), military expenditures on fixed assets were treated as GFCF only if they could be used for civilian purposes (e.g. airfields, docks, roads). The 2008 SNA, however, treats all military expenditures on fixed assets as GFCF regardless of the purpose. The US, of course, spends huge sums of money annually in this area.[96]

To simplify what can become quite a complicated and technical subject, the US is just not investing sufficiently in the nonmilitary physical infrastructure required to ensure it is domestically fit for purpose. This is an obvious and visible fact: numerous towns and cities have been hollowed out and left for dead as industry leaves the area. Meanwhile, crumbling roads and worn-out railways are an all-too-common sight. The US has a ranking of 13th globally for its domestic infrastructure – hardly indicative of "world leading" status.[97] A 2021 study by the

American Society of Civil Engineers found that 11 of the 17 infra-structure categories evaluated were graded in the "D" range. It is no surprise, then, to see the power and water failures caused by winter storms and extreme cold, with many infrastructure systems deemed increasingly susceptible to catastrophic failure.[98]

We can also examine the ability to travel successfully along the arteries of the country without incident by looking at the estimated number of road-traffic fatalities per 100,000 people. The WHO's 2018 report on road safety gives a figure of 12.4 for the US, which is more than double the rate in places like Canada (5.8), Australia (5.6), France (5.5), Germany (4.1) and the UK (3.1).[99] This is in part due to lax regulations on car-safety standards and seatbelts, as well as driving under the influence and speeding, but it's also due to the lack of viable alternative transport methods. Many sprawling US cities lack a well-operated mass transit system, so Americans are required to drive far more miles annually than their counterparts in other developed nations.[100] The network of crumbling roads, ridden with potholes, will not be helping to improve road safety in the US. Nor will the fact that 42 per cent of the 617,000 bridges in the US are more than fifty years old, and more than 46,000 of them are rated as structurally deficient.[101]

Finally, let's look at a key aspect of the social contract that ensures imperial stability, namely shelter. This fundamental human requirement – the ability to place a roof over one's head – is an area where the US scores above OECD averages. The figures for the US are as follows: the average home contains 2.4 rooms per person (against an OECD average of 1.7 rooms); 99.9 per cent of US dwellings have access to a flushing toilet (for the OECD, the average is 97 per cent), and American households on average spend around 18 per cent of their gross adjusted disposable income on shelter (putting the US in the top ten of OECD countries).[102]

According to a 2020 study, the US had an estimated 580,000 people without shelter (and therefore meeting a definition of being homeless), equating to 0.18 per cent of the total population.[103] While this is clearly a large number of people in real terms, as a percentage of population this figure is in line with OECD averages. The perception that there is a homelessness problem in the US that does not exist elsewhere is not accurate; this perception seems to stem from the existence of certain high-visibility areas that contain an increased density of homeless people. For example, the state of California hosts 23.47 per cent of all America's unsheltered homeless, and just four states (plus Washington, D.C.) contain 45 per cent of its total homeless, while only containing 20 per cent of the US population as a whole.[104]

Whatever the exact numbers at any one point in time, there is simply no excuse for the level of neglect and degradation as it relates to domestic infrastructure in the US today. Unfortunately, the congressional consensus required to address these issues, and adequately pay for solutions, is impossible to achieve in the current climate. This ensures that these problems, especially homelessness, are reduced to pawns in an ongoing political battle in which there are no winners.

Racial Equality

The American Empire has a complicated relationship with racial equality, built on a chequered history of slavery, violence, prejudice and suffering. This simple fact lies behind much of the animosity that exists within the US today, with violence erupting after regular occurrences of police brutality against minorities. This issue has now become so toxic, so problematic, that facts and statistics are no longer sufficient as analysis – they have been superseded by subjective "lived experience". To question or denigrate this worldview is to risk being labelled a racist, as debate is narrowed to fit within newly defined parameters – the lexicon is constantly updated and amended to reflect this new "anti-racist reality". This is dangerous for many reasons, which will be examined in this section with as much objectivity as possible.

The roots of the current problem of race within America are intertwined with a history of racial prejudice at state, national and individual levels of society. The very nation was forged through a genocidal conquest of the native inhabitants. Those not massacred were rounded up and forced to live on the margins of society within reservations that continue to be beset by the societal issues created by this apartheid existence and worsened by endemic substance and alcohol abuse.

This original sin of the American Empire was compounded by the importation of slaves from the African continent over a period of 250 years. Even after the official abolition of slavery, an ideology of white supremacy that was used to justify the abhorrent practice has not vanished from the continent. As with anything in history, a proclamation or stroke of a pen does not change entrenched attitudes overnight, and segregation and discrimination inflicted by a white majority on a non-white minority continued visibly for a further century and beyond.

The inability to accept this fact has created a festering wound in the national psyche; moreover, it has created the conditions for the emergence of a doctrine that does not espouse Dr King's dream of equality, but instead seeks something much more dangerous: revenge. It is now accepted dogma within many of the major institutions of the nation that there exists an institutional and systemic racism that must be rooted out and extinguished at all costs. This is not in itself problematic, but those espousing these views most vehemently – and acting as thought leaders in creating the new "anti-racist" reality – are actively promoting modern prejudice as a solution to previous prejudice.

While this viewpoint is currently spreading, it will not yield the desired results for one simple reason: a majority will never actively destroy itself for the benefits of a minority; and if dominance rather than equality is the aim, then this will require not only the support of the minority but also the continuing acquiescence of the majority. While there are parts of the majority who believe that the scales require rebalancing, this process will not continue when it dawns on them that this is a task that by its very design can never be sufficiently achieved. If the opinion of a member of the majority ethnicity is deemed invalid from birth, at what point will the members of this majority decide not to advance this cause any further?

George Floyd's death in 2020 provoked condemnation, outrage and an outpouring of anger that had previously been simmering under the surface, waiting for a flashpoint to ignite it. The resultant rush to anti-racism, with many believing they are acting nobly and striving for justice, has unfortunately had the effect of limiting the exchange of ideas. Sceptical or critical views are either deemed invalid, due to the ethnicity of the speaker, or labelled racist if they challenge the tenets of the new orthodoxy. Does this represent a post-MLK racial reality in the US, whereby it is not in fact the content of one's character that is to be examined, but rather one's ethnicity?

This situation is likely to endure until the inevitable backlash, spear-headed by those whose interests are best served by stoking the culture wars and fanning the flames of the "war on woke". Undeniably, progress has been made toward racial equality, but this progress is also too slow for those who are tired of living with its realities and restrictions. It is easy to speak of progress over 50, 100 or even 200 years, but this provides little solace to a black parent explaining to their child why they continue to be disproportionately stopped by police, sent to prison or condemned to living below the poverty line. The primary issue for American hegemony is that an empire cannot survive with its citizens constantly at each other's throats, focused on areas of divergence and difference rather than coalescing around shared values and common ground. The way to achieve this is not to demonize "whiteness" as an irredeemable original sin, but to encourage open dialogue and discourse. Attaching blame for slavery to a white child born in 2024 is not only discriminatory; it is simply counter-productive, and it will drive away far more potential allies than it generates.

So how racist is America in 2023? What can we deduce when we examine the statistics? If we look at poverty figures by ethnicity, we can see that there has been marked progress in reducing the poverty rate in the black population, and the Asian population now has the same poverty rate as the non-Hispanic white population.[105] The figures regarding Asian poverty are instructive as this reflects a more nuanced state of affairs rather than a purely "racist" nation that condemns all its non-white citizens to similar levels of poverty. Perhaps the reality is more that the conditions that allow certain portions of the Asian community to thrive do not exist for members of the black or Hispanic community, or at least have not existed in the past.

Much of this can be explained by acknowledging the openly segregationist "redlining" housing policies of the New Deal, and the subsequent refusal of insurance companies to underwrite properties owned by black Americans, or even near those owned by black Americans. This was mandated government instruction, with the *Underwriting Manual* of the Federal Housing Administration stating that "incompatible racial groups should not be permitted to live in the same communities".[106] The 1968 Fair Housing Act declared an end to this practice, but by this point the lack of entrenched or inherited wealth, and rising house prices, meant that houses in the more affluent suburbs were out of reach for most black Americans. It is clear that a child born into a less affluent, higher-crime neighbourhood, with a larger percentage of his or her potential male role models being incarcerated, will begin yards behind the start line. These limiting factors reduce the scope of these children not only to achieve a different future, but to even imagine one.

Can we take any solace in the trends in these areas, if they do after all point toward greater equality being achieved over time? The answer is a qualified yes. On the one hand it is clearly positive to see a decline from a poverty rate of around 40 per cent for black Americans in 1965 to 18.8 per cent, under half of that first figure, in 2019. This move toward racial income equality is welcome, but it does not change the fact that the current poverty rates for black and Hispanic Americans (15.7 per cent) still remain over double that of their Asian and white counterparts (both at 7.3 per cent). While a decline from 40 per cent is indicative of progress, a poverty rate of almost one in five black Americans indicates that this progress is too slow. If it takes another fifty years for the figure to halve again, it would still most likely remain above the poverty levels for Asian and white Americans.

Gender Equality

Gender equality is a positive societal outcome, allowing more members of a society to benefit from all of the opportunities available, rather than being restricted on the basis of gender. There are many ways in which a society may not offer equal opportunities to members of each gender; they range from the most obvious and draconian, like the Taliban banning female students or mandating male-only jobs, to more covert examples, such as traditional societal views that create an unspoken, self-reinforcing system where access to professions traditionally seen as "male" is restricted. This is a relatively modern construction, as during the eighteenth and nineteenth centuries female participation in the workforce was vital to the family and community. This is because a premechanized society relied solely upon physical labour to manufacture products for sale and produce surplus food for market. It was only once these activities were mechanized and moved outside the home, that female involvement in the workforce dropped dramatically, and the more stereotypical gender roles of child-rearing and homemaking began to be labelled as female tasks.[107]

These social stereotypes have persisted, even as women began to re-enter the workforce during the twentieth century. This re-entry was necessitated by the impact of both the first and second world wars, and the numbers of women in the workforce grew steadily throughout this period. This was driven in large part by a growing number of married women taking clerical roles and by the advent of information technology, and it was further fuelled by the rising number of girls completing secondary education. From the late 1970s to the early 2000s – the period labelled "the quiet revolution" by Harvard economist Claudia Goldin – there was a relatively small rise in female workforce participation, but arguably more important social changes were occurring. Due in no small part to the introduction of the contraceptive pill, young women began to take control of their futures and expanded their potential horizons to include fulfilling long-term careers that would not be curtailed or halted by childbearing.[108]

After 2000, however, there began a decline in female workforce participation, which, although modest, still proceeded at a faster rate than for their male counterparts. Interestingly, this is not mirrored in other OECD countries, and economists believe this is due to discrepancies in the provision of family policies such as paid parental leave, access to childcare and support for early childhood learning. In 2012, the US ranked 33rd out of 36 developed countries in these areas, signposting the issues that are likely to be at the heart of this participatory decline.[109] As discussed previously, the US remains the only developed country not to provide any paid maternal leave – a dismal statistic.

Harder to quantify is the impact of ingrained and continuing expectations of women to perform an inequitable amount of the unpaid, traditionally "female" tasks around the home, such as housework and childcare. This is by no means a US-centric issue; compared to other regions globally, North America actually has the smallest gender gap in unpaid care work.[110] In Europe, meanwhile, countries with more "traditional" gender roles, like Italy, seem to be widening the gap that more equitable countries, like Iceland, are narrowing. It should go without saying that the US, as the global superpower, should be aiming to emulate Iceland rather than Italy in this regard.

It is not simply the participation rates of females in the workforce, or the responsibility for unpaid labour, that contribute to gender imbalances in the world of work. Gender-related discrepancies in both remuneration and the number of positions in senior management also exacerbate the issue. In the US, the gender wage gap (defined as the difference between the median earnings of women relative to the median earnings of men) is notably larger (at around 17 per cent) than the OECD average (around 12 per cent).[111]

Put another way, while it may be positive to have a more equitable split in unpaid care work than in many other regions, if the gender wage gap is larger in the US than in their OECD peers, then gender inequality will remain. If a female is paid on average 82 cents for every dollar of similar work performed by a male counterpart, this is not gender equality. Again, this is not to say that progress has not been made – after all, in 1982 this figure was only 65 cents – but it is simply to state that more progress is needed.[112]

There are a variety of reasons why the gender pay gap has narrowed. Some, such as female gains in educational attainment and work experience, are clear and measurable, while others are more anecdotal and it's harder to assign specific numerical values to them. Examples of the latter include instances of remuneration discrimination, and denial of progression opportunities for mothers who have been deemed to not be fully committed to their work. So, while it may be a positive that the unpaid care-work gap is relatively small in the US, an ongoing issue is the fact that more mothers than fathers continue to believe that they have been passed over for promotions and important assignments.[113]

One quantifiable indicator of how much progress is being made in combating these problems is the gender diversity on the boards of top US companies. As of 2022, there were no all-male boards of S&P 500 companies, and 32 per cent of board members were women, a record high.[114] For *Fortune* 500 companies, the figure is similar (30.4 per cent).[115] Does this tell the whole story? As always, further investigation shows that while progress is undeniable, the actual representation of female board members remains low. Two per cent of S&P 500 boards contain only a single woman, and 37 per cent have three women – the average board size is 10.8 members. Interestingly, traditionally patriarchal OECD countries with strictly defined social gender roles, such as Japan, rank far worse than the US in this area.

These broad trends are also seen when we apply the microscope to female representation in politics. The most recent year for which relevant comparisons can be drawn is 2021. The percentage of female parliamentarians in the US in 2021 (27.3 per cent) was significantly below the OECD average (32 per cent), and way behind the leading OECD countries.[116] The Scandinavian nations of Norway, Sweden and Finland rank among the best nations for gender equality in this field, each with more than 44 per cent of their parliamentarians being female in 2021.

At ministerial level, we have data from 2023: the US has a similar percentage of female ministers (33.3) to the OECD average (35.7), but this is much less than the likes of Sweden (47.8), Norway (50) and Finland (64.3).[117]

A truly gender-equitable world of work and politics is unlikely to occur overnight, given that there are so many different areas to be addressed, but two things are certain. Firstly, the US should not be aiming to be average among OECD peers in this regard or any other. Secondly, it must take coherent policy action toward reaching this goal by emulating the OECD leaders. This action should encourage men and women to explore career or caring opportunities without viewing these spheres in traditionally gendered terms.

Finally, when examining questions of gender, it is worth going back to basics. The most fundamental aspect of gender equality is the relative safety of a country's female population, and this begins within their own homes. Let's examine this simple question: what percentage of women in the US have suffered physical and/or sexual violence from an intimate partner at some time in their life? With a figure of

26 per cent in 2023, the US clearly has a problem – this rate is higher than that of each country in the EU, for example – but some of its OECD peers are not all that far behind. Violence against women may be a lot worse in less developed nations, but the US should not congratulate itself on being better than Saudi Arabia (43 per cent) or Bangladesh (50 per cent); it should focus on swiftly becoming a safer, fairer, more just society for its female citizens.[118]

Of course, there are likely to be methodological and societal factors that affect these statistics, including how likely women are to admit to suffering abuse, but this is not sufficient to disregard what the data is showing us. Not only are US women more likely than most of their peers in developed countries to suffer domestic abuse; they are also more likely to believe that this abuse is justified under certain circumstances (13.9 per cent).[119]

The final matter in this discussion focuses on one of the starkest areas of gender inequality: control over one's own reproductive organs. This point is so important in the wider context of the divisions threatening the American Empire that it requires a far more detailed analysis than can be given here. This will be addressed more fully in chapter 4, when we examine the workings of the Supreme Court and the potential ramifications of the 2022 decision to overturn *Roe v. Wade*. The decision to restrict rather than enhance the right to abortion marks the US as an outlier internationally, with most countries increasing rather than decreasing abortion access.[120] Rather than lining up with its fellow Western democracies, the US now finds itself in the company of the developing world, where religious and patriarchal cultures continue to set the agenda.

4

Politics: The Cold Civil War

Debate. Negotiation. Compromise. These are the key tenets of a well-functioning democracy, ensuring the most beneficial outcomes for the citizenry and the nation by sharing ideas, modifying positions through discussion, and then implementing consensus-based outcomes. This is not politics in the American Empire of 2024. Bipartisanship is dead, ideology has replaced pragmatism and to compromise is to be "weak" or traitorous to your "side".

While differences of opinion between opposing parties have always been a feature of American democracy, politics is now a zero-sum game: there can be only winners or losers. Positions are entrenched and differences are magnified by a partisan media chasing ratings, clicks and outrage. The two-party system foists on voters a binary choice between equally compromised parties. This political theatre, heavily funded by outside interests and perpetuated by a complicit media, creates an illusion of choice while ensuring that the system continues to function as designed, enriching the oligarchy who maintain the status quo. Let us begin our analysis of the dire health of the US political system by examining the current state of the two major parties of the American oligarchy, before we look at the various branches of government in turn.

The Republicans

The Grand Old Party. The party of Abe Lincoln, Teddy Roosevelt and Dwight D. Eisenhower. The party of low taxes, small government and minimal state encroachment on personal freedoms. This is not the

Republican Party today. Fringe right-wing views and conspiracy theories are presented as fact by its representatives while Fox News, providing 24/7 propaganda in its capacity as the unofficial media arm of the party, forces such views into the mainstream consciousness.

Within the Republican Party and the conservative movement more broadly, there exists a fanatical adherence to the idea of individual freedom, which supersedes any notion of collective responsibility – a key component of any well-functioning society. This outlook is applied selectively and cynically. A powerful and influential undercurrent of fundamentalist Christianity also shapes Republican policy, even as fewer and fewer Americans attend church services. The very notion of "conservatism" within the Republican Party is oxymoronic, as these religious influences lead to policies that do not aim for coherence and continuity but impose radical measures that are often contrary to the views of the majority of the country.

Meanwhile, Republican donations to the National Rifle Association (NRA) and a cultish adherence to the Second Amendment right to bear arms ensure that any efforts to curb the epidemic of gun violence are defeated. This means that assault rifles designed for military combat are all too readily available and used to devastating effect in mass shootings that occur with predictable and depressing frequency. When James Madison proposed the Second Amendment in 1789, he was guarding against the potential transgressions of a tyrannical federal government, not ensuring that citizens with questionable mental stability could access weapons of war and wander around their schools killing indiscriminately.

Elsewhere, rivers of black dollars ensure that attempts to transition away from fossil fuels are stymied and delayed, as industry-sponsored reports spread lies and pseudoscience. Following the same path as Big Tobacco in the twentieth century, Big Oil and its Republican allies will continue using these methods to enrich themselves until the very last second, happy to sacrifice the future health of the nation and the planet.

The Republican Party's extreme interpretation of reproductive rights, propelled by evangelical Christians, masquerades under the misplaced moniker of "pro-life". "Pro-life" for unborn fetuses, but not for the victims of gun violence, nor the future generations who will have to live with the reality of climate change. "Pro-life" until the moment a child is born, but after this point they are on their own. Any state assistance that would improve the lives of these fetuses when they become children and then adults, be it parental leave or social security, is opposed, such is the party's ideological reflex. "Pro-life", then, in only very selective circumstances. The party of small government and personal freedom sees no contradiction in stealing bodily autonomy from women and forcing unwanted pregnancies to term – even after rape, in certain states.

This litany of contradiction and destruction was only the state of the Republican Party *before* it was hijacked by Donald Trump and remade in his image. After four years of enabling the worst impulses of Trump as he unravelled norms and conventions in his attempt to "Make America Great Again", the party of Lincoln has abandoned the ideals of accountability and democracy. The 2021 Capitol insurrection that led to the deaths of four Trump supporters, incited and cheered on by their leader, has been downplayed and characterized by Republicans as a "normal tourist visit", with efforts to investigate it labelled as harassment.[1]

It should be no surprise that the Republican Party is still happy to enable Donald Trump, even as he spreads dangerous lies about election fraud and undermines the entire democratic process; they have been doing the same for years using other, more covert methods. Facing the reality of demographic changes that could lead to a non-white majority in the next decade, the GOP has decided not to adapt and evolve to appeal to a more diverse voter base, but is instead concen- trating on efforts to subvert the democratic process itself. "Project Redmap", a brazen gerrymandering campaign conceived in 2010 behind locked doors and away from prying eyes, allowed Republicans to redraw voting districts and rig the democratic process to their advantage. With a conservative majority, by 2019 the Supreme Court had made it clear that there was nothing federal courts could do to stop even the most blatant and aggressive gerrymandering, ensuring that these nefarious tactics will not only continue, but increase in both scope and audacity.[2]

In the year that followed Trump's attempted coup, Republicans introduced at least 262 bills in 41 states which aimed to subvert the democratic process and tip the scales unfairly in their favour. One of the most widespread methods deployed has been the attempt to rewrite state election laws in order to give legislatures control over vote counts. Independent non-partisan election officials, subject to threats of violence after the 2020 election, are also being replaced by hyper-partisan adherents to the unfounded "stop the steal" conspiracy theory.[3] At every level, active Republican attempts are ongoing to undermine the integrity of the entire democratic process. Lincoln would surely be turning in his grave at what his party has become.

The Democrats

The party of Wilson, FDR and JFK. Champions of progressive policies designed to lift up the less fortunate. The party of "Hope" and "Change" that managed to convince the country to elect (and re-elect) a black president. As with their Republican counterparts, however, these cheerful initial observations do not reflect the state of the Democratic Party today.

The party is now riven by infighting – centrists attacking progressives and vice versa, consensus only seemingly possible when opposing Republican policies, not in making bold actions of their own. They exemplify inaction, excuses and empty soundbites, pursuing an electoral strategy so limited in scope that it is simply aimed at being "not the Republicans".

The ruling echelons of the party exist primarily to ensure that its most elite members are insulated from challenges, and that the status quo is preserved. This electoral protection racket was so brazen as to fix the results of the Democratic primaries in 2016, to ensure progressive Senator Bernie Sanders's campaign could not prevent the coronation of the "chosen candidate", Hillary Clinton. The glass ceiling of the Jacob K. Javits Convention Center in Manhattan, chosen rather hubristically to celebrate an expected victory against Donald Trump, remained unbroken as the obvious flaws of the Democrats' candidate were ignored by the party, but not the country.

The belief that an unfairly chosen, unpopular candidate would be guaranteed victory because she was female and not Donald Trump reveals the naivety and myopia of much of the party today: it is driven not by policy but by identity politics. Progressives clamouring for real change are sidelined and ignored, as the party elite simply assume that voters will have no choice but to hold their noses and vote for them in the face of a candidate such as Trump.

The elites remain wilfully ignorant of the anger felt by ordinary Americans when it comes to inequality and being the subject of derision from metropolitan commentators – better instead to simply label those who disagree with you as a "basket of deplorables" made up of "the racist, sexist, homophobic, xenophobic, Islamophobic – you name it".[4] For a member of the ruling elite, not to mention the wife of a former president, to label a significant proportion of the US population in this manner is electoral suicide and would surely lead to soul-searching and an examination of the entire party strategy? Not so. The Russian bogeyman was to blame, and Hillary was supposedly robbed.

Even during the Obama years, the Democratic elite's disconnection from reality was evident, as working people were ignored, maligned and incarcerated in record numbers. Although Trump was rightly criticized for caging children at the border and separating families, his predecessor, nicknamed the "Deporter-in-Chief", oversaw in this first term over 60 per cent more deportations than Trump, in the naive hope that it would persuade Republicans to agree to a bipartisan immigration bill.[5]

Elsewhere, it was not Donald Trump who sponsored the 1994 crime bill, but Joe Biden. Biden and the bill have come under repeated criticism for the disproportionate effect on the incarceration rates for black males, a point clearly illustrated by the differing punishments for arrests for cocaine in powder form (used by wealthier, white Americans) and crack cocaine (used by poorer black Americans). A point often forgotten is that Biden was supported by prominent members of the black community, who could see first-hand the damage that the crack epidemic was causing in their communities.[6] The recent moves by the Biden administration to decriminalize marijuana use, and expunge the criminal records of those convicted in the past for minor offences (again, disproportionately affecting black males), might be proceeding too slowly for some critics, but they are certainly a step in the right direction.

The most valid criticism of the Democrats today is that they lack the requisite determination and invention to counter the actions of the Republicans, and that they are too busy "going high" to address the long-term damage being done by an adversary content to keep "going low". The failure to use all tools available to challenge the decision to overturn *Roe v. Wade*, or to enact meaningful gun-control legislation, are two major examples of this predicament. If these issues really mattered to the Democratic elite, or if there was a genuine threat of supporters withholding their votes because of such inaction, then pressure would be applied at every possible point to find a solution. Instead, in the week after *Roe v. Wade* was overturned, it was straight back to business for Nancy Pelosi and Joe Biden, namely using the Republican bogeyman to tap up worried donors for more campaign donations, without any mention of a specific plan to counter the move and protect reproductive rights.[7] Even when action did follow in the form of an executive order, it was loosely worded, non-binding and generally underwhelming.[8]

The Executive Branch

President Biden promised to govern for everyone, regardless of party affiliation, after President Trump had pursued the opposite strategy for four years. He has quickly found that this is no longer possible: the days of working to find common ground with those across the aisle are over. Bipartisanship does not necessarily equate to good governance, as the Iraq War and Patriot Act illustrated clearly, but a political system so entrenched in opposing ideologies is not a blueprint for long-term stability.

Take the Trump presidency by way of example. Four years were spent attempting to unravel seemingly every policy enacted by the previous Obama administration. Sometimes this was for ideological reasons, such as Trump's decision to abandon the Paris Agreement on climate change. Sometimes it was simply petty and vindictive, such as the unilateral exit from the Iran nuclear deal which had no intended outcome except to destroy Obama's legacy. Now that the pendulum has swung back to the Democrats, these decisions are again reversed, ready to be reversed again in 2024 if a Republican president takes the White House.

This tragic farce of inefficiency is most often perpetrated via presidential executive orders, in effect ruling by diktat, a short-term solution to avoid intransigence within Congress and ensure immediate effect. Who better to illustrate the ludicrous nature of this system than Trump himself, who laid it out clearly while campaigning in 2016:

> [Obama] just goes along and signs executive orders for everything … because that's easy to do. I'll tell you the one good thing about an executive order is that the new president [can] come and with just a signature, they're all gone.[9]

Trump signed 220 executive orders in his single term of office compared with Obama's 276 over the course of his two terms. Biden, working faster than any other previous president to reverse the executive orders of his predecessor, had signed more than 100 by the middle of 2023.

Executive orders are not a new phenomenon: all previous presidents, except William Henry Harrison, have used them in varying numbers.[10] As William G. Howell argues in his book *Power Without Persuasion: The Politics of Direct Presidential Action*, the difference is that modern presidents are using them for far more "significant" actions.[11] What does this matter? Does it represent a slide toward fascism, ruling by imperial decree and circumventing the normal checks and balances of government? Possibly, but this is not the main issue. If we take a step back from party politics and partisan outrage, we can appreciate that the use of executive orders is simply not a coherent method of governing and will not produce outcomes that are beneficial for the nation in the long term.

To gain some perspective, let's compare the use of executive orders to two alternative models which are wildly different; but if viewed only in terms of long-term strategy, they might seem preferable to the current state of affairs. Firstly, in China, the American Empire's only viable competitor for hegemony, there is an ideological dictatorship. To be clear, this authoritarianism is not to be admired or held up as a model of good governance. China is currently subject to the whims of one man who is accountable to no one for the most part. But the inescapable reality is that the Chinese Communist Party can plan far more effectively for the long term than the US. While American presidents trade executive orders, the Chinese are implementing policies that are designed to supplant the American Empire and that are tailored not for a four-year cycle but for a forty-year one. This observation is not intended as a rose-tinted homage to Chinese autocracy, but rather a wake-up call to pay attention to how this rival is aiming to continue a relentless rise until it eventually replaces the American Empire. A Chinese-led technocratic global order is not an outcome to be desired by anybody who appreciates their individual freedom, but the ineffectiveness and short-term partisan nature of the current US political system makes this outcome more likely. We can agree that this Chinese model is best avoided, but what about the other alternative?

Democratic models of governance exist globally in various forms with differences in application and effectiveness, but let's look now at the example of truly pluralistic democracies and their multiparty coalition governments, which have little choice but to rule by consensus and compromise. Nowhere is this more evident than in Europe, where few of the parliamentary democracies have governments formed from a single party.

Coalition governments are not without their issues; paralysis is common and there may be periods without a functioning government as the various parties work toward compromise. The unwanted record in this area goes to Belgium, which experienced a staggering 541 days without a government in 2010–11.

In efforts to avoid this type of situation, different democracies have established different systems to "tip the balance" and create governing majorities, but these also create undemocratic outcomes. In the UK, the "first past the post" electoral system has created an effective two-party system, where smaller parties receive far less parliamentary representation than their share of the vote would suggest. "Safe seats" and marginal constituencies create an unbalanced weighting, where a vote in one area is in effect far more powerful than in another, fuelling voter apathy.

Many countries share the German model and have a minimum electoral threshold, to reduce fringe-party representation, while some, such as Italy and Greece, simply gift the winning party a number of seats to ensure a governing majority. These workaround solutions often fail to produce stable governments and also lead to disengagement from the democratic process as people feel their vote is wasted.

The "consensus democracy" models employed in Switzerland and Denmark, both different in their application but producing a similar pattern, could provide guidance for the American Empire, but either model would require a cultural shift that seems unlikely to be possible at present. The Swiss system is successful because the government is seen not as a single political entity, but instead as an amalgamation of all major parties and representative of 80 per cent of all votes cast. When issues are debated, movements or groupings can form safely within the coalition, resulting in far less entrenched ideology and far greater discussion and compromise. There also exists a backstop in the event that consensus cannot be reached: direct democracy via referendum. The opposite approach is taken in Denmark, where as few parties as possible are included in the ruling government, leading to successions of minority governments. In order to legislate effectively, these governments must use the parliamentary process to generate support for their policies. These two systems illustrate a way of governing that can be possible when nation is placed above party, progress is valued over ideology, and common ground is sought rather than shunned.[12]

What should the American Empire take from these differing methods of governance? Clearly, Chinese-style dictatorship is best avoided, but a lesson can be learned from this system: the importance of long-term strategic planning to advance *national* interests. Similarly, the multi-party systems of western Europe are often mired in paralysis, indecision and ineffectiveness, but there are clearly benefits for the longevity of the American Empire in aiming to move closer to consensus rule, and in appealing to a wider selection of the citizenry. Are such fundamental changes to the existing democratic system likely or even possible? Unfortunately, if history is our guide, such changes are unlikely to occur until a domestic crisis of great severity exposes the inadequacies of the current system and forces change from all sides as a matter of survival. Would Lincoln and Mandela have been successful at different times, under different circumstances, or was the turmoil caused by the American Civil War and apartheid South Africa the necessary factor in producing the conditions that enabled the unification of their nations? The Capitol insurrection of 2021, incited by a sitting president calling for the democratic process to be ignored and overridden, could have been this catalyst for the US in the present day. But party ideology and power have trumped national interest. The threat of an end to American democracy may have been narrowly averted, but the seriousness of that threat seems now to have been forgotten by many of the same policymakers who were building barricades behind locked doors and fearing for their lives.

It is not simply the partisan nature of US politics that is unfit for purpose, but also the very electoral mechanisms – questions of legitimacy have plagued the enterprise from its inception. The Electoral College was created as a way of ensuring that smaller states were given fair representation in the choosing of the president. The idea of an "independent" collection of educated men, deliberating and reaching consensus upon who should lead, was seen as preferable to trusting the will of the people through a popular vote.

This decision not to trust the popular vote continues to this day, with Donald Trump in 2016 becoming the fifth president to be elected while losing the popular vote (by almost three million ballots). In spite of this shortfall, Trump won by a margin of more than 70 Electoral College votes. Situations like this contribute to a problem of legitimacy within American democracy, fuelling the sentiment that the winner of the election is not endorsed by most of the nation; this was especially problematic with a candidate as divisive as Trump.

There is another problem with the Electoral College: the issue of "faithless electors". This is where representatives are permitted to vote in opposition to the decision of their state's popular vote. More than 160 electors have chosen this action over the course of US history, including the seven members of the "Hamilton Electors" movement in 2016, who aimed to prevent Trump from taking the presidency. Writing for the Brookings Institute in 2019 before the election, Darrell

West argued for a popular vote to maintain legitimacy and trust in democracy, presciently warning that:

> It is time to move ahead with abolishing the Electoral College before its clear failures undermine public confidence in American democracy, distort the popular will, and create a genuine constitutional crisis.[13]

Only Mr West can answer whether he believed such a crisis would occur the very next year, but his concerns were and are well founded.

I would go one step further and argue that these long-standing defects within the US electoral system are directly responsible for creating the circumstances that emboldened President Trump to believe he could subvert democracy and cling fascistically to power. This very much includes the efforts of the Hamilton Electors and the repeated allegations by the Democrats that Russian electoral interference was the principal reason for their defeat in 2016. Although defeat was officially accepted, unofficially any possible external reason was sought and widely propagated. Rather than address the shortcomings of Hillary Clinton as a flawed and unpopular candidate – or confront the proven and unpopular reality that the Democratic nomination was rigged in her favour – the Democrats sought to blame Russians for manipulating social media, thus rendering the election illegitimate in their eyes.

If 2016 was declared illegitimate by the losing party, why would 2020 not yield a similar outcome? If the popular vote has been distrusted and intentionally subverted since the days of the founding fathers, is it viable for commentators and politicians from the losing side to attempt to use this metric as a benchmark for legitimacy within the current system? If members of the Electoral College can ignore the wishes of those they are chosen to represent, and have done so many times before, is it a surprise that a losing president would aim to go further and instruct his vice president to nullify the results entirely? The system has created the circumstances where a losing candidate can brazenly pressure elected officials to find him more votes while using baseless accusations of voter fraud to build a false narrative of a stolen election.

Without a democratic system of unquestionable legitimacy, this kind of behaviour was inevitable. Trump was simply the person with the exact character traits to make this possible – a narcissist without equal, devoid of any discernible moral compass, and loyal only to himself and his desire for power. This is, after all, the same man who spent his years in power attacking almost every established norm; refused to divest his business interests when taking up that office; ran his nepotistic administration like an organized crime syndicate; and refused to commit to the peaceful transfer of power if he lost the 2020 election. The man is responsible for his actions, but the system is responsible for creating the circumstances that allowed his actions to occur. In the future, unless changes to this system are made, there will be a candidate, with greater intellect and cunning, who inspires less division and will attempt to subvert democracy – and quite possibly succeed. These are the troubling issues of legitimacy that exist within the executive branch of government and the electoral system of the American Empire. Let us now examine those within the legislative branch.

The Legislative Branch

We have already touched on the heart of the problem with Congress in its current form, namely the relationship between money and influence for these career politicians. To better understand exactly how this relationship manifests, let's look at the process by which laws are enacted.

In his book *The Great Derangement*, Matt Taibbi exposes how laws are actually made in the American Empire.[14] While the public are invited to sit in on inane sessions to name post offices, it is behind the closed doors of private rooms that laws of substance are actually made. Within these rooms and away from prying eyes, in committee, is where bills that affect millions of Americans are mangled and distorted as members of Congress do the bidding of their unseen paymasters. The resultant Frankenstein's monster that is passed back to the executive branch to be signed into law is often unrecognizable from the bill that passed the scrutiny of the House, containing provisions wholly irrelevant to the matter being addressed. This process is conducted in the knowledge that there will be no further oversight, as the executive branch requires laws to be passed and progress to be seen to be occurring. Meanwhile, the system continues to enrich everyone involved.

If the people do not know how the laws that govern them are made, apathy is the result and legitimacy is lost. The American oligarchy has perfected this process, creating an intentionally labyrinthian system that is designed to appear so complicated that the public have no interest in, or ability to decipher, its inner workings.

The Filibuster

Now let us run a thought experiment. You sit on the board of a large multinational corporation, and you are presenting your proposals for a new policy that you believe will increase productivity, raise employee morale and boost profits. As you finish your presentation, you notice that many heads are nodding in approval and the CEO raises a hand, declaring the matter closed and that steps should be taken to enact your proposals. Before the CEO finishes the sentence, however, one of your fellow board members, who has no requisite experience in your field and no direct involvement in the areas you are discussing, rises to his feet and is given the floor; this is a collaborative working environment after all. He starts with a superficial disagreement with your proposals but then proceeds to discuss at length his favourite recipes, quote hip-hop lyrics and ramble incoherently for a full 24 hours. Your fellow board members try to interrupt, questioning the relevance of this diatribe, but they are silenced as tradition dictates that any member can be heard without interruption for as long as they wish. The nodding heads soon change to stifled yawns and slumped shoulders as members struggle to remain awake after so many hours of irrelevant white noise. The boardroom door opens, a janitor enters and he asks those assembled if they are aware that it is now the weekend, which is followed by a public holiday on the Monday. Exhausted, the members of the board look round at each other and the CEO yawns, stretches and declares, "I guess that means it is time to head home." He slowly rises to his feet, followed by the rest of the room, who begin to file out the door. "What about my proposals?" you angrily declare, as months of preparation evaporate in front of your admittedly tired eyes, hours upon hours now seemingly wasted. "Let's talk about it another time; I think we could all do with some sleep" is the response. You feel a pat on your back and turn to see your antagonist smiling broadly. "Don't you just love the filibuster?" he says as he suppresses a chuckle and strides past you toward the door.

This scenario, although ludicrous at first glance, is the filibuster in action. Unfortunately, the best intentions of allowing unlimited healthy debate have been frequently hijacked by those who use this tactic to prolong debate in the Senate with the intention of delaying or even preventing a vote on a bill. Before 1917 there was no way to end this farce and force a vote on a bill. After 1917 the procedure known as cloture was introduced to allow for a forced end to a filibuster attempt, provided a two-thirds majority in the Senate agreed. In 1975 this requirement was further reduced to three-fifths, or 60 senators from the 100 elected.

Due to the increasingly partisan nature of Congress and the often razor-thin majorities in the Senate, filibuster attempts are often successful. Strom Thurmond, a South Carolina senator, who died in 2003, holds the record for the longest filibuster, speaking for over 24 hours in 1957 in an attempt to delay the vote on the Civil Rights Act.

His efforts only succeeded in delaying the vote; the legislation was subsequently passed.

The tactic has since been adopted with great success by many senators, predominantly while representing the minority party, thus preventing votes on important issues in the national interest. While many of the most publicized recent examples of filibustering are efforts by Republican senators to stifle debate on polarizing issues like gun control and abortion, its use is actually fairly evenly split between the parties. Between 1991 and 2008 there were 152 filibusters, 63 by Democrats and 89 by Republicans. From 2009 to 2021, this figure was far higher: 1,266 filibusters were recorded, 657 by Democrats and 609 by Republicans.[15] In one congressional term alone, spanning 2021–22, a record-breaking 336 cloture motions were filed, and more such motions have been filed in the last twenty years than in the previous eighty.[16] Much like the increased frequency of executive orders, this massive rise in the use of the filibuster reveals a democratic system that is not functioning correctly.[17]

Why is this situation permitted to continue? In the nineteenth century many efforts were made by both parties to abolish the filibuster, but these were simply filibustered themselves. As the use of the filibuster has increased, and politics has become more partisan and divided, the motivation to abolish it has also waned. There is undoubtedly a fear that today's majority party will soon become tomorrow's minority, and that the abolition of the filibuster would remove a powerful weapon from the limited minority arsenal. Blaming filibustering by the minority party for the failure of a bill is also a useful tactic, deflecting focus from a policy that does not enjoy universal popularity within the majority party. There also exists a perverse reverence for the rule itself – much as there is for certain constitutional amendments – and so the filibuster is often portrayed as unassailable and immovable, regardless of the resulting legislative gridlock. Democratic senator Joe Manchin embodied this attitude when opposing a proposal by his own party for filibuster reform which would change the threshold of sixty votes to a simple majority. He declared:

> That's never happened in the history of our country … You know, basically, there's never been a simple majority vote to basically get off a debate…I don't know how you break a rule to make a rule.[18]

With reform unlikely, this problem will persist. While the Chinese plan for decades in advance, the American Empire lurches from party to party, mired in political gridlock. There is no need to simply take my word on the subject; let's hear from a keen advocate of filibuster reform back in 2011 – a freshman senator whose demand to "fix the filibuster" was one of the 12 pillars of a bold proposal to "Make Congress Work":

> We have become paralyzed by the filibuster and an unwillingness to work together at all, just because it's an election cycle … We couldn't even get the horse in the start gate, let alone to run the race. That's the problem here … It's political and it's being played absolutely unmercifully at the highest level.[19]

That senator's name? You guessed it … Joe Manchin.

The Debt Ceiling and Government Shutdowns

Another method used to stifle progress and hold the ruling majority hostage is the cynical use of the debt ceiling, a frequent subject of discussion by the political commentator Robert Reich. In essence, it is an arbitrary limit imposed on what the government can borrow to pay for what is already owed on bills that have been agreed and enacted; the limit does not apply to legislation currently being debated. If the ceiling is not raised, the government defaults on payments and ceases to function.[20]

While the debt ceiling originated in 1917, a federal law in 1974 reorganized the United States budgeting process, transferring power from the executive branch to the legislative, thus preventing the federal government from spending money without congressional approval. This led to clashes and funding gaps of 28 days in 1977 (over whether Medicaid should be used to pay for abortions) and 17 days in 1978, when President Carter took exception to an expensive bill for public works and defence spending.[21] These shutdowns were not as severe as those that occur today, as most government agencies continued to function on the understanding that, although funding bills had not been passed, they were likely to be in the future. This could be viewed as a pragmatic, common-sense approach to the situation, but this practice was deemed illegal by Attorney General Benjamin R. Civiletti in 1980 and 1981.[22] This led to the politicization and weaponization of the debt ceiling and government shutdowns.

In 1981, President Reagan set a precedent by ordering the furlough of 241,000 government employees as leverage in a clash with Congress over his request for $8.5 billion of budget cuts. This shutdown cost taxpayers between $80 million and $90 million, and subsequent furloughs in 1984, 1986 and 1990 cost an estimated $128 million.[23]

As time has passed and the political atmosphere has become more polarized and cynical, the regularity and severity of government shutdowns has increased. In 1995, the Clinton administration was subject to a shutdown of five days and then a further 21. In this instance, Republicans aimed to use the tactic to force Clinton into signing a bill designed to limit Medicare spending, and also to make the president delegate control of Medicaid and other welfare programs to individual states.

In 2013, the Obama administration endured a 16-day shutdown similar in nature over funding for "Obamacare". The president stated at the time that "We have to get out of the habit of governing by crisis," but this advice has not been followed by either party.[24]

In 2018, the Trump administration set the record for the longest shutdown – 35 days – over opposition to his plan to enact his signature campaign pledge of building a border wall with Mexico.[25] The Congressional Budget Office estimated that this shutdown cost the American economy at least $11 billion.[26] Whether you agree or disagree with the issues that have caused these shutdowns, no sensible person can claim that this is a sensible use of precious taxpayer funds, nor a shining example of a well-functioning democracy. Occasions such as these also provide perfect ammunition for authoritarian regimes worldwide, legitimately able to decry the inefficiencies and wastefulness of a democratic system.

The actual level of US government debt should be discussed at this point, as in fiscal terms it is the largest in the world, north of $33.68 *trillion* in October 2023.[27] For context, this represents more than 120 per cent of the national GDP; back in 1996, it was around 60 per cent.[28]

Compared with certain other countries, America's level of debt might seem tolerable. Japan's national debt is more than 260 per cent of its GDP, the highest in the world by some distance. We might note that Japan, Greece and Italy have larger debt-to-GDP ratios than the US among OECD countries.[29] It should go without saying, however, that a Japanese economy plagued by decades of deflation should not be used as a guide.[30] The same can be said for Europe's two worst-performing economies, regularly described as "basket cases" that endanger the economic security of the entire Eurozone.

To better understand the scale of the problem when it comes to US national debt, we might consider the cost of simply servicing the national debt: net interest payments are around $400 billion annually, or almost 7 per cent of all federal outlays. If that is still too abstract, this $400 billion is more than the federal government spends on elementary and secondary education, science and space programs, disaster relief, agriculture, foreign aid, and natural resources and environmental protection *combined*.[31]

Economists are split on how serious a threat to US stability is posed by the size of the national debt. From 2009 to 2020 the US experienced a cycle of record low interest rates and a corresponding stock market boom that was the longest bull run in history. Debt "doves", lenient in their attitude to public debt, even created an economic theory to justify record borrowing levels during this time and coined the term "modern monetary theory".[32] The theory, assuming that governments could simply create money without inflationary consequence, seems misguided at best and deluded at worst as the US battles with the rest of the world to bring down inflation levels of over 8 per cent per annum.[33] A more sobering assessment is available from Ray Dalio, the billionaire founder of the world's largest hedge fund, Bridgewater Associates. In September 2023 he warned that a serious debt crisis is on the near-term horizon, and he also predicts an economic slowdown, with growth falling to almost zero. For the growth-centric capitalist model that is the backbone of the American Empire, this would be disastrous.[34]

Another interesting point is the amount of debt owned by foreign states, notably China – it owns around $1 trillion. For some analysts, this represents a genuine threat to US national security, but others maintain that China could never call in the debt, as it is issued in the form of treasury bonds that do not mature all at once. The Chinese economy has more to lose than to gain by a total US debt default, as the global economic shocks would have dire ramifications for China as well as for the entire global community.[35]

Let's end this section by asking some very obvious questions: will the US debt ever be paid back? *Can* it even be paid back? The figure is so vast, and the steps needed to eliminate it are so massive, that they would most likely be impossible to implement without there being a real danger to the ongoing stability of the American Empire. Huge tax hikes and draconian spending cuts would devastate the already degraded social fabric in the US. More radical options have been suggested, including opening the borders to encourage greater immigration and thereby stimulating the economy through increased entrepreneurialism and consumption.[36] But in a climate of domestic protectionism and vocal unease about immigrants coming north through Mexico, this seems a highly unlikely scenario.

As debt ratios continue to spiral upwards around the world, it is more likely that a global solution will be sought, potentially in the form of a global agreement on debt cancellation. This is not without precedent, as the crippling debts of the poorest countries within the developing world were forgiven in 2005 after a concerted campaign by NGOs.[37] It is debatable whether such an action would be considered fair if applied to the developed world, which has profited handsomely by running huge deficits, but the question of fairness is not always a priority for richer nations.

Wise Old Heads or a Lack of Options?

There are very few companies in the modern world that would allow a 78-year-old to serve as CEO, but age is no impediment when assuming the role of commander-in-chief and custodian of the American Empire. That's how old Joe Biden was when he was sworn in as president in 2021.

While his countrymen of a similar age are settling into retirement, perhaps playing golf and travelling the world, Biden is in charge of managing the world's only hyperpower. If he is lucky enough to win a second term, President Biden will be 82 at the start of it and – if he stays alive and in power for the full term – 86 at the end. His possible opponent in 2024, Donald Trump, will be a positively sprightly 78 years old on the day of the vote.

While age should not be an inhibiting factor for many of life's experiences, is it sensible that the only choices available to the American electorate are people who are clearly past their prime? Even the keenest mind suffers deterioration as time marches on, and presidents are no exception. How is a nation to plan for decades into the future if its citizens can only vote for candidates who will only be around to see a fraction of it? The idea that the two most suitable candidates for the role of president in 2020, out of millions of eligible adults, were both white men in their seventies who have unsurprisingly both shown signs of cognitive decline, stretches credibility to say the least. Controversial billionaire Elon Musk agrees with this line of thinking, suggesting that anyone over the age of 70 should not be able to run for political office.[38]

These observations are not intended as an ageist slight. Nor are they meant to disparage or undervalue years of experience, but it simply does not make sense to give a role of such domestic and global signif-icance to the eldest members of a society. Wise old heads should be using their experience to the full, namely by advising younger, more headstrong and inexperienced colleagues – not the other way round.

Too Much Democracy?

Is it possible to have too much democracy? We might not think so, but our assessment may change when money and influence complicate matters. When controls on campaign funding are lacking, the system becomes corrupted. Take the 2020 US election, which was the most expensive in history, with over $14.4 billion spent, double the cost of the 2016 election and the same as paying an annual salary to more than 170,000 nurses.[39] We have already examined the issues surrounding where this money comes from and what is expected in return, but now we must question the value for money of all this political theatre.

While the citizens of the American Empire slip into food insecurity and poverty, ever-increasing sums are funnelled into campaign dona-tions and the purchase of influence. Should a democratic society reward candidates whose primary skill seems to be the ability to attract corporate donors? Research by the Center for Responsive Politics has shown that in elections to the House of Representatives between 2000 and 2016, more than 85 per cent of the candidates who spent the most emerged victorious.[40]

While this suggests that outspending an opponent can lead to victory, further insight from the Stanford professor of political science Adam Bonica, presented by Maggie Koerth for *FiveThirtyEight*, indicates that it is usually not the deciding factor. The relationship is more accurately described as "winning attracts donations", especially from big donors and special-interest groups who can sense the way the wind is blowing in a particular race and wish to ensure that they have influence over the winning candidate during their term of office.[41]

Bonica also notes that, in general elections, 80–90 per cent of congressional races are effectively predetermined by the partisan composition of the district in question. The fact that vast sums of money are donated, even with the result in no real doubt, shows that the goal is to ensure future favours or loyalty on issues important to the donor. By way of example, in the 2016 campaign for Wisconsin's 1st congressional district, Paul Ryan spent $13 million defeating a candidate who spent $16,000. Nationally in 2016, 129 members of Congress were elected after spending varying sums – from hundreds to millions – while their opponents reported spending nothing.[42]

Koerth also suggests that the biggest effect of money in politics is not to ensure campaign victories, but to raise a profile sufficiently, and so effectively determine who is capable of running in the first instance. We might ask how democracy benefits from a situation in which the only candidates who become viable are indebted to outside interests before they even begin to campaign. Why would a candidate prioritize representing their constituents when their political survival seems to depend more on the actions of donors than of voters?

It is not just the effectively predetermined nature of many races that causes voter fatigue, but also the reality of too much democracy.

Decreasing voter turnout at all levels suggests this is a recurring theme. There are 519,682 elected officials in the whole American Empire, including those occupying 537 federal offices, namely those of the president, vice president, 100 US senators and 435 voting US representatives.[43] In presidential elections over the last hundred years, between 50 and 60 per cent of the eligible population have ordinarily voted, with a recent spike to almost 70 per cent in the 2020 election – likely due to the fact that Trump was the most polarizing candidate in living memory. In midterm elections the participation figure hovers closer to 40 per cent, spiking at 50 per cent in 2018 as voters made their voices heard regarding the conduct of President Trump.

The average turnout in OECD countries is around 70 per cent, greater than both national and midterm participation rates in the US.[44] US senators serve six-year terms, with one-third of them up for election every even-numbered year. US representatives serve two-year terms, with the entire House up for election every even-numbered year. This constant electioneering, at the vast costs noted previously, cannot result in officials concentrating on the tasks at hand. There are also almost 20,000 state officials who must be constantly elected. In most states, these offices include governor, lieutenant governor, secretary of state, attorney general, state supreme court justices, comptroller, treasurer, state senators, and state legislators.[45] Finally, local officials make up the vast majority (96 per cent) of elected officials in the US and number over half a million people, including mayors, town or city council members, school board members, county officers and special district members.[46]

In almost every area of public service, elections are held constantly, ostensibly so the public can choose the best candidate for the position. While nations such as China and Russia suffer from the problems caused by too little democracy, the American Empire suffers from the opposite. How can a regular citizen, busy with their professional, family and personal interests, be expected to devote the requisite time to focus on this constant deluge of democracy? Apathy is the all-too-common result, and one that serves the interests of the elected officials who participate in this constant political theatre.

The Judicial Branch

The third and final branch of government in the American Empire is the judiciary. The Supreme Court represents its highest level, under which there exist district courts and 13 courts of appeals, which are subject to precedent set by the Supreme Court. The Supreme Court is the only part of the judiciary that is specifically required by the US Constitution. Rather than holding trials, the Court is tasked with interpreting the meaning of a law, deciding whether a law is relevant to a particular set of facts, or ruling on how a law should be applied.

This is also the sole branch of government whose members are not directly elected by the public; rather they are appointed by the president and confirmed by the Senate. Unless they retire, Supreme Court justices may serve until their deaths, ostensibly independent from the temporary political passions of the public and of the other two branches of government. These judges are meant to be able to interpret the law free of electoral or political concerns. After oral arguments are heard in any particular case, the deliberation among the judges is carried out in private before a ruling is provided, often after a period of many months.

In theory, an apolitical body whose chief purpose is interpretation of the law should provide a steadying influence to guide the American Empire through choppy political waters. Theory, however, is not always reflected in practice. The Supreme Court is currently composed of nine justices, and has been since 1869, but the number itself is actually decided by Congress. Prior to 1869, the number of justices was subject to alteration by Congress as a method of furthering partisan political goals, with as few as five under John Adams and as many as ten under Abraham Lincoln. Currently only the Republican Party seems to be playing to win when it comes to the Court, while the Democrats uphold supposed "accepted" norms of decency, demonstrating breathtaking naivety to the realities of history. The Republicans have been playing a very long game, while the Democrats wring their hands and navel-gaze as the Court has marched to the right.

Conservatives have created a system that nurtures and advances lawyers (and therefore future justices) who adhere to the "originalist" interpretation of the Constitution.[47] Within this movement, the Federalist Society, founded in 1982, has been most influential, succeeding in rebranding originalist interpretation: rather than archaic or backward, the originalist approach is presented as traditionalist, safeguarding the ideals of those heralded demigods, the founding fathers. As the majority of the country seems to have moved to the left on many issues, the Republican Party has moved to the right, adopting this originalist interpretation of the Constitution and skilfully using their legislative power to influence the confirmation process for Supreme Court nominees. This has resulted ultimately in a conservative majority on the Supreme Court.[48]

Delaying and obstructing nominations to the judiciary are tactics used by both parties, but far more successfully and more often by the Republicans. In 2016, after taking control of the Senate, Republicans effectively vetoed Democratic nominations to the judiciary, refusing to even meet with Obama nominee Merrick Garland, who was supposed to fill the seat left open by the death of conservative justice Antonin Scalia. Citing the Senate's "constitutional right to act as a check on a president and withhold its consent", Mitch McConnell and his party simply ignored all criticisms and waited for Republicans to retake control of the presidency.[49]

When minority Democrats filibustered Trump's nomination of Neil Gorsuch in 2017, McConnell was able to remove the ability to filibuster Supreme Court nominations. And in 2020, only a week after the death of liberal icon Ruth Bader Ginsburg, and 38 days before the election that would remove Trump from office, he nominated conservative Amy Coney Barrett to the Supreme Court.[50] She was confirmed by the Republican-controlled Senate and installed a week before the election, with the Republican Party described by Democrat Senate minority leader Chuck Schumer as "lighting its credibility on fire".[51]

Herein lies the issue. One party, which is moving away from the views of US society in the main, understands how to use the system most effectively to achieve its goals, while the other does nothing meaningful to combat these moves, simply sitting on its hands and calling foul play. Why does this matter, and how could it hasten the decline of the American Empire? In the current political climate of hyper-partisanship, how long will it be before a divide becomes a chasm? Secession is a scenario rarely considered as a realistic ending for the American Empire, but it's one that has historically proven to be a catalyst in the decline of many empires.

If the "apolitical" Supreme Court is seen to be nothing of the sort, and therefore believed to represent an extreme interpretation of the Constitution – contrary to the views of a majority of Americans – then discussions around the possibility of secession will increase in their sincerity and plausibility. In general, the legal musings of the judiciary are largely ignored by the public, but the decision to overturn *Roe v. Wade* has brought the Supreme Court into the spotlight. Few subjects in the US generate more polarization than the question of abortion, and the decision on 24 June 2022 to effectively strip women of the right to abortion, which was enshrined since 1973, could come to be seen as a leading cause of any future breakup of the union.

It is not hyperbole to make this claim, and comparisons to the Taliban and the fictional Gilead from *The Handmaid's Tale* are not without merit. Removing the government from decisions about abortion was never the primary intention. Years of building a conservative majority ensured that the Supreme Court's decision removed reproductive rights from 40 million American women who live in states that had trigger laws in place, designed to limit abortion rights the instant that *Roe v. Wade* was overturned. Within a week of the ruling, the real-world ramifications had already begun to filter into public consciousness. A 10-year-old victim of rape in Ohio was unable to obtain an abortion in her home state, having to travel instead for hours into neighbouring Indiana for the procedure. Ohio state representative Jean Schmidt suggested that, in cases such as these, the victim should instead view the pregnancy as an "opportunity".[52]

Political bias is not the only issue eroding public trust in the Supreme Court, as accusations of corruption also cast a shadow over the independence of some of its members. The Court has traditionally policed itself in matters of ethics, and the unimpeachable character of its members was taken as a given. No longer. Justices Clarence Thomas and Samuel Alito have both been accused of accepting gifts from the ultrawealthy who happen to have interests being decided upon by the Court. As Michael Waldman, head of the Brennan Center for Justice, puts it: "This court majority has put in place a radically diminished notion of what corruption is." Kedric Payne of the Campaign Legal Center adds: "The hallmark of a democratic society is for the public to have trust in their institutions ... When you start to chip away at what corruption means, then you chip away at public trust."[53]

5

Media: The Erosion of Trust

An empire's fortunes depend in no small way on the speed and quality of the information it is able to disseminate among its citizens and subjects. Its fate can also rest on the extent to which it can control the dominant narrative via what is known as information hegemony. In empires of the past, the information disseminated might have taken many forms – perhaps a warning about the impending dangers posed by invaders, or propaganda proclaiming the glorious rule of the current leader and his dynasty. As time has passed, methods of communication have evolved – from an Incan runner hand-delivering a message to 24-hour live coverage of a war zone. There are both positive and negative aspects of this evolution, as the world has become ever more closely connected. Communication now moves at the speed of thought, and the ability of a state to maintain information hegemony has become increasingly difficult.

This chapter will examine how the relationship between the American Empire and the media has evolved over time. We will look at how this evolution has affected the level of control that the state has been able to maintain over the presentation of its viewpoint as the official, unchallenged narrative. There is also a constantly changing landscape concerning the level of trust that the citizenry places in both the state and the media, with widespread and increasingly destabilizing effects.

Establishing Information Hegemony

For the British Empire, precursor to the American, state control of information allowed the authorities to quash dissent and censor in the media the unsavoury realities of imperial rule. The notion that the British Empire was an engine of free speech is inaccurate; like every empire beforehand, its survival depended on its ability to control the narrative.

In India, this took the form of the Press Act of 1857 (which became known as the Gagging Act) and the Vernacular Press Act of 1878, which censored any media content that could be seen as potentially seditious. The Press Act of 1910 went even further, forcing newspapers and publishers to deposit large financial securities with the British authorities; these sums could be confiscated at any moment if critical content was published which the British deemed a threat to the stability of their rule. Similar laws existed in Trinidad and other British colonies, where not just written information but also cultural imagery was monitored and restricted in the attempt to control minds and curb unrest.[1]

In 1922, the British Broadcasting Corporation was created as a quasi-autonomous media outlet, but throughout its history it has been accused of being less an independent broadcaster and more a state mouthpiece. Witnessed most notably during the Iraq War in 2003, this criticism was also levelled at almost the entirety of the US media, and it will be examined further in this chapter.

In the 1940s, in the twilight of the British Empire, any coverage of political parties in India was forbidden, though the writing was very much on the wall by this point. After the Second World War, the empire collapsed: India gained its independence in 1947 and a scramble for decolonization elsewhere began to gain pace. Overt censorship practices, however, continued as late as 1978: the government of Ian Smith in Rhodesia (now Zimbabwe), informed by the white-supremacist model of the British Empire, prohibited any reporting that contradicted the official narrative of the ongoing civil war.[2]

The American Empire could not and cannot be as overt as its predecessor when attempting to control the media and shape the narrative, but this does not mean it has been inactive in this regard. In the modern world, the dissemination of information is the responsibility of a multitude of journalists, editors, analysts, presenters, bloggers and amateur videographers, who make up the fourth estate. As information availability has exploded, first with satellite television and then with the internet, the independence, reliability and reputation of the fourth estate has increasingly been called into question.

The rest of this chapter will look at both the successes and failures of the American Empire in controlling the narrative in an evolving information landscape. We will examine in particular how the failures have occurred, how distrust has grown and what effects this has had on the political and media landscape. The potential impact of this on the American Empire will then be considered. This will all be viewed through the prism of conflict reporting while bearing in mind that, in the present day, conflict is increasingly internal and domestic as well as external and foreign.

The Loss of Information Hegemony

In the years directly after the Second World War a victorious American Empire was basking in the afterglow of having defeated fascism. At the same time, it was preparing its citizens for the ideological struggle against a new foe, the communist Soviet Union. The friendly wartime ally "Uncle Joe" was no more – Stalin was rebranded, much more accurately, as the dictatorial ruler of a totalitarian state. The creation of NATO in 1949 signalled the beginning of the Cold War, as containment of the communist threat became the primary policy objective of the American Empire. During this period, the US attempted to control the narrative globally, with varying success, and worked tirelessly to spread and perpetuate the Hollywood image of righteous American exceptionalism battling the evil Soviet empire. In the Korean War of the early 1950s, with the backing of the UN, the US intervened to support South Korea against assault from their estranged northern brethren. In an act of strikingly similar verbal gymnastics to Vladimir Putin's talk of a "special military operation" in Ukraine in 2022, President Truman sidestepped the requirement for a congressional declaration of war by branding the intervention a "police action".[3] After the armistice of 1953 the war was widely forgotten in the US; those who did remember it portrayed it primarily as a noble act – executed successfully and with minimal US casualties – to protect innocent South Koreans against the communist threat.

The next major foreign intervention by the US would occur in Vietnam, and would begin with its own deceptive linguistic foundation: US troops were labelled not as combatants, but merely "observers".[4] Although the conflict would famously be labelled the first "television war", successive administrations were initially able to control the narrative by exerting pressure on network executives, shaping the public mood by exploiting national security concerns and by appealing to patriotism. In 1968, in the context of the Tet Offensive, this all changed as the US government lost hegemonic control of the reporting of the conflict. Viet Cong guerrillas attacked and breached the US embassy in Saigon, and the reality of the conflict, rather than the sanitized White House-approved version, was reported for the first time and seen by millions of Americans on their TV screens. This prompted a visit to Vietnam by Walter Cronkite, the most trusted man on television, who asserted that the war was unwinnable and would lead to an inevitable stalemate.

The importance of the "Cronkite moment" in the overall context of the war is still debated, but what is certain is that it signalled the first real delineation between the media and the White House with respect to conflict coverage. This separation continued in earnest when journalist Seymour Hersh exposed the 1968 Mỹ Lai massacre of some 500 innocent Vietnamese as well as the subsequent 20-month attempt by the US Army to hide the true nature of the events.[5] The loss of information hegemony would prove to be a decisive factor in the turning of public opinion against the war, but it also laid the foundations for an evolving relationship between the media, the public and US civilian and military leadership.

One might imagine that the condemnation and public outrage generated by the atrocities of the Vietnam War would lead to a change in direction for the American Empire, especially regarding foreign interventions. The real change, however, was that the authorities newly appreciated the importance of information control and began developing the methods required to secure it. The overt became the covert, with paramilitary actions increasingly co-ordinated or conducted by operatives of the CIA, providing a veneer of separation between White House policy and events on the ground, not to mention plausible deniability. Between 1898 and 1994, the US was partly responsible for at least 41 regime changes in Latin America, 17 of which involved direct intervention and 24 indirect. During the Cold War these interventions involved a large variety of methods: direct CIA involvement in coups, employing local militias to further US interests, offering support to local actors to destabilize leftist regimes, extensive propaganda and the waging of information warfare against the local population.[6]

Modern sensibilities have evolved away from the glorification of war and conquest, and this has occurred at the same time as an explosion in the availability of information, albeit in combination with the loss of hegemonic control over it. These changes necessitated the covert nature of many American actions abroad, and their secrecy ensured that these actions were subjected to far less media scrutiny – and public opposition – than the Vietnam War. The majority of these interventions went widely unreported until the Iran–Contra Affair engulfed the Reagan administration. The scandal, and its connection to the president himself, showed that information hegemony, even relating to covert operations, was no longer possible. The years after the Mỹ Lai revelations and the Cronkite moment saw a steady decline in public trust in US authorities, but a belief was also growing among the public that the US media should objectively and fearlessly hold leaders to account. The events of 9/11 and the war on terror would open a new chapter in this story.

The Loss of Objectivity and Trust

The 11th of September 2001 was a pivotal moment in the history of the American Empire, with seismic ramifications for the entire world. The day's shocking events were soon followed by a rare show of global unity – with some exceptions – as nations around the globe offered condolences and support to the wounded superpower. The subsequent invasion of Afghanistan to hunt the perpetrators was the first time that NATO had triggered Article 5, and the mission began with widespread approval among the US public and media.

The impact of the 9/11 attacks on the public psyche was so profound that the distance between the media and the government, which had opened up gradually between 1968 and 2001, instantly evaporated. There were few dissenting voices within the US regarding action in Afghanistan, and the Bush administration's move to invade Iraq in 2003 began in a similar manner – the media, functioning increasingly as state broadcasters, were in lockstep with the government. This period is of vital importance. The collective failure of the media to challenge the official narrative has had long-lasting effects on the relationship between the public and the media. This period can be viewed as the beginning of the end of public trust in traditional media. The post-9/11 wars were the first to be fought in the age of the 24/7 news cycle, and the early seeds of conspiracy theory were sown onto fertile ground.

Twenty years after the invasion of Iraq, the facts and falsehoods of the justification of the war are now well known. The Bush administration had decided to invade and needed to find reasons of sufficient emotional heft to persuade the public to support its actions. Attempts to tie the Saddam Hussein regime to Al-Qaeda were unlikely to stand up to serious scrutiny, as the Baathist regime was no real friend to Islamic terror. The regime's survival was predicated on the ruthless elimination of any attempts to unite Muslims under a single banner, and as a result Iraq was almost as despised by bin Laden and his followers as the US itself.

Human rights abuses in Iraq were well documented – just as they were in numerous other countries – but were deemed unimportant with regard to US national security. The Bush administration realized that, to achieve widespread support for the invasion, the public's remaining trust in the media would need to be skilfully exploited. Hussein would need to be both Hitler and Stalin – a threat to the very survival of the United States, to freedom and to the world as a whole. Spurious claims about WMDs were trumpeted by administration officials and repeated by the media, with Secretary of State Condoleezza Rice most famously warning that "we don't want the smoking gun to be a mushroom cloud".[7]

Competing cable news networks, desperate for content to fill 24/7 schedules, abandoned journalistic scrutiny and simply aimed to be first rather than factual, ensuring their continued access to administration sources. As the war progressed and WMDs were never uncovered, the invasion was rebranded as an exercise to spread freedom and democracy.[8] The "noble" nature of this endeavour was undercut somewhat by the decision to abandon the rule of law – America fought terror with terror, restricting or destroying numerous freedoms in the process.

Without proper scrutiny from the media, the worst impulses were unleashed: human-rights abuses became enshrined as government policy – with torture rebranded as "enhanced interrogation" – as events at Abu Ghraib prison and Guantanamo Bay would illustrate. These revelations, much like Mỹ Lai almost forty years prior, made it clear to the media and the US public just how skilfully they had been manipulated and misled.

It was also revealed, over the course of 2005 and 2006, that the use of subterfuge to create a justification for war was nothing new. The release of more than 200 previously classified documents showed that the Gulf of Tonkin incident, which had been used in 1964 to justify escalation of the conflict in Vietnam, had been misreported: some of the events had simply not happened.[9] One disastrous intervention was revealed to be based on lies, just as another was undergoing similar scrutiny.

Why is this important for our analysis of the American Empire and its potential demise? In simple terms, the lies and revelations of this period have served as a formative learning experience for many American citizens, creating conditions that are conducive to conspiracist thinking in the present day. A healthy distrust of – and ability to question – state authority is a crucial and protective aspect of a liberal society. When this distrust becomes a reflex, however, and when the public begin to turn away from media they see as complicit in selling them lies, alternative sources of information will be sought.

The Curse of 24/7 Coverage and Partisan Media

With Barack Obama's election in 2008, the US aimed to move on from the "war on terror" and begin extricating itself from the conflicts in Iraq and Afghanistan. This process would not be straightforward, illustrating clearly that it is far easier to begin a war than to end one. The public and political appetite for fighting wars in foreign lands had evaporated, a reality keenly appreciated by Obama when he authorized airstrikes in Libya in 2011 without congressional approval. After Syrian government forces used chemical weapons in 2013, he sought the backing of Congress to take military action, but avoided putting this to a vote – and potentially losing, given significant legislative and popular opposition to intervention – by agreeing a deal which required Syria to join the Chemical Weapons Convention.

During this period, the media were no longer complicit in the way they had been in the immediate aftermath of 9/11. Over Obama's two terms, the media landscape continued to evolve as domestic division was increasingly stoked in the absence of credible external threats. Actions (or perceived inaction) were increasingly analysed and attacked through a purely partisan prism: the actor, rather than the action itself, became the subject of greater attention. Obama received criticism for taking military action in Libya that was viewed as illegitimate, and yet he was also attacked by some for not immediately authorizing airstrikes in Syria in 2013: a lose–lose situation.

A subtle shift in the American psyche was being illustrated, as political tribalism increased and people seemed to prioritize their party identities as Republicans or Democrats over their shared identity as Americans. This tribalism was exacerbated by the continued evolution of news media and its consumption by the population. The rise of the 24/7 news cycle in the 2000s marked an increasing shift from factual reporting to infotainment, and in the 2010s this evolution continued as objectivity was replaced by opinion.

This change, although gradual, has important consequences. Opinion, unlike fact, is designed to appeal to a predetermined cross-section of society, and controversy and vitriol are far more popular than balance and nuance in the ongoing quest for ratings. Whereas Walter Cronkite achieved celebrity status because of his perceived impartiality and trustworthiness, Tucker Carlson in the present day has become famous despite exhibiting the exact opposite of these traits. This is not to single out Republicans for particular criticism – media outlets representing both the left and right are deeply flawed, biased and compromised; hypocrisy abounds. Both sides are happy to ignore the transgressions of their standard-bearers, while attacking the actions of the other side. We must note the mass hysteria within the liberal media in 2016 after Donald Trump's election, expressed in the desperate, obsessive search for any possible method to delegitimize the man and his presidency. Any attempt at political introspection, or analysis of the flaws of the Democrats, was shut down with accusations of betrayal and handing "wins" to the other side. For the right, meanwhile, outright falsehoods and conspiracy theories have become mainstream, propagated by elected representatives, such as QAnon-adherent Marjorie Taylor Greene, and their media mouthpieces.

The Age of Social Media, Fake News, Alternative Facts and Conspiracy Theories

Why are apparently intelligent, reasonable Americans increasingly believing in convoluted conspiracy theories that are often clearly illogical, contradictory or demonstrably false? The simple answer is not that these people are all mentally deficient or prone to fantasy, but that they have been repeatedly lied to by the traditional arbiters of truth within the American Empire. In Vietnam, the media exposed what the public may have suspected, namely that political and military leaders lie regularly to further their own goals. During the war on terror, it was revealed that the public could trust neither their country's leaders nor the traditional media. Individuals within these groups seemed to coalesce, in the eyes of the public, into one amorphous, untrustworthy mass which was labelled "the establishment". Donald Trump exploited this to great effect in his 2016 campaign for the presidency: the establishment, composed of elites from both parties, was castigated as the cause of America's misfortunes, while everyone else (including the billionaire presidential candidate himself) ranked as the good guys.

In this changing landscape, many Americans distrust anyone within this perceived establishment, seeking answers and reassurance instead from those with webcams and YouTube channels. On the rise, this alternative media provides both pitfalls and potential. A move away from a siloed, hyper-partisan media whose content is driven by vested interests has the potential to be transformative, but this depends on what replaces it.

A growing number of people are receiving their news from YouTube and social media, whose algorithms are specifically designed to provide content that will appeal to each individual. The problem is that such content is likely to reinforce existing beliefs and create an even more siloed experience: an echo chamber. Furthermore, the algorithms have deduced that the more extreme the viewpoint expressed, the more likely the individual is to view that content – not a healthy development for balanced discourse.[10] If the public chooses instead to seek out balanced, independent-minded, factually accurate journalism within the alternative media, then this will improve public discourse and could prove beneficial to the country at large. The best example of this is the rapid success of the podcast and YouTube channel *Breaking Points*, the brainchild of Krystal Ball and Saagar Enjeti. Although from ostensibly different sides of the political divide, they are united in holding the powerful to account and in objectively reporting the facts through a bipartisan lens. As Enjeti stated in the first episode:

> What are we doing here? ... We truly believe in making everybody really hate each other less and hate the corrupt ruling class more.[11]

This premise clearly touched a section of the population and made *Breaking Points* the most-streamed political podcast when it launched in 2021, at a time when viewing figures for traditional cable-news networks were in decline.[12] CNN's recent struggles to shore up its ratings, including the attempt to win back right-of-centre viewers – which was the goal of CEO Chris Licht before he was forced to leave the network in June 2023 – testify to the challenges faced by traditional media in the current environment.[13]

It is difficult to predict how the media will continue to evolve, but this matter is of vital importance to the survival of the American Empire. Facts themselves are no longer seen as objective. Previously, facts were simply facts, and it was only the interpretation of these facts that could be clouded by prior beliefs and bias. Now, the very idea of objective facts is disputed – an incredibly dangerous development for any society that hopes to remain cohesive.

This problem of subjectivity has been exacerbated by Donald Trump and his epithet of "fake news" – a derisory catch-all description of any facts that prove to be inconvenient to him or his agenda. While attendance figures at presidential inaugurations are not a matter of life and death, Kellyanne Conway's reference to "alternative facts" on this matter in January 2017 set a dangerous precedent.[14] Meanwhile, foreign powers with their state-sponsored bot farms have already realized how to manipulate reality to weaponize the divisions within US society, and this will only become more dangerous as deepfake technology continues to generate fake content that is increasingly hard to detect. In a society where a significant number of citizens seem ready and willing to take up arms against the government, what would happen if they were instructed to do so by a deepfake version of their leader, be it Trump or someone else?

In the same manner that Trump weaponized the concept of fake news, the Biden administration and its cheerleaders have done the same with the term "conspiracy theory". To question the official narrative on either Covid-19 or the war in Ukraine is to be labelled a conspiracy theorist, have your reputation tarnished and see your arguments ignored. Jeffrey Sachs, a distinguished economist and professor at Columbia University, has discovered this to his cost. After he was asked by *The Lancet* to chair a commission on Covid-19, Sachs came to the view that, while uncertainty still exists, the virus may well have been the product of gain-of-function research, and that there was a real possibility it could have leaked from a lab in Wuhan. He was instantly criticized and accused of fuelling conspiracy theories.[15] Sachs experienced similar treatment when he expressed the idea that NATO's eastern expansion (despite repeated warnings from Russia), along with US behaviour during Ukraine's political upheaval in early 2014, was bound to provoke a Russian response.[16]

Attempts to stifle dissent and suppress questioning of dominant narratives are eerily reminiscent of the atmosphere during the early stages of the war on terror, and of the media complicity that helped justify the invasion of Iraq. These recent developments regarding Covid-19 and Ukraine show that government attempts to control the media and the narrative are more akin to a game of cat and mouse than a progression through distinct and predictable stages. This game will continue to evolve as technological advances further blur the lines between fact and fiction.

PART THREE

External Threats

6

The Changing Nature of War

In empires of the past, the idea of imperial expansion through military force was a glorious endeavour for the victors and a lamented fact of life for the vanquished. It would have been pointless to explain to a Roman caesar, Aztec emperor or Mongol warlord that a time would come when the glory of empire would be disputed and disparaged – these rulers might have responded to such a suggestion with utter incomprehension, lofty amusement or a swift beheading.

Of course, it has always been known that the conquered were not happy about their fate, but the realist maxim of "might is right" has been the driving force behind geopolitics for the majority of human history. The move away from the image of glorious conquest began during the First World War, owing to its scenes of industrial slaughter, enabled by modern weaponry, at a level unprecedented in previous times. The scale and pace of this change in perspective cannot be overstated; as this was a truly global conflict, the effects were felt worldwide.

After the conclusion of the conflict, hopeful nations, scarred by such wanton carnage and loss of life, sought to consign bloody conquest to the history books, referring to the slaughter as "the war to end all wars". This hope would prove to be naive, as the world would be at war again in little more than two decades. The eventual Allied vanquishing of Imperial Japan and Nazi Germany, the latter of which had been striving for nothing less than global domination, continued the move away from notions of imperial glory via foreign conquest, supporting instead the claims of individual national sovereignty. The Second World War also signalled the beginning of the end of the last global empire, with the bankrupt British paying a heavy price for their victory. The cost to maintain the empire was simply too great to bear, but also the clamour for individual nationhood was too difficult to ignore, especially after these subject nations had themselves spent years fighting the threat of tyranny and subjugation.

The end of the Second World War confirmed the existence of two young empires in North America and the USSR respectively, although they did not refer to themselves as such (but they would certainly tar their opponent with the term). Rather than view itself as a stronger power inflicting its will on weaker states, the Soviet Union aimed to depict its domain as one of shared fraternal bonds and mutual prosperity in the communist tradition. The American Empire, on the other hand, promoted the ideas of democracy, free-market capitalism and individual liberty far and wide to entice other nations into its orbit. Both empires continued to wage war in different areas of the globe, but they attempted to package their military activities as efforts in "spreading democracy" or "maintaining order" rather than as glorious imperial conquest.

When the Berlin Wall fell in 1989 and the Cold War drew to a close, the only remaining challenger to the global hegemony of the American Empire disintegrated. In bygone eras, this unchallenged military superiority would have led inevitably to territorial conquest. Not so for the American Empire: modern sensibilities and evolved views on warfare required that any military activities be presented as "humanitarian intervention". Unassailable military superiority, influence over all major global institutions, and enormous financial and commercial clout made territorial conquest and occupation unnecessary.

This new state of affairs does, however, provide a check on the ability of the American Empire to exert its will – a constraint not placed on any of its predecessors. The fierce public resistance to the Iraq War, and to any suggestion of long-term occupation and extraction of the natural resources of the country, is the perfect example of this constraint. While the protests in 2003 did not stop the war, the carefully crafted, benevolent image of the American Empire evaporated. The misadventures in Iraq, and in Afghanistan, had a profound effect on US citizens, severely diminishing the national tolerance for suffering casualties in far-flung lands.

This change in attitude would hamper the ability of the US to shape events in Libya and Syria in the 2010s. In Syria, the decision to not get deeply involved handed the far less circumspect regime of Putin's Russia free rein to behave without any such restrictions. American reluctance to intervene overseas has without doubt emboldened regimes such as Putin's to act with far less regard to how the American Empire may respond. US actions to stem the expansion of ISIS were the exception to this rule, as global condemnation of the Islamist group provided the necessary cover for spending taxpayer dollars to combat the threat.

If we consider potential future conflicts, and the recent past as regards the Russian invasion of Ukraine, we can see that the aim of conquering one's neighbours cannot, for the time being at least, be used to justify military action and loss of life. The justification given by Putin for his disastrous invasion of Ukraine was not conquest for its own sake, but the spurious pretext of "de-Nazification" of the neighbouring state. In reality, he aimed to regain territory ceded by the Soviet Union, the collapse of which he has labelled "the greatest geopolitical disaster of the twentieth century".[1] Elsewhere, China considers Taiwan to be a part of the motherland, which it intends to retake, by force if necessary. While Russia and China make claims about uniting ethnically similar peoples under the rule of Moscow and Beijing respectively, the US would struggle to use similar arguments to justify military action. Its borders seem settled now. A march north into Canada would be unthinkable.

However, nobody can accurately predict how future events may shape attitudes to warfare in the decades and centuries ahead. In a possible future of resource scarcity, will current sensibilities fade away, leading to a return to the belief that "might is right"? This cannot be known; but if the current trajectory of America's evolving attitude to warfare continues, many will raise a key question: what is the benefit of possessing unparalleled military superiority if you are not able to use it?

Let's explore this matter further with reference to the ancient Greek historian Thucydides, who studied the Peloponnesian War between Athens and Sparta in the fifth century BCE. In the 2010s, the American political scientist Graham Allison coined and popularized the phrase "the Thucydides trap", outlining why it was, in his view, highly likely that a dominant empire will launch a war against a state looking to overtake it – or it will be attacked itself.[2] In the ancient Greek world following the Persian Wars, Athens was the dominant empire and Sparta was its suspicious rival. Allison's analysis of 16 historical scenarios showed that 12 of them resulted in conflict (including the Greek example). This conflict can be driven by a rising power that has no course of action but to attack and usurp the hegemon if it wishes to continue to increase its influence, territory and resources. The conflict can also be driven by a hegemon that has no choice but to attack its less powerful rival before it becomes vulnerable to usurpation.

We might describe this Thucydides trap as a catch-22 situation, where war becomes an inevitability rather than a choice. But is this logic still valid today? It is no secret that China has global ambitions that ultimately include the replacement of the US as the world's hegemon. Until this goal is reached, China wishes to promote or maintain multipolarity in the international order. Most commentators would agree that this point has already been reached, as the US no longer enjoys the unique position it held from 1991 as the world's sole superpower. There is also a strong argument that, through its actions during the disastrous war in Ukraine, Russia has sown the seeds of its own demise and the world will move swiftly from the current state of multipolarity to bipolarity. With its military depleted and economy in shambles, Putin's Russia has now become the junior partner in the Sino-Russian relationship, and Russian influence will continue to wane as Putin's kleptocratic regime enters a death spiral. So, if a world of bipolarity seems likely in the next 10–20 years, will the conditions exist for the Thucydides trap to be sprung, and is war an inevitability? Let's begin our analysis with the reasons why a rising China may or may not engage in conflict with the US as it attempts to attain dominance.

Will China Attack the US?

The Chinese geopolitical strategy is one with patience at its heart, mindful that a direct military conflict with the American Empire would end in defeat. Instead, China has been building global influence through its "Belt and Road" initiative, a twenty-first-century revival of the Silk Road trading network. The initiative involves the financing of vast infrastructure projects in areas where US influence is in decline, specifically Africa and Eurasia. By providing manpower and funds to assist in the industrializing of these regions, Xi Jinping intends to spread Chinese influence without resorting to physical conquest. He is also working to establish a Chinese-led bloc of states, mainly authoritarian or autocratic, as an alternative to the Western-led international order. If this seems familiar, it should. It was the tactic used by the British to subvert the Portuguese and Spanish empires in the sixteenth and seventeenth centuries. And more recently it was used by the American Empire after the Second World War, as the US ensured subservience through its domination of multinational organizations.

It is not surprising that US officials loudly deride China's schemes and warn of the dangers to the host countries; it is hypocritical, absolutely, but game quietly respects game. However, is there a point when this expanding influence reaches a level where the Chinese decide they can no longer continue to expand their reach without resorting to military conflict? It is possible that this point could be reached and a direct assault on the US or its forces would occur, but this seems improbable. The more likely scenario is that Chinese military action against US allies or its interests would provoke a military response – a hot war between the two superpowers might then ensue. The likely flashpoint is Taiwan (which will be discussed further in a moment), but there are many potential locations where conflict could originate, including states in mineral-rich Africa.

The key aspect in all this is demographics. Attempts to prevent over-population and also the drive toward rapid urbanization have led to a demographic disaster in many states; China in particular is going to suffer acutely. The problem is not too many people but too few, and the Chinese population is expected to shrink from around 1.4 billion at present to perhaps as little as 600 million people by 2100.[3] Not only that, but of these 600 million people, far too few will be in the age 20–60 category and able to contribute economically to society. Furthermore, the modern Chinese state is underpinned by an ethno-nationalist ideology that prevents its leadership from using mass immigration to plug the gap that will be created by its declining population. All these pressures and uncertainties – and the ruling party's fear of domestic unrest as Chinese society undergoes such changes – may force President Xi to abandon strategic patience and take the step of engaging the US militarily long before the American Empire has itself collapsed.

Fear of population collapse also lies behind the huge Chinese investment in robotics and AI, as the productive members of its society will need to be replaced somehow. But this forgets the other side of the demo-graphic argument: productive members of society do not simply produce goods and services – they also consume them. The current global model is growth-centric and relies upon both production and consumption to stimulate the economy and drive progress. If China is to succeed in surpassing the US, it will require a global shift away from a focus on growth. As a 2009 book of the same name explained, China will need "prosperity without growth".[4] This is not impossible, as other states are also experiencing the same demographic issues, and a consensus is growing that endless growth is neither possible nor desirable, especially due to the environmental impact of such a strategy. Initiatives like the four-day working week and experiments in universal basic income are steps toward this goal, but there is much more road to run. For China, the question is how long this pivot takes to occur, and whether it will still be a realistic challenger to the US by that point.

Will the US Attack China?

The other side of the coin is to ask under what conditions the US would act militarily against China, halting its rise before it can surpass the US as the global superpower. The answer to this question is informed by the changing attitudes to warfare that were described earlier in the chapter. In Thucydides's time, it was a perfectly logical, acceptable and predictable action for the dominant power to wage a preventative war against an upcoming rival to prevent their rise and postpone its own decline. Due to evolving attitudes to warfare, this is no longer the case.

For the US to act militarily in this manner, attacking China first, the rationale would have to be utterly overwhelming. If it were not, global condemnation would follow swiftly and the moral high ground that the American Empire claims to hold – however dubious that claim might seem to outside observers – would be lost. As outlined above, Xi Jinping is unlikely at present to threaten the world with nuclear blackmail or promise to destroy militarily the Western, US-led order in the same manner as his ally Putin. The difference is Putin is desperate, and Xi is not. This may change, of course, especially as the realities of China's demographic imbalance begin to bite.

The US might choose to exploit a Chinese military action, probably an attempt to retake Taiwan, to provide the pretext for an overwhelming (yet non-nuclear) US military response which hobbles its challenger. The threat that a Chinese seizure of Taiwan would pose to the global semiconductor industry might be sufficient to rally global support for a US military response, as might a similar threat to the supply of any number of potential raw materials in the future.

But in all such scenarios the presence of nuclear arsenals will always loom large: the use of such weapons, especially after Putin's threats regarding Ukraine, is now unfortunately more conceivable – but not necessarily inevitable – in any military conflict between major powers. The US and China, not to mention the world, have much to lose in the event of a nuclear war. Self-interest may preserve peace for a while longer, but nothing is ever guaranteed.

The Cost of War

Let's turn now to simple economics and whether the US can continue to spend the vast sums required to maintain its global empire and military dominance. If the cost of maintaining hegemony causes US imperial power to implode, this would not be the first time that an empire collapsed under the weight of its military spending commitments; both the Roman and British empires faltered for this reason. For the Romans, the taxes required to ensure military pre-eminence and imperial expansion were met with such hostility that revolt and disintegration ensued. Domestic concerns had been ignored for too long in favour of imperial expansion. For Britain, no internal revolt was necessary – its political leaders realized that the country simply could not afford to maintain its empire after the financial outlay required to achieve victory over Germany and Japan in the Second World War.

What does this mean for the American Empire? The US maintains a huge network of military bases around the world at a huge annual cost of around $55 billion.[5] Moreover, its dominant presence in the

Atlantic and Pacific through its unassailable naval superiority now requires an annual outlay of over $200 billion.[6] There is growing opposition within the American Empire to performing, and paying to perform, the role of global police officer; this was exemplified by President Trump's constant demands for US allies to pay for their own protection. As globalization seems to be unravelling in the wake of the coronavirus pandemic, as states become more inward-looking and often nationalistic, seeking to control immigration and protect their citizens from disrupted supply chains, this opposition will only continue to grow louder and more difficult to ignore.

It is not simply these direct costs that are required to maintain the military dominance of the American Empire, as the Russia–Ukraine War has highlighted. Unable to engage Russia militarily without a descent into World War Three and possible nuclear Armageddon, the US has instead led a global effort to support the Ukrainian war effort through money and materiel.

American taxpayers have already contributed multiple billions of dollars to this proxy war.[7] This funding of Ukraine was largely backed by US citizens and received bipartisan support in Congress at first. But as inflation rampages through the economy, Americans are increasingly asking why they should support Ukrainians thousands of miles away when they can't afford to pay their own bills, feed their own children or heat their own homes.

The sense that US support for Ukraine represents a blank cheque is only reinforced by the manner in which reasonable questions are dealt with by those who support the action. When legitimate concerns are voiced, most notably by Senator Rand Paul of Kentucky and representative Tulsi Gabbard of Hawaii, these are not addressed or debated but instead dismissed, with the accusatory smear of "Putin apologism". Is it not sensible to ask where billions of dollars of support are actually going to be spent, especially in a country widely known to suffer very high levels of corruption? Time is of the essence, but an extra day to show that these concerns are being addressed would most likely keep the public onside for a little longer.

While Paul and Gabbard (and Jeffrey Sachs) are not incorrect, the reality is that the current situation with regard to Ukraine was unfortunately always likely after the end of the Cold War and the collapse of the Soviet Union. As nobody suffered a complete military defeat, Russian and American viewpoints on geopolitical realities were always likely to differ. As the Cold War's victor, and like many empires before, America believed that it could reshape the world as it saw fit. Russia, after internal disarray led to a kleptocratic regime, was always going to feel marginalized and seek to regain its former might. On the one hand, American actions have unquestionably stoked the embers of Russian dissatisfaction, whether through neoconservative design or simply arrogance. On the other, it is unrealistic for the victor to allow the defeated to dictate geopolitical realities. Simply because the Russian regime does not wish for a neighbour to embrace closer ties with the Western world, that does not justify a brutal war of aggression costing thousands of lives.

The idea of utilizing a third-party state in a proxy-war effort to avoid direct engagement while weakening an enemy is also nothing new; also known as "buck passing", it's a tactic used by many of the empires we have examined previously. The American Empire is no different, as the Cold War was defined by a succession of proxy wars all over the world. In purely financial terms, though, there is still a strong case to be made that supporting Ukraine furthers American strategic interests at a fraction of the cost of waging war directly. The estimated $2.3 trillion spent by the US in Afghanistan over two decades provides a salient point of comparison, and there are obvious benefits to not being involved in direct conflict with a nuclear-armed Russia. It will not be a surprise, then, to see this tactic used in future in the event of Chinese aggression in the South China Sea.

The Changing Nature of Warfare

It is not simply attitudes to warfare that continue to evolve; the methods of waging it are changing as well. Empires have always sought out the most advanced military techniques and technology, and the US is no different today, but the importance of sheer military superiority and firepower has been somewhat reduced in the globalized interconnected world that emerged after the Second World War.

Recent events in Ukraine and the global Covid pandemic seem to be accelerating a retreat from globalization, but this will not be instant and the world remains intrinsically linked via the intricate networks required for modern life in the twenty-first century. The spread and entrenching of these networks in commerce, finance, knowledge and raw materials has powered the march to industrialization and prosperity for many states, creating a global, multifaceted, mutual dependency.

This mutual dependency has often served as a preventative measure, reducing the chance of direct conflict between states. It can also serve to level the playing field for a less powerful state in conflict against a more powerful adversary. This can provide an additional level of security for states threatened by the predatory actions of larger neighbours, as is the case with the global dependence on Taiwanese semiconductors.

The importance of the Taiwanese semiconductor industry in global civilian and military applications is colossal – so colossal in fact that the Biden administration has abandoned the long-standing "strategic ambiguity" surrounding US commitments to the defence of the island and has stated explicitly that any attack will be met with a US military response.[8] Will this policy still be relevant if the US is able to fulfil its ambitions to boost domestic semiconductor production to the level required for independence in the years to come? The $280 billion in

161

funding provided for semiconductor research and manufacturing in the 2022 CHIPS and Science Act shows how significant this issue is in the long-term strategic thinking of the US. Biden's words upon signing the act into law on 9 August 2022 are very telling of the current decline of the American Empire:

> This bill is about more than chips ... It's about saying, decades ago we used to invest 2 percent of our GDP [in research and development] and led the world in everything. We lead the world in everything from internet to GPS. Today, we invest less than 1 percent [of the nation's GDP].[9]

In the current climate, the US never wants to be too reliant or dependent on any foreign actor or supplier. Dependencies can and will be leveraged and exploited by adversaries, but even ostensible allies will do so in certain circumstances. After the assassination and dismemberment of the journalist Jamal Khashoggi in 2018, the Saudi regime of Mohammed bin Salman (MBS) was heavily criticized in the US. But this criticism seemed to evaporate instantly when the Russian invasion of Ukraine threatened global energy supply. MBS is acutely aware of this situation and willing to not only exploit it, but also advertise it. America is not alone in looking the other way when it is convenient to do so. British prime minister Boris Johnson visited Saudi Arabia in March 2022 days after the announcement that a record number of 81 people had been executed by the state; to bludgeon home the point, a further three people were beheaded on the first day of his visit.

States that would have no chance against a more powerful adversary in a direct military conflict are able to exploit global interdependency to reduce the importance of military superiority and create opportunities to further their own aims. Even Russia, far more powerful militarily than Ukraine, has adopted this strategy to exploit the globalized system and exert additional pressure on Ukraine and its allies. Chastened by the shortcomings of the conventional Russian military and its unexpected losses in the war in Ukraine – and by the staunch support of Ukraine by the West in the form of materiel, training and intelligence sharing – Putin quickly turned instead to global blackmail. Control of the Black Sea and of the Ukrainian port of Odessa gave him the ability to throttle the global food supply, as shipments of grain were not only prevented from leaving the country, but also stolen or simply bombed and destroyed. This threatened to have a devastating impact on global food supplies, as Russia and Ukraine account for 14 per cent of global wheat supply and 30 per cent of the world's wheat exports, and they produce 60 per cent of global sunflower oil.[10] The Black Sea Grain Initiative, agreed in July 2022, was a positive development, but it collapsed before a full year had elapsed. The future of grain supplies remains uncertain. Meanwhile, the ability to choke off other supplies has also been utilized, as Russia has restricted exports of potash, phosphate and nitrogen-containing fertilizer – it provides 13 per cent of global supplies.[11]

It is not only food and chemical supplies that Putin can exploit, as the dependence on raw materials from both Russia and Ukraine is also vital to global markets. Russia controls 44 per cent of global palladium supplies, 13 per cent of platinum, 23 per cent of titanium and 34 per cent of vanadium, while Ukraine produces 50 per cent of the global supply of neon used in semiconductor manufacturing. Russia is also the world's third-largest supplier of nickel, which is used for electric vehicle batteries, and it also produces vast quantities of stainless steel, which is a crucial commodity in modern industries.[12]

This is all before we even begin to discuss Putin's most potent weapon: not nuclear warheads or chemical weapons, but control over fossil-fuel-based energy supplies to Europe. As President Trump rightly warned in a speech to the UN in September 2018, the European (and specifically German) dependency on Russian energy was a clear and present threat to their security.[13] The derisive laughter from the German delegation could be interpreted more as a reaction to the messenger than the message, but the ramifications of Russia's invasion of Ukraine have since demonstrated that the message was not unwise. In 2021, before the invasion, three states (Bosnia and Herzegovina, Moldova and North Macedonia) were completely dependent on Russia for their gas supplies, a further three (Latvia, Serbia and Austria) had over 85 per cent dependency, two (Bulgaria and Finland) over 75 per cent, four others over 60 per cent, and three (including Germany) were close to or above 50 per cent.[14]

Putin has been able to use energy blackmail as a method of sowing division among Ukraine's European allies simply by turning off the taps. The decision not to open the Nord Stream 2 pipeline was actually made by Germany, not Russia, in an unprecedented display of political unity against Russian aggression. This unity, however, has its limits, and the fact that Russia can influence so many other nations with its control of energy supplies highlights the potential dangers of interconnective globalization, and the importance of energy independence in the US.

It is not only energy blackmail that Putin has at his disposal, but also two varieties of nuclear blackmail. The first, and most obvious, is the repeated threat to deploy the Russian nuclear arsenal against any state deemed a danger to Russian security. The second and less widely predicted variety involves the military assaults on nuclear power stations in Ukraine, which carry a dual threat: this applies pressure on Kyiv by attacking Ukrainian energy sovereignty, but it also raises the spectre of a deliberate repeat of the Chernobyl incident. Direct shelling or occupation and mismanagement of the nuclear plants could result in a catastrophic power failure and reactor meltdown.

All of the above scenarios and options being leveraged by Putin might appear to be unique to this particular conflict – due to the energy, food and raw-material realities of the region, and the prevalence of nuclear power in Ukraine – but they might occur elsewhere. In the future, when resources are likely to be scarcer, this type of asymmetric warfare could become more commonplace and potentially threaten the traditional military superiority of the US. That being said, the US is almost uniquely positioned in terms of geography and resource availability to ensure that these tactics can never be used effectively against it.

The term "hybrid warfare" is often misused or misinterpreted to suggest a novel development hitherto unseen, but warfare is always evolving and always waged using a variety of direct and indirect methods. Putin's limiting of exports of food, chemicals and raw materials to assist his war in Ukraine is an inversion of the age-old tactic of starving a population into submission. Control of the seas allowed the British to use naval blockades to great effect to restrict the ability of their adversaries to import and resupply. Putin uses his forces to restrict the flow of goods the other way. Standard imperial practice for invasion was to terrorize and pillage a civilian population, spreading terror and starvation to destroy morale and hasten defeat. The difference today is that globalization has increased the potential range of such attacks, with an enemy nation's allies also feeling the impact rather than just the population of the country under attack. This is essentially an evolution of the notion of collective punishment, a method of warfare as old as war itself.

Even the idea of economic warfare is nothing new: it has been one of the most potent tools used to secure the dominance of the American Empire. This was possible through de facto leadership of the levers of global finance, via supranational bodies like the IMF and World Bank and via control of the global reserve currency. This granted an ability to essentially control a nation's money supply – the lifeblood of any nation state. Displeasing the US could impact your terms of trade with the international community, limit your access to borrowing, or increase the cost of doing so. These levers were used effectively and regularly to destabilize uncompliant regimes in South and Central America during the Cold War; they were part of a multi-method approach to fomenting coups and achieving regime change.

Even "assistance" from these financial institutions in relation to infra-structure projects was designed to promote vassalage, creating consumers for the American Empire; and if the vassal state also benefited, then this was a bonus – but not crucial.[15] If more direct action was required against a state that refused to comply, sanctions could be used as a modern equivalent of burning crops or blockading ports. The use of sanctions is the definition of collective punishment, with the poor disproportionately affected by increased mortality and morbidity, displacement and psychological damage, as was most recently illustrated in Venezuela since 2017.[16]

In the twenty-first century, then, warfare comes in many forms, from the deaths caused slowly by economic sanctions to the sudden drone strikes that instantly eliminate their targets – along with anyone else in the vicinity. Beneath drone-dominated skies local populations exist in a state of constant fear of death from an all-seeing, invisible enemy high overhead – another example of collective punishment.

Hybrid Warfare: Evolution, Not Revolution

Hybrid warfare entails an interplay or fusion of conventional as well as unconventional instruments of power and tools of subversion. These instruments or tools are blended in a synchronised manner to exploit the vulnerabilities of an antagonist and achieve synergistic effects … The objective of conflating kinetic tools and non-kinetic tactics is to inflict damage on a belligerent state in an optimal manner. [A key characteristic of hybrid warfare is that] the line between war and peace time is rendered obscure. This means that it is hard to identify or discern the war threshold. War becomes elusive as it becomes difficult to operationalise it.[17]

This November 2021 definition of hybrid warfare by the scholar Arsalan Bilal is a useful means of examining the concept and how it may relate to the military superiority of the American Empire in the future. Bilal also states, quite accurately, that although the concept is very much in vogue, many practitioners (and commentators like myself) contend that it is as old as war itself. He also places emphasis on "the use of non-state actors and information technology to subdue [adversaries] in the absence of direct armed conflict". The use of non-state actors to blur the lines between war and peace is again nothing new, as empires in the past have often employed mercenaries and partisans without insignia to further their goals.

Bilal's analysis also reflects the time it was written, as less than three months later Putin would invade Ukraine using traditional, kinetic and (as it turned out) rather outdated methods. Columns of tanks advancing single file toward Kyiv do not represent a novel or ingenious approach to warfare. As Bilal states in his analysis, Russia's previous actions in Crimea in 2014 were far more indicative of hybrid warfare, as they "achieved its objectives by virtue of conflating 'deniable' special forces, local armed actors, economic clout, disinformation, and exploitation of socio-political polarisation in Ukraine".[18]

Only one man can explain why he abandoned this previously successful approach in 2022. Was it arrogance or ill health that forced a more direct approach in order to achieve his goals within a swifter time frame? It also remains to be seen whether Putin's disastrous invasion will reinforce the idea and appeal of hybrid warfare, as states look on and learn from his mistakes, or will the conflict serve to emphasize how important more traditional, kinetic military capabilities continue to be? For the purposes of this study, let's examine various aspects of modern non-traditional warfare to see how less powerful states might use these methods to gain a competitive edge over the American Empire.

Cyber

Cyber warfare is often cited in support of the supposed novelty or modernity of hybrid warfare, but this type is again very much indicative of the evolution, not revolution, of warfare. The primary goals of cyber warfare are the disabling of military and civilian infrastructure; psychological warfare against a civilian population; and industrial espionage. Bots may have replaced Bond, as it were, but the goals are the same, and the grey area in which attacks are conducted continues to offer the cover of deniability, however implausible. Technological advances have improved the potency and sophistication of cyber attacks, and these attacks will become all the more dangerous as algorithms improve, AI comes into its own and quantum computing yields untold breakthroughs.

China, America's main challenger, is counting on all this as it now leads the world in data collection and quantum computing.[19] This does not change the current reality, however, and the US remains the most powerful state actor in cyberspace today. But in some areas China, and to a lesser extent Russia, has surpassed the US. A 2020 Harvard study used a mathematical formula – a National Cyber Power Index – to rank the ten most powerful cyber nations in the world in its benchmark report.[20] The researchers identified seven national objectives that states pursue using cyber means:

- Surveilling and monitoring domestic groups
- Strengthening and enhancing national cyber defences
- Controlling and manipulating the information environment
- Foreign intelligence collection for national security
- Commercial gain or enhancing domestic industry growth
- Destroying or disabling an adversary's infrastructure and capabilities
- Defining international cyber norms and technical standards

The researchers then measured the "comprehensiveness" of a particular state as a cyber actor by its ability to achieve multiple objectives. The US is duly listed as the "most comprehensive country that has (1) the intent to pursue multiple national objectives using cyber means and (2) the capabilities to achieve those objective(s)".[21] The US is ranked highest in four out of seven of these objectives, but China is present in the top five of every objective. China also leads in several categories: cyber surveillance power, cyber power in commerce and cyber defence power. Especially with regard to the first two, this is due in no small part to China's willingness to pursue these objectives through both legal and illegal means, and also its ability to exert far greater levels of control over the civilian population than is possible, or even desirable, in its democratic competitors. It must be remembered that the Chinese cyber-warfare doctrine has not emerged in a vacuum; it is a response to the actions taken by other powerful states – primarily the US, as the benchmark setter. It is also important not to overstate China's current capabilities, as this could become a cause for conflict between two nuclear-armed superpowers that already share a deep (and growing) mistrust of one another.

Biological

The pattern of America's adversaries focusing on developing new technologies at speed, with little regard for legality or safeguarding, is also playing out in the realm of biological science, which could have a significant impact on how war will be waged in the future. In the West, ethical concerns are purported to stifle development in cutting-edge areas of biological research, but this may not reflect the reality on the ground – secretive research projects, as yet unknown to the public in the Western democracies, may yet come to light.

China, meanwhile, is relatively explicit about its fusion of civilian and military life as the regime searches for any possible competitive edge. Chinese scientists are experimenting with the building blocks of life, aiming to master DNA's double helix and gain an advantage in the nascent field of genetic warfare. Various high-ranking officials have explained this doctrine. In his 2010 book *War for Biological Dominance*, Guo Jiwei, a professor with the Third Military Medical University, highlighted the potential impact of biological weapons in future conflicts.[22] In 2015, the then president of the Academy of

Military Medical Sciences, He Fuchu noted the 2014 establishment of the Biological Technologies Office by the US Defense Advanced Research Projects Agency (DARPA) and sought to champion rival efforts by the Chinese:

> As the understanding of the living world continues to deepen in the future, biodiversity, complexity and intelligence provide unlimited room for imagination for national defence technological innovation, which will open a new chapter in the era of intelligent and biological military revolution.[23]

Fuchu goes on to describe numerous different avenues of this revolution, including bionics and biomaterials; biosensing technology; and "brain-controlled weapons and equipment that can interfere with and control human consciousness".[24]

If this does not paint a sufficiently dystopian science-fiction picture, the aim of this new biological frontier is to allow the controlling of the human brain, "expanding warfare from the physical domain and information domain to the cognitive domain". This will not be limited to individual brains: a linked network, an "Internet of Brains", will supposedly make biological intelligence fully integrated into modern information technology.[25]

These aims and methods, although Chinese in origin, are not dissimilar to those of the US since the Second World War, with the infamous MK ULTRA mind-control experiments springing to mind as but one example. The difference today is that technological advances mean these goals have a better chance of actually being achieved. We should also be wary of taking assurances from the US at face value when it comes to the extent of ethical restrictions placed on military research and development, especially given the paranoid "prisoner's dilemma" environment of the modern day. If there was little compunction in breaking the rules during the Cold War, why would now be any different?

This is especially true when we consider the mind-boggling amount spent on "black budget" projects, i.e. those that are not subjected to oversight or scrutiny. Their secretive nature means we only have estimates as opposed to exact numbers, but a figure of more than $50 billion per year is likely, although some administrations request more money than others.[26] Depending on one's perspective, the existence of secretive programs might be a comfort – the US is most likely pursuing similar research activities to its adversaries – or it might be a concern: a potentially dangerous arms race could be exploring untested, unregulated areas of research. Of course, it is not simply China that is willing to push ethical boundaries in the aim of achieving a competitive edge against the US, as states like North Korea, Russia and Iran are probably all running similar programs.

Air and Space

Before the First World War, there were but two potential theatres of conflict: land and sea. From the moment the Wright brothers first slipped the bonds of earth with their 1903 flight, the path to a third theatre was clear. Although the First World War was the first major conflict where air power was utilized, it cannot truly be described as the first air war. The use of aircraft was limited to reconnaissance of enemy positions and the delivery of bombs, grenades or gas onto targets below. Still, aircraft undoubtedly added a new element to battlefield strategy, as previous conflicts, over thousands of years, had all been fought closer to the surface of the earth.

The interwar years saw rapid advances in military aeronautical capabilities, and by the outbreak of the Second World War in 1939 a nation's air force was a major component in its ability to wage modern warfare. This led to the possibility of "total war" – one state could attack the cities and civilians of another from the air, without a single soldier stepping onto enemy territory. Previously, empires aiming to sow misery and destruction had to lay siege to cities with massed troops, but now no longer.

The evolution of air combat involved two tools of kinetic warfare: long-range bombers and the smaller, nimbler aircraft whose task was to prevent the bombers from reaching their target. This led to air-to-air dogfighting between enemy aircraft. Another development during the Second World War was the use of jet engines rather than propellers in German aircraft. These aircraft were so technologically superior to their predecessors that, had the Axis powers been able to prolong the war and manufacture them at scale, the balance of air power would have been entirely one-sided – and the war's duration and outcome might have been rather different.

A further development that had the same seismic potential was the world's first long-range guided missile: the V-2 rocket system. After the war, as part of Operation Paperclip, the architect of the V-2, German engineer Wernher von Braun, developed rocket technology for the US, creating intercontinental ballistic missiles (ICBMs). This gave the American Empire the ability to strike enemy territory thousands of miles away. From this point to today, major advancements have been made in missile delivery and defence, and for strategic warfare planners the world has become a lot smaller.

In the last two decades, unmanned aerial vehicles, capable of hovering unseen above enemy territory and delivering precision-guided missiles, have yet again changed the game. But even this development, however important, did not add a further theatre of war. On 11 January 2007, a fourth theatre was introduced to the world. It was on this day that the Chinese successfully demonstrated their ability to shoot down a satellite orbiting the planet. It is in no doubt that the US and other military powers will have been developing this capability, but the success of the test, and the fact that it was not the dominant superpower that had conducted it, sparked a new space race.

It was previously accepted (in public at least) that space was a domain free of militarization and it belonged to all the peaceful peoples of earth. That is no longer the case. President Trump's response to this new reality was the creation in 2019 of the fourth branch of the US military: the United States Space Force. As with many of Trump's actions, the unpopularity of the messenger overshadowed the message as memes and derision swiftly followed, but his was a logical and unavoidable course of action.

Why is this new space race important in the context of our inquiries, and how might it impact the military pre-eminence of the American Empire? While it is not possible to predict the outcome, it is possible to speculate about the potential ramifications if the Chinese were to gain an upper hand. A modern military is reliant on its satellites for every aspect of warfare; as technology improves, this reliance increases. If the US cannot guarantee the security of its satellites, it would have a devastating effect on the ability to project force around the globe.

The data provided from satellites is also used to carry out enemy reconnaissance, provide telemetry and targeting information to allow precision-guided missile delivery, and even to relay real-time battlefield information and enemy troop locations for soldiers on the ground. This new theatre of warfare is in its infancy, but it will develop rapidly with wide-ranging and unpredictable effects. It will not be long before the first satellite is equipped with a kinetic offensive capability that would prove more difficult to defend against than even hypersonic missiles. To ensure continued military dominance, the US will need to ensure that it does not allow any adversary to take control of this fourth domain.

Developments in Traditional Warfare

There are also some developments in kinetic warfare technology that are worthy of mention briefly as they are altering how modern wars are fought, but they are unlikely to have a significant impact on the military superiority of the American Empire. One example is the attack carried out on the Saudi oil refineries in 2020 by Iranian-backed Houthi rebels. This operation used a cluster of small, readily available civilian drones equipped with ordnance, thereby creating miniature, difficult-to-detect missiles. This methodology could be used in future conflicts to strike US interests overseas, but it is unlikely to pose a direct threat to the mainland for many years to come.

It remains to be seen whether advances in this technology, specifically further reductions in drone size, could pose a threat to US aircraft carriers, which are huge floating targets. The use of such drones by Ukrainian forces has also been notable in the effort to stop the Russian advance, a perfect example of a traditional warfare strategy being blunted by modern methods and technologies. Again, the likelihood of this impacting future warfare operations by the much more tech-nologically astute US military is difficult to gauge, and questions are rightly asked as to why the Russian air force has not managed to secure the aerial theatre of war. Similarly, the ability of the Ukrainians to seize and recycle military materiel from their Russian invaders is most likely specific to this conflict, due to the shared Soviet-era tech-nology, and this is unlikely to be a problem for the US in any future conflict. One thing is certain: all aspects of the conflict in Ukraine are being studied by military strategists across the globe for any lessons that can be learned.

Conclusion

The changing nature of warfare and the evolving attitudes toward it are both limiting factors on the ability of the American Empire to leverage its military superiority in the same manner as previous empires. Evolving global norms and moves toward peace and away from violence can only act as a restriction on the world's leading superpower, as inferior challengers are able to avoid direct military conflicts that they would surely lose. In this respect, the state with the most to lose is the one with greater (and more costly) military might.

Changes in how war is conducted follow the same pattern. The US enjoys traditional military superiority, so any evolution in new theatres of war or technological advances can only be viewed as providing more problems rather than opportunities. The past provides valuable insights, as empires have fallen when new technologies rendered pre-existing military superiority obsolete. The clearest examples are found in the Spanish conquest of the Aztec and Inca empires: the conquistadors with their horses, gunpowder and steel rendered the methods and equipment of the indigenous empires useless overnight. European germs were also a kind of biological warfare, devastating those populations without immunity, but the Spanish did not know the truth of this at the time.

At what point, then, is it irresponsible for the American Empire to continue to operate within restrictions that are not adhered to by its adversaries when it comes to developing new weaponry or making advances in potentially dangerous fields such as genetics and AI? Do we even know if the US is adhering to such restrictions? Is the US simply paying lip service to the kind of ethical principles that are normally championed by Western democracies? At what point is it foolish for the US not to act pre-emptively to halt the rise of a rival power, especially if the US falls behind in a new technological arms race? Would the American Empire even survive in the event it became an outright aggressor rather than self-styled global protector? The answers to these questions are likely to become clearer in the next 20–30 years, as technology continues to provide breakthroughs previously seen only in science fiction.

7

International Relations

Democracy is integral to the continued existence of the American Empire. Much like the hamburger, democracy did not originate on American soil, but the American Empire considers itself responsible for exporting it around the globe. After the Cold War ended, democracy was widely (though not universally) perceived as the best form of government for nation states, assisted by multinational institutions with lofty goals of international cooperation and global peace. Belief in the virtues of democracy stemmed from liberal democratic theory, which posited that the spread of democracy would lead to increased peace, as democracies would be less likely to attack one another. This theory has been the guiding force of American foreign policy for much of the last century, and it has often been used – as in the case of the Iraq War in this century – to justify illiberal actions.

The period of certainty about the primacy of democratic government has, however, come to an end, as democracy is now in decline, with many states that were previously democratic inching closer toward authoritarianism or autocracy. This pattern is also evident in the US itself, as the peaceful transfer of power has come under genuine threat. The attempted insurrection on 6 January 2021 was a gift to authoritarians and autocrats, who could point to the US and argue that democracy itself was a failing institution. At the same time, global cooperation is also in decline, as the world moves away from liberal institutionalism and returns to realism and the primacy of the nation state.[1]

A vital element of American power is the creation and exportation of the "Hollywood myth" that is the American Dream. This rests on the premise of American exceptionalism – a divine right to pre-eminence – but this power is only to be used benevolently rather than to conquer and dominate in the manner of former empires. The power of this myth cannot be overstated, but cracks have begun to appear. Successive foreign policy errors are to blame. The disastrous wars in Vietnam, Iraq and Afghanistan illustrated the limits of American military power while human rights abuses committed in each conflict have tarnished the carefully crafted Hollywood image. The Iraq War and the failure to install a functioning democratic government led directly to the rise of ISIS, which filled the resulting power vacuum. In Afghanistan, a disastrous evacuation in 2021 gifted power back to the Taliban, whose repression has begun anew. Intervention in Libya has served only to create a failed state marred by internecine violence and civil war, and any possibility of influence in Syria has been yielded to Russia. Four years of chaotic foreign policy during the Trump presidency reduced American influence, weakened multi-national institutions and left scores of ambassadorial and diplomatic posts vacant. Intransigence from the Republican Party has not helped since Trump's departure, stifling Biden's efforts to fill these roles. This partisan point-scoring has a material impact, hampering the ability of the US to exert influence globally.

Beginning with the important topic of diplomacy, this chapter will consider the numerous areas in international relations where US effectiveness and influence has already waned or is now being challenged. It will also touch on the behaviour, alliances and institutions of America's adversaries to provide context and a clearer sense of what is at stake.

Diplomacy

There are many ways a nation can exert influence globally, and one of the most long-standing and effective ways is through a well-functioning diplomatic corps, led by ambassadors. Historically, the American Empire has exerted considerable influence in this manner with its 167 embassies and high commissions around the globe. Only China has more, with a total of 171.[2]

An embassy is not simply a home away from home; it is a vital cog in the influence machine, ensuring that interests are pushed and information is gathered from every corner of the globe. Even in the age of instant communication, there is no substitute for the presence of trusted representatives on the ground, with experience of the ever-changing realities and multifaceted factors that might influence the actions of the host nation.

As the scholar and former diplomat Kishan Rana asserts, diplomacy is, at its core, about "trust-based communication between authorised state actors, and that trust is a product of relationships constructed and nurtured with foreign interlocutors".[3] This trust is not quickly earned, and these relationships require both "predictability and integrity", with the embassy playing a vital role in grounding such relationships. This view is not one shared by Donald Trump, who saw ambassadorships simply as a method of rewarding donors and supporters with little or no experience in diplomacy.[4]

It is not simply gaffes and inexperience that harm the reputation and effectiveness of the US. In practical terms, dismissals of experienced diplomats from senior positions are also significant.[5] The disregard Trump had for this area of foreign policy is best illustrated by the number of positions left vacant during and after his presidency. After almost two full years of his administration, 18 countries were without a US ambassador, including Australia, Saudi Arabia, Turkey and Mexico.[6] There were many reasons for this failure, including Trump's disdain for the process leading to nomination delays, and the choosing of unsuitable candidates leading to nominations being blocked by both Democrats and Republicans.[7] President Biden has also struggled to fill these roles, but he has not proposed unsuitable candidates – partisan intransigence has stifled the nomination process. This opposition has been led by the Republicans Ted Cruz and Josh Hawley, both harbouring presidential ambitions and happy to frustrate the Democrats.[8]

With the multinationalism of the post-Cold-War era now in decline and with international relations returning to traditional realism, bilateral diplomacy is only going to become more important. The American Empire needs to ensure it puts country over party and restores an effective diplomatic corps. This reality was articulated best by Eric Rubin, the president of the American Foreign Services Association, in 2021:

> No other country doesn't send ambassadors on a regular, timely basis, and no other country in history, including ours, has ever had this many vacant jobs for this long … The world is changing. It is by no means in a stable state and we have to work out and defend our role in this new world. The time has passed when the world is just going to tolerate our peculiarities. "The US doesn't fill half its ambassadorships for a year? Oh, well, that's the US."[9]

What is the solution? In a country beset by political division and infighting, the current system is clearly not serving the interests of the American people. Perhaps there needs to be a requirement for appointees to be apolitical in nature, in a similar vein to the British civil service. If there were also a requirement to serve for a specific term of eight years, this would serve two functions. Firstly, it would be long enough to build trust and confidence in the host country and ensure an effective exertion of US influence. Secondly, it would also ensure that positions are filled by long-standing diplomats and not simply donors looking for a few years of glamorous Ferrero Rocher receptions before returning to their careers back home.

The United Nations

Another aspect of America's continued global dominance is its position as first among equals in the numerous multination organizations that shape global affairs, most notably the United Nations. This position has allowed the US to wield influence over many areas where brute military strength cannot, but many of these organizations and institutions are in decline, and some are simply unfit for purpose. This has a direct impact on the position of the American Empire as global hegemon. It is accurate to suggest that President Trump's disdain and disrespect for these institutions was detrimental in many cases, but he is not the first president to act in this manner, and many of these institutions were in decline before he took office. Let's take a look at the biggest and most obvious example first: the United Nations.

The UN was created with the lofty goals of promoting international cooperation and conflict resolution, but it has descended into a talking shop afflicted by politicking as member states trade votes for favours. The UN is simply not fit for purpose, unable as it is to enforce global norms of human rights, security and territorial integrity, as veto powers are constantly used to counter these efforts. UN backing is sought when it is deemed convenient, but the more powerful members see fit to act unilaterally when such support is not forthcoming. Great powers do not wish to be restrained by anything, be it weaker states or multinational institutions.

The US is very much guilty of this and has a complicated relationship with the organization that it had a key hand in creating. The true nature of the US relationship with the UN is summed up in a single word: expedience. In 2000, before the events of 9/11 and the war on terror, Senator Jesse Helms articulated this clearly in a speech to the UN Security Council:

> The American people want the UN to serve the purpose for which it was designed: they want it to help sovereign states coordinate collective action by "coalitions of the willing" ... they want it to provide a forum where diplomats can meet and keep open channels of communication in times of crisis; they want it to provide to the peoples of the world important services, such as peacekeeping, weapons inspections and humanitarian relief.[10]

He continued to outline, in language strikingly similar to that used by Donald Trump two decades later, that the US was the leading source of funding for the institution and does not wish to be restrained by it:

[If] the UN seeks to move beyond these core tasks, if it seeks to impose the UN's power and authority over nation-states, I guarantee that the United Nations will meet stiff resistance from the American people ... They see the UN aspiring to establish itself as the central authority of a new international order of global laws and global governance. This is an international order the American people will not countenance.[11]

As global hegemon, the American Empire views itself as the central authority on global laws, as the arbiter of right and wrong, and any nation or body encroaching on this position is deemed illegitimate. America's military superiority, following the Cold War, effectively guarantees this position – this is realism in a multilateral world. Helms argued that the actions taken by the US during the Cold War, direct or indirect, were fully justified: "In none of these cases ... did the United States ask for, or receive, the approval of the United Nations to 'legitimize' its actions." With uncanny foreshadowing of the invasion of Iraq three years later, he went on:

It is a fanciful notion that free peoples need to seek the approval of an international body (some of whose members are totalitarian dictatorships) to lend support to nations struggling to break the chains of tyranny and claim their inalienable, God-given rights. The United Nations has no power to grant or decline legitimacy to such actions. They are inherently legitimate.[12]

This is an honest appraisal of the relationship between a hegemon and a collection of weaker nations. When it is convenient to garner support to lend legitimacy to an action, then the UN is used to this effect; otherwise, the institution is ignored and disregarded. The invasion of Iraq in 2003 is the perfect example of this reality.

The US has acted to diminish the authority of the UN in other ways. It has used its veto on the Security Council more than eighty times, around half of which have been to support Israel against the Palestinians. This allows Israel a free hand for unilateral action, creating an apartheid state and open prison through land seizures and punitive military incursions, secure in the knowledge that any attempts to halt these actions via UN resolution will be vetoed by the US. A perceived "chronic bias against Israel" led the Trump administration to withdraw from the UN's Human Rights Council (UNHRC) in 2018, further weakening the effectiveness of the institution.[13] This stood at odds with the position of the previous administration. As ambassador to the UN under Obama, Susan Rice had rightly declared in 2009 that "working from within, we can make the council a more effective forum to promote and protect human rights".[14] The administration of George W. Bush had previously refused to join the UNHRC, which was perhaps unsurprising as many of these same rights were being violated during the war on terror.

President Trump's first speech to the UN in 2017 was notable for ruffling the feathers of the international community, but it must be appreciated for its candour. Saying he would always put America first, Trump argued that the UN needed "strong, sovereign nations" as members if it was to have any hope of success in troubled times. While he was criticized at the time for championing his own nation's immense power and influence, he is certainly not the first president to prioritize American interests – simply the first to articulate it so brazenly.[15]

Russia has acted with similar arrogance, maintaining a great-power mindset even during its decline. The opinions of other states or institutions like the UN are deemed irrelevant when they run contrary to policy objectives of the nation state. The destruction of Grozny during the war in Chechnya, and support for Assad in murdering his own citizens in the Syrian civil war, were condemned internationally, but Russia ignored the outcries. The impotence of the UN over the past two decades played a significant role in convincing Putin that there would be no repercussions for the invasion of Ukraine in 2022. Similar Russian actions in Georgia in 2008 and Crimea in 2014 were met with condemnation but little in the way of a meaningful response. In a similar fashion to Helms before him, Russian prime minister Dmitry Medvedev disregarded the territorial integrity of Ukraine after the illegal annexation of Crimea in 2014: "We don't have to guarantee anything to anyone, because we never took on any commitments concerning this."[16]

This disdain is unsurprising. Russia has long seen the UN as simply a way for it to disrupt international goals of collective action. Russia has used more than 120 vetoes of UN resolutions, and has increasingly acted in concert with China to block US-led initiatives that are contrary to its own foreign-policy goals.[17] A notable indignity was inflicted in April 2022 when Russian missiles were launched at Kyiv during a visit from UN Secretary-General António Guterres. This was an overt and brazen affront to the UN and the ideas it claims to represent.[18]

Meanwhile, China has been far less active in the use of its veto at the UN, deploying it 17 times – the least of any of the permanent members of the Security Council, although with more frequency recently. This latter development is due to a number of factors: the adoption by Beijing of a more assertive foreign policy; recognition of the increased role that China has within the UN as the second-largest contributor to both the regular and peacekeeping budgets; and an increasing move away from the West and toward an East-centric power bloc with Russia.

The nature of China's 17 vetoes at the UN is also instructive, as 14 of the 17 were joined with Russia, ten of which were to block Security Council action on Syria since 2011. A further three were regarding draft resolutions in Myanmar (2007), Zimbabwe (2008) and Venezuela (2019). The purpose of these vetoes is simple: the drafts condemned governmental behaviour which violated human rights, and China sees these condemnations as unacceptable interference in the internal matters (and therefore sovereignty) of other states.[19] Once again, it is interesting to note the similarities in the objections of the US, China and Russia regarding this issue of sovereignty.

Concern for its own sovereignty also informs Beijing's thinking in its actions against the Uighur minority, described by the UN Human Rights Office as amounting to crimes against humanity involving arbitrary detention and repression in Xinjiang province. Once again, the limitations of the UN are clearly illustrated: a motion to debate the issue in 2022 was defeated by 19 votes to 17, with 11 abstentions. Hua Chunying, China's foreign affairs spokesperson, tweeted in response to the vote at the UN's Human Rights Council:

> This is a victory for developing countries and a victory [for] truth and justice ... Human rights must not be used as a pretext to make up lies and interfere in other countries' internal affairs, or to contain, coerce & humiliate others.[20]

Elsewhere, Saudi Arabia has learned lessons from the actions of the superpowers, namely that the UN is a paper tiger whose opposition is immaterial to the pursuing of foreign-policy objectives by unpopular means. Opposition to the war in Yemen is frequently raised in the UN and summarily ignored by Mohammed bin Salman, who appears to care little about war crimes, starvation and mass displacement. This is unsurprising: a ruthless operator, happy to dismember journalists, will pay little heed to a body without any power in a realist world where "might is right". MBS has gone even further, using a mixture of incentives and intimidation to shut down a UN investigation of human-rights violations committed by both sides in the conflict.[21] Indonesia, home to more Muslims than any other nation, was allegedly warned that access to Mecca would be restricted if it did not vote against an October 2021 resolution, while Togo announced the opening of a new embassy in Riyadh and the receipt of financial support for antiterrorism activities. John Fisher, then the Geneva director of Human Rights Watch, described the situation perfectly:

We understand that Saudi Arabia and their coalition allies and Yemen were working at a high level for some time to persuade states in capitals through a mixture of threats and incentives, to back their bids to terminate the mandate of this international monitoring mechanism ... The loss of the mandate is a huge blow for accountability in Yemen and for the credibility of the human rights council as a whole. For a mandate to have been defeated by a party to the conflict for no reason other than to evade scrutiny for international crimes is a travesty.[22]

Less powerful states have long realized how to leverage their limited power by supporting larger states in key votes in exchange for investment or deeper ties, and this is simply the latest example. Realism triumphs as each nation state acts in its own interest, and so the illusory promise of multinational institutionalism is exposed yet again.

There have been UN successes, but these were mostly consigned to a time when international cooperation seemed genuinely possible. Efforts to smooth the process of decolonization after the Second World War are certainly to be viewed as successes, as is the material assistance provided to starving, displaced and vulnerable people around the world. The World Food Programme provides food and monetary assistance to over 80 million people, and the UN provides aid to 69 million displaced people who have fled their homes due to persecution, conflict or human-rights violations. UN agencies also supply 45 per cent of the world's children with vaccines, saving an estimated 2–3 million lives each year.[23] Peacekeeping operations have enjoyed successes, but there have also been notable failures. The failure to prevent genocides in Rwanda and Bosnia was largely due to the UN's institutional shortcomings, and both catastrophes left its reputation much diminished. As one analyst has explained:

First, UN peacekeepers are held to a strict mandate to only use force in self-defense or to help evacuate foreigners. Second, the UN failed to train peacekeepers to negotiate with perpetrators of violence against civilians. Similarly, there existed a cultural disconnect between the training peacekeepers received and the reality of local communities … More generally, peacekeeping is limited in that intervention requires the consent of the host government and other parties to the conflict which makes swift action more difficult.[24]

Will the UN continue to exist in fifty years? As the world moves further away from multinational cooperation and toward populist nationalism – and as an East–West power struggle intensifies between authoritarian and democratic states – will the UN have any real influence? At what point will it be declared extinct, a creation and tool of the US that no longer serves its purpose in furthering the interests of the American Empire? It is entirely conceivable that a future US president, driven by domestic interests, will go even further than Trump and withdraw from the UN completely, rather than simply some of its agreements and agencies. More than $12 billion is, after all, a large annual bill to pay when you decide that it no longer serves your foreign-policy objectives.[25]

The World Health Organization

The World Health Organization (WHO) was established in 1948 as part of a global effort to combat disease and ensure preparedness for future outbreaks of it. Although not perfect, it has continued to function through a variety of international crises, and it is a rare example of long-term international cooperation.

This changed in 2020, at the height of the global Covid pandemic, when President Trump blindsided his aides and advisers by announcing that the US would be leaving the WHO. In place of membership of the WHO, Trump wanted to focus on direct aid to various countries to assist in the same areas that the WHO operates within. This represented another step away from US-led, often US-created, multinational institutions. To make this decision at the height of the Covid pandemic was widely attacked as being irresponsible and likely to lead to further loss of life as well as leaving the US vulnerable to future global outbreaks.

While these accusations are accurate, there were also valid reasons behind Trump's action. Trump's main contention was that the WHO was under Chinese control, both overtly via the number of Chinese nationals involved in the agency and covertly through the influence that Beijing had over its decision-making. This assertion is not without merit, and Trump correctly stated that the possibility of a leak from the Wuhan Institute of Virology had not been examined with sufficient thoroughness by the WHO. The fact that the institute was actively studying coronaviruses within bats at the time of the outbreak is certainly noteworthy. The refusal to properly investigate the "lab leak hypothesis" was and is most likely politically motivated. In the US, Trump's political enemies could not be seen to be entertaining one of his pet theories, and any who wished to investigate further were labelled conspiracy theorists, MAGA members or pseudoscientists.[26] In China, meanwhile, Xi Jinping was keen to avoid any possible question of Chinese culpability for a global pandemic that killed millions and cost the global economy trillions of dollars.

Soon after Joe Biden became president in 2021, he reversed the Trump decision and the US has rejoined the WHO. So does this mean a return to business as usual? Not necessarily. US participation in multinational institutions, such as the WHO, is obviously a useful way of ensuring US interests and influence are furthered globally. This has been a given for almost a century. The "soft power" gained by continuing to assume this prominent role cannot be underestimated; and yet, if the US is seen as an unreliable partner, this power will be diminished.

G6 to G7 to G7+1 to G8 to G20 to GZERO

If NATO represents the military arm of the American-led global order, the G7 is the economic counterpart. The organization was originally established as the G6 in 1975; it was an informal gathering of the leaders of the six largest industrialized economies, convened to discuss a coherent strategy to recover from the oil shock and resultant global recession, which had also led to the collapse of the exchange rate mechanism established at Bretton Woods. A year later Canada joined, creating the G7, comprising the US, UK, Italy, France, West Germany, Canada and Japan. A year later they were joined by the President of the European Commission, and thus a representative for what is now the EU has joined every year since that time.

This informal grouping ostensibly concentrated on economic matters, but during the 1980s it expanded its remit to include foreign policy and security issues, including the Soviet Union's war in Afghanistan. This evolution is no surprise: economic stability is intrinsically linked to geopolitical events, and war has the potential to create the most significant shocks to this stability.

In the heady days of 1991, with the Cold War at an end, Mikhail Gorbachev was invited to attend, creating the G7+1, which continued until Russia's official entry and the creation of the G8 in 1998. During this period there existed a sense that Russia could become "western-ized" by embracing the twin pillars of capitalism and democracy. This ended in 2014 as Russia annexed Crimea, and so the planned G8 meeting in Sochi was moved to Germany and became a G7 again – this state of affairs continues to this day.[27]

Rapid globalization and increasing wealth in the 1990s led a number of developed nations to demand a seat at the table, and the G20 was created in 1999.[28] The G7 continues to meet alongside the G20, but the reality is unavoidable: the ability of seven nations, led by the US, to steer global economic policy was dissipating even before Russia's exclusion. The events of the Covid-19 pandemic have weakened this ability further, as international cooperation faltered and states turned inward, many embracing nationalistic populism. This new reality is accurately dubbed the "G-Zero" by the political scientist Ian Bremmer, and it most likely signals the end of globalization and the beginning of a process of deglobalization.[29]

This process may not be rapid, but it is likely to lead to reduced international cooperation, increased nationalism, and onshoring of industry and manufacturing. The Covid pandemic laid bare the limitations of the just-in-time supply model that relies so heavily on imports, especially when the Chinese sought to pursue a zero-Covid strategy. The pandemic also illustrated how future geopolitical problems between China and the US could easily lead to actions that would benefit neither and potentially cripple both economies – and the global economy with it.

Bretton Woods or Belt and Road?

The International Monetary Fund (IMF) and the World Bank were both created toward the end of the Second World War. Nestled in the White Mountain National Forest of New Hampshire sits the resort and hotel of Bretton Woods, the site of an international conference of the 44 Allied nations in July 1944. This conference would play a vital role in the creation of the American Empire, as the US sought to claim the spoils of a war it looked likely to win, using its position as a superpower to create the structures and processes required to shape a new international financial order.

Bretton Woods established the US dollar as the reserve currency of the world, and created a global monetary system built around what became the International Monetary Fund and the World Bank. The two organizations would work in tandem: the fund would seek to eliminate exchange controls and export subsidies, while the bank would provide the capital to assist in rebuilding devastated countries after the war, and also bring developing nations into the developed world. The Soviet Union was represented at the talks but refused to later ratify the agreements, accurately describing the newly created institutions as "branches of Wall Street" and declaring that the World Bank was "subordinated to political purposes which make it the instrument of one great power".[30]

Although the British managed to obtain preferential voting rights, the conference represented the final throes of the British Empire as the American Empire rose in its place. They were allies on the battlefield, but there was no question as to who would lead the post-world order. What had started with the Lend-Lease program during the war was finalized at Bretton Woods: a bankrupt empire quietly put out to pasture by the new global superpower.

Lend-Lease, described by Franklin Roosevelt as "lending a neighbour a hosepipe to put out a fire", served three interests of the ascending American Empire. Firstly, it allowed the US to ensure its ideological allies would not suffer defeat against the tyrannical dictatorships of the Axis powers. Secondly, it allowed FDR to postpone entry into the war until it was politically viable to do so. Thirdly, it ensured that the British Empire would pass into history, saddled with huge sums of debt. Although the empire had unravelled long beforehand, the final payment of the debt incurred during the war would not be made until 2006, more than sixty years after the borrowing occurred.[31]

This lending of a "hosepipe" illustrates how an empire can actually be replaced by an ally rather than an adversary, without any direct conflict between the two. Since the ratification of the Bretton Woods agreements after the Second World War, the institutions created have, as predicted by the Soviet Union, been utilized incredibly effectively as the instruments of the American Empire. Behind the façade of independence, these institutions have ensured that struggling states become vassals of the American Empire, in need of capital to drive economic advancement and bring their societies into the twenty-first century. For the US, unofficial influence is guaranteed in its role as creditor to these states, while US firms are awarded lucrative contracts in processes labelled as "development".[32] This point is not raised as an accusation or slight, merely to acknowledge the reality of a hegemon ruling over a multinational system, using all tools available rather than resorting to physical, territorial conquest. Nobel Prize-winning economist Joseph Stiglitz, a renowned critic of what he deems "the Washington consensus", puts it as follows:

> International institutions go around the world preaching liberalization, and the developing countries see that means open up your markets to our commodities, but we aren't going to open our markets to your commodities. In the nineteenth century, they used gunboats. Now they use economic weapons and arm-twisting.[33]

If the US-led institutions of Bretton Woods have economically controlled the post-war era, what does the future hold and can this dominance be challenged? China, with its "Belt and Road" initiative, would seem to believe so.

Announced in 2013 as "One Belt, One Road", this initiative involved a Chinese mirroring of the actions of the World Bank, underwriting billions of dollars in infrastructure investment in developing countries. At first, these countries tended to be located on the path of the old Silk Road trade route, which first connected China with Europe over 2,000 years ago. The initiative then expanded, notably into Africa. Xi Jinping had clearly been watching the Bretton Woods institutions closely and seen the benefit of this particular brand of economic influence. In 2017, China was spending around $150 billion per year "assisting" the 68 countries that were members of the Belt and Road scheme.[34] By September 2021, researchers had analysed 13,427 Chinese development projects, across 165 countries and 18 years, costing $843 billion. Annual international-development finance commitments by Beijing are now worth around $85 billion per year, which means that China is outspending the US by a ratio of 2:1. Taking a leaf out of the Bretton Woods playbook, this is primarily through debt rather than aid – a 31:1 ratio of loans to grants since the start of the Belt and Road initiative.[35]

It is interesting to see critics of the initiative accusing China, without any recognition of the apparent hypocrisy, of practising "debt-trap diplomacy".[36] Likely mindful of his nation's looming demographic crisis, Xi has broken from Deng Xiaoping's dictum to "hide your strength and bide your time", instead aiming to supplant the American Empire using the same tactics that ensured the latter was originally able to thrive.[37] The huge sums involved suggest that Beijing increasingly realizes that time is not on its side, and that biding its time is no longer viable. This strategy is not without risk, as much of the capital is invested in high-risk, unprofitable ventures, with Chinese businessmen in Central Asia labelling the initiative as "One Road, One Trap".[38]

There are some, such as the American scholar Yasheng Huang, who believe it is the Chinese, not the recipient countries, who may end up trapped as unreliable debtors seek to renegotiate the deals struck in the past, or they simply default.[39] Clearly cognizant of this predicament, Xi is shifting the focus of infrastructure investment projects to the growing clean-energy sector, aiming to make China a "clean energy superpower". In March 2022, this was officially unveiled as Chinese policy with the publication of a key policy document authored by four Chinese ministries, entitled "Opinions on the Joint Implementation of Green Development in the Belt and Road Initiative".[40] The move to lead the world in renewable energy ticks many boxes, both domestically and abroad. Its international reputation, harmed by accusations of human rights abuses, is improved by establishing China as a global leader in the fight against climate change. Relations with other nations are cemented through partnerships to smooth the transition to clean energy, a goal to which every nation has committed itself. Chinese investment can be poured into a burgeoning sector, with less inherent risk than in many of the traditional Belt and Road projects. And any influence over global energy supplies could be an incredibly useful geopolitical tool – just ask Vladimir Putin or MBS.

Challenges to the Dollar

At Bretton Woods, the designation of the US dollar as the global reserve currency was a masterstroke. It has since ensured that the US has been able to borrow money at a lower cost than its rivals and essentially control the global money supply. Conversely, it has harmed exports and contributed to the hollowing out of the US manufacturing economy, but this was an inevitable result of globalization and a focus on minimizing costs and maximizing shareholder profit.

Most global trade is conducted in dollars, and this has allowed the US to wage economic warfare using coordinated global sanctions – this is the collective punishment discussed in the previous chapter. The overuse of these sanctions has led to efforts to circumvent the dollar, most notably by the other signatories of the Iran nuclear deal after Trump's decision in 2018 to unilaterally abandon the treaty. Finding an alternative to global dollar dependence is a key aspect of any rival state's plan to challenge the American Empire. Up to this point, such efforts have been unsuccessful, and the nearest challenger to the dollar is not the Chinese renminbi but actually the euro. These "challengers" can barely be described as such, as they are minnows competing with a killer whale.[41] More than 85 per cent of global foreign exchange transactions are conducted in dollars.[42] Around 60 per cent of central bank currency reserves are in dollars, with about 20 per cent in euros and about 3 per cent in renminbi.[43]

The speed at which most of the developed world coalesced around US-led sanctions of Russia in 2022 suggests that the dollar-dominated global reality is unlikely to change any time soon, although the development and widespread adoption of cryptocurrency and blockchain technology has the potential to pose more of a threat than any existing state-issued currency. A decentralized banking system that eliminates the requirement for dollar transactions is the anarchic dream of the early crypto pioneers, but it is one possible future. This threat to the dollar has been publicly recognized by the Federal Reserve:

> A shifting payments landscape could also result in a challenge to the U.S. dollar's dominance. For example, the rapid growth of digital currencies, both private sector and official, could reduce reliance on the U.S. dollar. Changing consumer and investor preferences, combined with the possibility of new products, could shift the balance of perceived costs and benefits enough to overcome some of the inertia that helps to maintain the dollar's leading role.[44]

The scale of the threat, at least in the short to medium term, remains negligible. The report concludes by stating that "the dollar will likely remain the world's dominant international currency for the foreseeable future".[45]

The most likely challenger to dollar dominance could come from the BRICS bloc of developing countries, who agreed in August 2023 to admit six new members. Once these states have officially joined, the member list will read: Brazil, Russia, India, China, South Africa, Argentina, Egypt, Ethiopia, Iran, Saudi Arabia and the United Arab Emirates. At the summit President Lula of Brazil called for the bloc to create a common currency to challenge the dollar's dominance in international trade. While this remains a long-term possibility, it will be much more difficult to dethrone the dollar as the global reserve currency, simply because of how easily it can be bought and sold worldwide.[46]

NATO before and after the Russia–Ukraine War

The North Atlantic Treaty Organization (NATO) was formed in 1949 and for much of its existence was primarily a defensive alliance with one enemy in mind: the Soviet Union. The key tenet of NATO is the concept of collective security, as enshrined in Article 5 of the North

Atlantic Treaty: an attack on one is an attack on all. After the collapse of the Soviet Union, NATO had two choices – evolve or die. Rather than sign off victorious, its enemy vanquished without a shot fired, the alliance pivoted toward humanitarian intervention. Throughout the 1990s, this newly evolved NATO moved away from a purely defensive role and became a security community that was comfortable using military force to protect Western ideals of human rights and democracy. In the 2000s, the alliance was involved in multiple actions in the Middle East and Afghanistan, but there were numerous short-comings. For the US, the commitment of other NATO allies was insufficient, as Defense Secretary Robert Gates articulated in 2011 during the war in Afghanistan:

> The mightiest military alliance in history is only 11 weeks into an operation against a poorly armed regime in a sparsely populated country – yet many allies are beginning to run short of munitions, requiring the US, once more, to make up the difference.[47]

The reality was that, for many NATO members, the raison d'être of the alliance had collapsed with the Berlin Wall and they had other spending priorities. Gates went on to warn:

> If current trends in the decline of European defence capabilities are not halted and reversed, future US political leaders – those for whom the Cold War was not the formative experience that it was for me – may not consider the return on America's investment in NATO worth the cost.[48]

This warning proved accurate, as President Trump railed against the alliance for his entire presidency, berating allies for their underfunding, and threatening to leave if this situation did not change. Although unpopular, Trump's views on NATO were more honest than many of his predecessors; in the absence of any direct threat to the US, it had become a grouping of weaker nations that he believed should be paying America for their continued protection. NATO barely survived the

Trump presidency, and it began to look eastwards to China to provide an enemy that would be of interest to the American Empire.

This situation changed in February 2022 when Putin inadvertently rescued NATO by invading Ukraine. Finally, the alliance which had been sliding toward irrelevancy for thirty years was reinvigorated by the return of its original foe and the launching of a war in mainland Europe. It is one of history's true ironies that the man who hated NATO the most turned into its saviour.

Instead of their contributions and enthusiasm dwindling, NATO member states have reaffirmed their commitment in word and deed, and Sweden and Finland abandoned neutrality to seek immediate membership, which seems likely after the diplomatic wrangling is concluded. NATO itself has strengthened its commitment to assisting Ukraine via the Comprehensive Assistance Package and numerous training and assistance programs.[49] Member states have provided direct assistance with massive provision of military equipment, munitions and training to the tune of billions of dollars. Regardless of the validity of Putin's accusations regarding NATO's encirclement of Russia, its eastern expansion and its broken promises, the result is the same: NATO is back and more committed than ever. While Ukraine remains a non-member state and therefore not eligible for Article 5 protection, in every other meaningful regard the country is now a member of the alliance.

It is difficult to look beyond the current crisis to predict what future direction NATO will take. If Ukraine falls, NATO will focus squarely on the Russian threat to its Eastern European members. If Ukraine remains independent, the alliance will be buoyed by victory and will most likely revert to the pre-war focus, moving to counter Chinese expansion in the Pacific. If this occurs, it will be no surprise to see the membership continue to grow, with Japan and South Korea likely to be high on any list of future candidates. If the US is losing influence in many multinational institutions, which are themselves losing relevancy, within NATO the opposite is occurring. This arm of the American Empire is rejuvenated, with previously reluctant members now concerned for their own security and therefore fully committed.

Military Alliances

In contrast to the prevalence of military alliances in the period before the First World War, the current adversaries of the US are not deeply embedded in such arrangements. This feature of twenty-first-century geopolitics should hopefully prevent any single conflict escalating into a global war. Instead of formal alliances between America's adversaries, there exist many arrangements for cooperation, both formal and informal. The most significant of these is the "friendship without limits" declared by China and Russia on 4 February 2022 at the beginning of the Winter Olympics in Beijing. The veracity of this statement was tested almost immediately by Putin's decision to invade Ukraine, an important trading partner for Xi's China. No doubt assured of a swift Russian victory in the "special military operation", Xi was seemingly content to let Putin launch his war of aggression – as long as it did not overshadow the games.

The resulting military fiasco in Ukraine has both positives and negatives for China. The humbling of Putin's military undoubtedly means that Russia is the junior partner in the alliance, for the first time in history, and it gives Xi the advantage in negotiations. Putin himself seemed to acknowledge this reality, describing in September 2022 how "our Chinese friends are tough bargainers".[50] Given that Western sanctions have reduced the markets available to Russian exports, Putin relies on China to import Russian commodities, with Beijing exploiting this vulnerability to demand significant pricing discounts.[51]

While Xi is keen to maintain a united front against the West, this has become more difficult following Russian actions and failures in

Ukraine. Cracks in the "friendship without limits" began to show at the Shanghai Cooperation Organization (SCO) summit in Uzbekistan in September 2022 as Putin was forced to address Chinese "questions and concerns" over the conflict.[52] If Putin decides at some point to use nuclear weapons, then the limits of the friendship with China will truly be tested, as Beijing's insistence against such action is seen as a major factor in preventing this outcome.

Even Russia's relationship with Iran, the perennial adversary of the US, is limited to trade, arms sales and rhetoric, with the Iranian regime realizing that a direct conflict with the US would lead to its destruction.[53] Iran's regional adversary Saudi Arabia is meanwhile undertaking a newly assertive foreign policy, and the decision to side with Putin regarding OPEC production in October 2022 was seen as an effort to humiliate the Biden administration. MBS may have overplayed his hand here, however, as this action has led to bipartisan calls for a recalibration of the US–Saudi relationship, namely one that is indispensable to Saudi national security and cannot be replaced by closer ties to an ailing Moscow. This reckoning has been a long time coming, with US support of the Saudis surviving 9/11, the Yemen conflict and the consistent repression and human rights abuses within the kingdom.

Russia's most important partnership outside China is with Turkey, led by a fellow authoritarian who calls Putin his "dear friend".[54] Erdoğan has managed to play both sides during the Ukraine conflict, and his good relations with both Putin and Zelensky mean he could be a vital participant in any negotiations to end the war. For Ukraine, Turkish military aid and especially drones supplied were vital in holding back the Russian assault on Kyiv in the early stages of the conflict. Turkey is also perfectly placed geographically to exert influence in the conflict, and it has used its naval influence in the Black Sea to play a leading role in creating humanitarian corridors for the exporting of grain. This unique position has allowed Ankara to avoid Western sanctions as it continues to welcome Russian business and tourists.[55] There are limits to this balancing act, however, and if the conflict were to escalate and directly involve NATO members, there is no scenario where Turkey would act against the US-led alliance of which it is itself a member.

Collective Security Treaty Organization (CSTO)

Established in 1992 as a post-Soviet alternative to NATO, the CSTO currently consists of Armenia, Belarus, Kazakhstan, Kyrgyzstan, Russia and Tajikistan. In 2002, Azerbaijan, Georgia and Uzbekistan withdrew from the alliance, leaving just the six aforementioned nations.

While the CSTO might seem to be some kind of successor to the Warsaw Pact of the Cold War, it is simply not a credible competitor to NATO. Whereas the CSTO has lost members in recent decades and may yet lose more, nobody looks likely to leave NATO any time soon – its membership is likely to swell with the imminent additions of Finland and Sweden, taking the total up to 32 states.

Of the existing CSTO members, only Belarus, led by the dictator and Putin puppet Alexander Lukashenko, has supported Russia in Ukraine. Even this support has been limited in nature and primarily logistical: allowing Russian troops to attack Ukraine from Belarusian territory; providing supply lines and medical care for Russian soldiers; and sending shipments of Belarusian tanks and ammunition to occupied Donbas and Crimea.

The CSTO remains a fractured, imperfect union held together only by pressure from an increasingly distracted Russia. Kyrgyzstan and Armenia have each criticized inaction from the bloc during deadly border violence with, respectively, fellow member Tajikistan and former member Azerbaijan. Would any of the other CSTO members follow Lukashenko in helping Putin in Ukraine and thereby risk the threat of Western sanctions? It seems more likely that leaving the bloc would be a more attractive proposition than becoming entrenched in a failing Russian enterprise against the West.

Shanghai Cooperation Organization (SCO)

Established in 2001 to rival the Western-led military and security alliances, the SCO comprises China, Russia, India, Pakistan, Iran and the ex-Soviet Central Asian nations of Kazakhstan, Uzbekistan, Kyrgyzstan and Tajikistan.[56] They remain loosely affiliated, bound more by arms sales and opposition to the US-led global order than a concrete shared commitment to action in the manner of NATO's Article 5. Shared military drills do not amount to alliances that could be relied upon in the event of war against the American-led Western order with all of its military might. While the ex-Soviet minnows could most likely be pressured into supporting Russia in such a scenario, India, China and Pakistan are simply not going to follow suit, correctly prioritizing their own national interests.

Conclusion

Militarily, the US currently has no realistic competitor that might act alone or as part of a multinational grouping. China, America's most likely adversary, does not enter into formal military alliances and is not yet in a position to challenge US military dominance. The Russia–Ukraine War has exposed the fragility of Putin's ailing nation, and Russian-led groupings are no match for the US or NATO. The resurgence of NATO in the aftermath of the Ukraine invasion only serves to further enhance US military dominance. It remains to be seen what action would be taken by both the US and NATO in the event of a Chinese invasion of Taiwan, but the actions taken in support of Ukraine could prove to be a playbook. The spectre of nuclear war seems closer than at any point since the end of the Cold War, but enduring horror of the potential casualties and consequences ensures that any state resorting to nuclear weapons would become a global pariah, shunned by allies and enemies alike.

Economically, there exists no real competition to Western-centric economic institutions, and any attempts to challenge this have been insignificant. Efforts to replace the dollar as the world's reserve currency have all failed, and the Ukraine crisis has shown the devastating reach of the US-led Western economic order, with its ability to freeze or seize Russian assets. Even Switzerland, harbourer of Nazi gold and stalwart of neutrality and investor anonymity, abandoned the latter policy and complied with sanctions on Russian money held there.

While the vigour of US leadership of multinational organizations seems to be waning, the influence of these organizations is also in decline. The future may well see a battle of ideologies between a democratic West and an authoritarian East, with a reinvigorated NATO acting as the military arm of the US-led Western alliance. However, this outcome may not come to pass if the US continues to move away from liberal democracy, as without its standard-bearer and most powerful practitioner the remaining Western democracies might lack the courage to stand up for themselves.

8

Environmental Threats

It is not just the actions of human beings that can cause an empire to collapse, as changes to the ecosystem, or unexpected events within it, can also fulfil this role. This chapter will examine briefly the possible environmental factors that could bring an end to the American Empire. We will look at some factors which have a local origin (i.e. within the continental United States) and some of a more global character. A localized event may well affect countries beyond the borders of the US, but it would probably have the greatest impact within them. In the same vein, a global event would not necessarily impact the American Empire more than any other state, so the relative impact should be considered. Of course, there will be many issues, dangers or threats that are not covered in this chapter, as it is not intended to be exhaustive; it seeks instead to provide some notable examples of how empires are sometimes ended by non-human factors.

Seismic Activity

The US is home to many fault lines that present a significant earthquake risk, but California's San Andreas Fault is by far the most dangerous. Catastrophe modellers believe another huge earthquake in this region is a matter of when, not if. This would cause widespread destruction and disruption to the millions of people living on and around the fault line. Although it would inflict a huge amount of suffering, injury and property damage, it would be unlikely to necessitate the end of the American Empire. There is even less risk of an empire-ending earthquake event originating in the Pacific Northwest or in the New Madrid Seismic Zone.[1]

Elsewhere, the Yellowstone Caldera in Wyoming is one of the largest calderas in the world and has erupted three times in history, at intervals of roughly 650,000 years. A common misconception is that this means that an eruption is now "due" or imminent, and that it would definitely take the form of a "supervolcano". In this worst-case scenario, the entire US would be impacted by the eruption, with states in the immediate vicinity – Wyoming, Montana, Idaho, Utah and Colorado – being buried under three feet of volcanic ash. This event would cause catastrophic damage to the American Empire; although it would most likely survive in some form, it would be unrecognizable from what it is today. The effect of such an eruption would also be felt around the world as global weather systems would transport the ash cloud to every continent. While not impossible, it remains statistically far more likely that smaller eruptions could occur at Yellowstone without triggering a super-eruption. As the US Geological Survey stated in 2014, "Yellowstone is behaving as it has for the past 140 years … Odds are very high that Yellowstone will be eruption-free for the coming centuries."[2]

If this does not provide sufficient reassurance, even if Yellowstone was erupting on a regular cycle, the odds of an eruption in any given year are still 0.00014 per cent.[3] This provides a helpful segue, as these odds are lower than those for the earth being struck by an asteroid of sufficient size to destroy a civilization.

Celestial Events

An asteroid hitting the US directly would of course cause greater damage to the US than if it were to strike elsewhere, but any impact of material size would cause truly global problems: every country would be affected. The estimated frequency of a civilization-ending impact is one in every 100–200 million years, which is fairly remote. In such an event, the destruction would be so catastrophic and so widespread that any talk of geopolitics, empires and states would be meaningless – survival of the human race would become the only priority.

The US is actually better prepared than most to survive such an impact, due to the network of underground tunnels built to withstand a different type of disaster: nuclear Armageddon. NASA's successful DART mission in 2022 also marked a historic breakthrough that could ultimately prevent an asteroid impact. The Double Asteroid Redirection Test involved a spacecraft being intentionally crashed into the Dimorphos moon of the Didymos asteroid, thereby altering its orbit. This was the first planetary defence exercise that has been successfully carried out.[4]

Another kind of celestial event is far more likely to endanger the American Empire, as well as the modern world as we know it: coronal mass ejections from the sun. These solar flares are relatively commonplace, and our protective ozone layer shields the earth from the worst effects. The great concern, however, is that a coronal mass ejection (CME) of sufficient strength could collide with our magnetosphere and wreak havoc on the electrical circuits that power modern human society. The largest CME in recorded history was the Carrington Event in September 1859, which caused widespread damage to the telegraph network. As human society has progressed, our reliance on electronics has become far greater than it was in 1859, and any similar event occurring now would cause far greater damage.[5]

Pandemic

As the events of 2020 illustrated, the potential impact of a global pandemic is massive. The Covid-19 pandemic represented perhaps the first truly global event in recorded human history. The same cannot be said for any previous plagues, famines, pestilence or wars. The recent pandemic was of a relatively low lethality, primarily causing the deaths of the old and the infirm, or those with underlying respiratory conditions. This did not prevent it from ravaging every inhabited continent on the planet, killing millions and leading to widespread panic and economy-ravaging lockdowns to prevent the spread of the virus.

The question remains: what would happen if a more lethal pandemic were to occur? It can be argued that the lessons learned during the Covid-19 pandemic would assist in the efforts to counter this hypothetical threat. A counter-argument, especially relevant for the US, is that any attempt to implement such extreme public-health measures as lockdowns or mandatory vaccination programs would be resisted, and so the pandemic would run wild. With trust in authority figures at record lows and with conspiracy theories in wide circulation, any efforts to counter a future pandemic in this way in the US would be likely to lead to mass civil disobedience.

A previous parallel to consider: at the height of the Cold War, the warring Soviet Union and US were able to eradicate smallpox by a mandatory vaccination program. In the current world of fake news and government distrust, would this be possible if a similar effort were required? Even the authoritarian Chinese government had to abandon a policy of draconian lockdowns and zero-Covid in the face of a public backlash. Of further concern is the lessening of the international cooperation that is required to react to global events such as pandemics, as countries are increasingly looking inward. This is best illustrated by China's refusal to cooperate with the Western vaccination effort, insisting instead on deploying the ineffective Sinopharm vaccine.

Antibiotic Resistance

Since Alexander Fleming's accidental discovery of penicillin in 1928, antibiotics have become an integral part of modern medicine, responsible for adding some twenty years to the average human lifespan.[6] However, widespread use (and misuse) of antibiotics, especially as a growth supplement in modern farming methods, has led to the current crisis of antibiotic resistance. In 2011, a national survey of infectious-disease specialists found that more than 60 per cent had seen a pan-resistant, i.e. untreatable, bacterial infection within the past year.[7]

The problem is exacerbated by the reluctance of pharmaceutical companies to develop new antibiotics. The companies cite economic viability as the reason, and this is not inaccurate: a cost-benefit analysis by the Office of Health Economics in London calculated that the net present value of a new antibiotic is only about $50 million, compared with approximately $1 billion for a drug used to treat a neuromuscular disease.[8] If this trend continues, the resulting impact on modern medicine and modern society would be catastrophic. The CDC declared in 2013 that the human race is now living in the "post-antibiotic era", and MRSA now kills more Americans annually than HIV/AIDS, Parkinson's, emphysema and homicide combined. Annual global deaths from antimicrobial resistant (AMR) infections are estimated at 700,000, but could reach 10 million by 2050, with a further 24 million people driven into extreme poverty, if no action is taken.[9] This is a truly global problem that could reset many of the improvements made in medicine over the past century.

It is not all doom and gloom, however, and one of the unexpected benefits of the Covid-19 vaccination effort was the evolution of the mRNA vaccine platform technology used by Moderna and Pfizer. This platform offers potential advantages in developing an AMR vaccine due to the "plug and play" methodology used, which reduces potential R&D costs and is also perfect for the development of multi-component vaccines; this is vital as AMR pathogens comprise many species and strains.[10] This is by no means a silver bullet and further work is required, but these promising developments show how human ingenuity often finds a way to overcome seemingly insurmountable problems.

Soil Degradation

There are many potential dangers arising from man's abuse of the natural world, but one that seems to be underappreciated is the global degradation of soil quality. The importance of soil quality cannot really be overestimated, as it is vital for ensuring humankind can continue to grow the various crops that are required to sustain life.

Degradation happens when the soil loses the physical, chemical or biological qualities that underpin its capacity to support plant and animal life. It takes hundreds or thousands of years to form a single inch of topsoil, and many further centuries before it is fertile.[11] Unfortunately, human activities have sped up the process of soil degradation in recent decades, most notably the intensive agriculture of modern farming, as well as the conversion of forestry to farmland. The urbanization of modern cities and use of tarmac and cement also worsens the problem as these surfaces prevent water from being absorbed into the ground, leading to the death of millions of micro-organisms, water run-off, flooding and erosion in other areas.

Soil degradation is not a US-specific problem, and the vastness of the continental United States clearly gives it an advantage over smaller countries, but as one of the main proponents of industrial farming methods, and also as a major exporter of foodstuffs globally, this is an issue that needs to be addressed domestically. The increasing frequency of extreme weather events is also further exacerbating the problem.

Around the world, the equivalent of one soccer pitch of soil is eroded every five seconds, resulting in the loss of food crops and livelihoods.[12] This rate of degradation is clearly not sustainable, in the US or elsewhere, and so awareness and education are the necessary first steps to prevent this problem becoming irreversible.[13]

Extreme Weather and Climate Change

In the interests of brevity, we are not going to be examining this subject in the depth that it deserves. The reason for this is simple: any rational individual is already acutely aware that planet earth is in the midst of a climate crisis that has been exacerbated by human activity since the Industrial Revolution. What is worthy of brief discussion is how an undoubtedly global issue may specifically affect the subject of this study: the longevity of the American Empire.

Extreme weather events can be short, sharp and violent or gradual, sustained and punishing. An increase in both the severity and frequency of hurricanes and severe storms, examples of the former type, are unlikely to precipitate the demise of an empire. What could lead to more problems in the future is the increasing number of severe climate events, such as spells of sapping heat. Since the beginning of this decade, temperatures in the US have hit record highs, and this is likely to keep happening as the planet continues to warm.[14] In the longer term, it may become increasingly difficult for certain areas of the US to sustain human life.

The American Empire would not be the first to fall due to environmental factors, as shifts in climate have hastened the demise of previous empires, rendering previously hospitable locations hostile and forcing populations to relocate. It is true that none of the empires of the past possessed the technological and scientific knowledge that we now possess, but to pin one's hopes on a scientific breakthrough would be breathtakingly naive. If the US, or the world more generally, does not address the issues in this chapter which are preventable or which can at least be mitigated, then the planet that future citizens find themselves struggling to inhabit may not be one worth living in at all.

Conclusions

While it is impossible to predict when the American Empire will end, it is inevitable that at some point it will. This study has examined a number of threats to the empire, both internal and external, avoidable and unavoidable, self-inflicted and involuntary. In this penultimate chapter, I will consider the most likely scenarios for the empire's demise, and then provide in the final chapter some recommendations to reduce their likelihood and postpone the inevitable for as long as possible.

External Threats

Nuclear war

A nuclear war is often described as one that "can never be won and should never be fought", but the Russian invasion of Ukraine has made this scenario far more likely than has been the case for many years. Russian political figures and commentators have threatened Ukraine and its Western backers with just this possibility, and it cannot be claimed with any certainty that this is merely sabre-rattling or the making of empty threats. A nuclear war could indeed cause the end of the American Empire, be it from a direct strike on the US or the fallout from a nuclear war elsewhere, thereby creating a nuclear winter in which there would be no winners. The size and sophistication of the US nuclear arsenal means it would be well placed to "rule the ashes" if it survived as a viable political entity, but this would be an empty victory.

Traditional war with peer competitor

The invasion of Ukraine has shifted Western attention from China back to Russia, after years spent ignoring the threat from a country that Barack Obama dismissed in 2014 as only a "regional power".[1]

It remains unlikely, though, that a direct conflict fought with traditional (non-nuclear) weapons would occur between Russia and the US, and even less likely that the US would not emerge victorious.

The threat posed by a rising China makes it a more likely future adversary, with a Chinese invasion of Taiwan being a potential flash-point that could ignite a wider conflict. The long-standing US policy of "strategic ambiguity" has seemingly been replaced by an ironclad guarantee to defend Taiwan militarily in the event of a Chinese inva-sion. It is probable that a confrontation over Taiwan would be localized and unlikely to lead to a direct Chinese assault on the US, which would be suicide for the Chinese. Once the US completes its efforts to onshore the semiconductor industry, Taiwan will hold far less strategic importance and the US commitment to defend the island is likely to be dialled down or forgotten.

Elsewhere, Chinese efforts to undermine the US will continue via non-military means, using economic and cultural warfare for this purpose. China is running out of time as its demographic time bomb steadily counts down, a result of the one-child policy (which was only ended in 2015) and the favouring of male over female children. Estimates on just how quickly China will unravel vary anywhere from 10 to 75 years,[2] and we can expect Xi Jinping to lean even further into nation-alism as this unravelling occurs and he struggles to maintain order. Any future war between China and the US is likely to be waged via proxies rather than directly, as suggested by the US response to Russia's invasion of Ukraine. If a 2022 poll is to be believed, this might be essential for American survival, as almost 40 per cent of respondents claimed that they would rather flee than fight to defend their country if it were attacked.[3]

The size of the US and its relative strength in demographics, labour supply and raw materials mean that a direct competitor would most likely need to be the size of a *continent* rather than a country. Now the world's most populous country, India has the potential to emerge as a possible competitor in the future, and a united Africa or South America might also become a powerful antagonist. If a united South American continent were ever to emerge as a threat, the US would need to hope that their adversaries have short memories, given the extent of US interference in the region in the twentieth century. Access to both the Atlantic and Pacific oceans would be militarily useful for this rising continental power – a benefit shared with the superpower to the north – but there are so many obstacles to cohesion that would need to be overcome before this scenario becomes remotely possible.

Environmental threats

As discussed in the previous chapter, climate change and extreme weather events are not specific to the US and are likely to affect other nations in a similar manner. Adapting to the new realities caused by these changes to the natural environment will be of vital importance to not just the US but every nation on earth. Coastal cities will be under threat from rising sea levels, and food production will be under threat from soil degradation and extreme weather. A future pandemic or the failure of antibiotics against resistant microorganisms would be a global phenomenon and not US-centric. Overall, the environmental threats that the US and the world are facing are real and significant, but the US would be better placed to weather such crises than many other states because of its size, wealth, technological sophistication and abundance of raw materials.

Technological developments

Firmly in the realm of speculation is the threat posed by technological developments leading to unpredictable consequences. This might involve advances in genetics, cybernetics, quantum computing and AI, as well as other areas of inquiry that our twenty-first-century brains may be unable to fully comprehend. The US is already a key player within many of the above-mentioned fields, spending billions of dollars on both overt and covert programs, but the external threat of other countries being the first to develop powerful technologies or weapons is not to be dismissed. As with all speculation, however, predicting

211

how a technological development could alter the global balance of power and bring about the end of the American Empire remains little more than guesswork.

Internal Threats

Secession

In theory, and sometimes in practice, the secession of certain areas from an empire can be relatively peaceful and orderly, but more often it leads to violence as the wounded empire acts to reassert its dominance and preserve its territorial integrity. This was the case in the American Civil War, which began with the secession of seven slave states in the South, thereby forming the Confederate States of America. Four more states joined the CSA after the Confederate attack at Fort Sumter on 12 April 1861.

If secession were to occur in the United States of the twenty-first century, would the result be the same, and how likely is this scenario? Notwithstanding the usual caveats regarding polls and their comparability, support for secession seems to be fairly constant. A 2014 Reuters poll found that 23.9 per cent of respondents would favour their state seceding from the rest of the country, with more Republicans than Democrats holding this view.[4] A recent 2023 poll found that around 20 per cent of Americans supported a "national divorce", whereby Republican-leaning states would form a separate country from Democratic-leaning states – again more Republicans (25 per cent) than Democrats (16 per cent) favoured this course of action.[5]

Under what circumstances could secession occur, and how would it be conducted and reacted to? Whether it would be violent or peaceful would depend on the states involved, with Republican secessionists more likely than their Democratic counterparts to be willing to use violence to achieve their goals. Regarding motive, as discussed in chapter 4, populations of liberal states increasingly feel their views are no longer aligned with those of the Supreme Court, especially on emotive issues such as abortion. After the decision in June 2022 to overturn *Roe v. Wade*, the number of Americans with almost no confidence in the Supreme Court reached 43 per cent, and members of the Court were not unaware of this worrying trend. Shortly after the decision, Associate Justice Elena Kagan said: "If, over time, the court loses all connection with the public and with public sentiment, that is a dangerous thing for democracy."[6]

If California and New York decided to peacefully secede from the union and form a liberal confederacy, would this decision be respected? What would happen if a group of Southern Republican states decided they could not accept the results of a future election and decided instead to secede? Modern attitudes on warfare, bloodshed and self-determination might suggest an alternative to violent conflict is possible, but this would be an exception to the general rule based on previous history. Could the US survive this kind of fracture, or would it fire the starting gun on the disintegration of the union and the end of the American Empire as a whole?

Civil war due to ethnic divisions

The most violent and worrisome internal outcome for the American Empire would be civil war, especially in a country that contains more privately owned guns than people. For many of the empires we have studied, civil wars have been caused by a failure to completely assimilate conquered peoples. These groups remain loyal to their tribal or ethnic roots and wait for the opportunity to rise up, exploit political instability and reclaim their independence from the empire. In the case of the American Empire, this cause of civil war is highly unlikely to occur, as we shall see. The relevant groups to consider are represented by the descendants of the following:

- Indigenous American peoples conquered during the Indian Wars.

- African slaves transported across the Atlantic.
- Hispanic peoples living in the US after the Mexican–American War of 1846–8 and the Mexican Cession of 1848, or such people who immigrated into the US thereafter.

Let's look at each group in turn to gain a better idea of why they are unlikely to generate the conditions for a civil war on American soil.

Indigenous Americans

Indigenous or Native Americans have been partially assimilated into the American Empire and this process is increasing. If this group is defined as people who have any ancestry relating to the original populations of North, South or Central America, and who maintain tribal affiliation or community attachment, the total figure was 9.7 million people in 2020 – 2.9 per cent of the total population of the US.[7] Of these, only around 13 per cent continue to live on the reservations their ancestors were forced onto many years ago, in conditions that lead to lower life expectancy, lower median household income and poorer quality of life as compared with their white counterparts. It is no surprise that 87 per cent have chosen to live outside of tribal areas and strive for a life with more opportunities than those offered on the reservations.

Whether this economic neglect of reservations is intentional strategy or accidental, the result is the same: gradual exodus and eventual assimilation into the wider population. For the majority of Indigenous Americans, their identity is specifically linked to one of the nearly 600 federally recognized tribes rather than to a single homogenous grouping, further reducing any chance of these Americans coalescing along ethnic lines into a constituency that could launch a violent uprising in the future.

African Americans

A similar process of subjugation has occurred with regard to the descendants of African slavery. Slaves were originally imprisoned not on reservations but on plantations, first for the production of tobacco and then cotton. Although slavery was never widespread in the Northern states, and was mostly abolished between 1774 and 1804, many Northern businessmen continued to grow rich on their investments in southern plantations. Congress outlawed the African slave trade in 1808, but the domestic trade expanded rapidly, with the enslaved population nearly tripling over the next 50 years to reach almost 4 million people in 1860.[8] President Lincoln would begin the end of the practice with the Preliminary Emancipation Proclamation in September 1862, followed by the official Emancipation Proclamation in January 1863, thereby freeing some 3.5 million slaves and depriving the Confederacy of the majority of its workforce and hastening its defeat.

The Thirteenth Amendment was passed in 1865 after the end of the Civil War, officially ending slavery in America. This did not lead to overnight equality, and prejudicial and discriminatory treatment of African Americans has continued to this day, both overt and covert. The Great Migration of the twentieth century saw millions of black Americans move out of the South in search of better prospects and fairer conditions, but the discriminatory policies discussed in chapter 3 created and sustained areas of deprivation across the nation. The reaction to this treatment has been largely peaceful and non-violent, and for the vast majority of African Americans the goal is equality achieved through peaceful means rather than violent struggle or supplantation of the white majority. Also, as time has passed and immigration has increased, so has the number of people who identify as black in the US without a direct connection to the history of slavery that originally led to the term "African American".

The response to the killing of George Floyd in 2020, however, illustrated the depth of feeling of many black Americans, whatever their ancestry. Racism based on skin colour is still a problem with the potential to disturb, disaffect and harm black Americans, and efforts to achieve equality must continue. Yet whereas oppressed ethnic groups in previous empires often did not feel they were part of the empire in which they were living, the crucial point for the American Empire is that, while they are understandably frustrated and angry at continued inequality, black Americans do ultimately identify as *Americans*.

Hispanic Americans

Descendants of Hispanic people living in the US after the Mexican–American War of 1846–48, or those who immigrated into the US thereafter, often have a complex relationship with racial identity and one that defies conventional classifications used in the US. Various Spanish terms exist to describe people of Hispanic, mixed, and non-Hispanic ancestry, and some of these are controversial or considered offensive.

The question of how to measure who is Hispanic and how big this population is – and will become – has been the subject of debate and analysis that we need not recapitulate here in detail. In terms of a general overview, however, recent figures from the Pew Research Center indicate that in 2022 nearly sixty-four million people in the US could be classified as Hispanic, which is around a fifth of the total population. The absolute numbers have been rising for decades – in 2000, for example, there were some thirty-five million Hispanics – and they look set to increase in the decades to come.[9]

Does this pose a threat to the US and its social cohesion? In the short term, it seems unlikely that Hispanic Americans will group themselves together and foment internal uprisings or civil war based on their ethnic identity. What is more likely is that Hispanics, as their numbers increase, will seek greater representation and exert greater political and cultural influence. In the long term, it is impossible to know whether a rising Mexico might encourage the growth of secessionist ideology and appetite in America's southern states, where the Hispanic population is highest, but it cannot be ruled out.

The American Empire, then, need not fear violent uprisings or civil war based on ethnic divisions at the present time, but racial or ethnic tensions can always be suddenly inflamed, provoking protests and riots. And these tensions can always grow steadily stronger and more dangerous over time, especially if problems such as inequality and discrimination are not adequately addressed. Complacency on these questions would not be wise if the US is to keep its citizens, of all backgrounds and skin colours, together and united over the long term.

Civil war due to political divisions

The US has experienced civil war once in its short history. The human cost of the conflict was staggering, a fact that should be more keenly appreciated by those within both politics and media who are intent on stoking divisions and mistrust. Approximately 620,000 American soldiers lost their lives during the Civil War of 1861–65. This figure is roughly equal to the total fatalities of the Revolutionary War, the War of 1812, the Mexican–American War, the Spanish–American War, the First World War, the Second World War and the Korean War combined. The death rate (incidence in comparison with the size of the population) was six times that of the Second World War and has been aptly labelled a "harvest of death".[10] If this rate (around 2 per cent) occurred in a future US civil war, there would be 6 million fatalities. If this sobering statistic does not give pause for thought about the shared responsibility of all Americans to calm the hateful rhetoric and invective, nothing will.

How close exactly is the US to a new civil war? In August 2022 a poll by YouGov and *The Economist* reported that a significant proportion of US adult citizen respondents thought that a civil war in the US was "very likely" (14 per cent) or "somewhat likely" (29 per cent) in the next decade. For this to be a larger proportion (43 per cent) than those who believed it was either "not very likely" or "not likely at all" (35 per cent) is alarming. Arguably more alarming are the answers of those who describe themselves as "strong Republicans": 21 per cent thought civil war was "very likely" and 33 per cent believed it was "somewhat likely".[11]

A similar survey of 8,620 American adults conducted by Garen Wintemute from the University of California also reported sobering findings in 2022. Fifty per cent believed that "in the next few years, there will be civil war in the United States". Within the 78.5 per cent who considered violence to be at least sometimes justified to achieve political objectives, 12.2 per cent were at least somewhat willing to use violence to "threaten or intimidate a person", 10.4 per cent to "injure a person" and 7.1 per cent to "kill a person". Four per cent of all respondents thought it was at least somewhat likely, in a situation "where you think force or violence is justified to advance an important political objective", that "I will shoot someone with a gun".[12]

While the importance of these figures should not be dismissed, it must be remembered that polls are not representative of society as a whole, and so simplistic extrapolation is misleading. For instance, it is highly unlikely that, of the 200 million or so adults in the US currently, 8 million (4 per cent) think they would shoot someone if it came down to it. It is also unlikely that 100 million or more US adults genuinely believe a civil war is likely to occur in the "next few years". Most American adults are too busy with their daily lives to take the time to respond to polls, and those who do are more likely to feel strongly about a subject than those who do not. There is also a big difference between *saying* you are likely to shoot someone and actually *following through* with the action. I may enjoy playing *Call of Duty*, but I am not likely to enjoy the reality of an urban war zone. Are these figures the result of resignation to a horrendous outcome, despair at the current situation, or motivation to actually wage civil war in a misguided attempt to "save America from the other side"?

Barbara F. Walter, author of *How Civil Wars Start and How to Stop Them* (2022), argues that a second US civil war, if it does happen, would not resemble the first, and the widespread miscomprehension that it might is creating a blind spot to the likelihood of it occurring.[13] Walter explains that the blueprint for a second US civil war not only exists, but is also hiding in plain sight. *The Turner Diaries* was published in 1978 by William Luther Pierce, founder of the neo-Nazi National Alliance, and pages of the novel were found in Timothy McVeigh's truck after the Oklahoma City bombing in 1995. Pierce's ideas were regurgitated in 2019 in the manifestos of alleged El Paso Walmart gunman Patrick Crusius and accused California synagogue shooter John Timothy Earnest. More recently, a Proud Boys member can be seen on video, during the Capitol insurrection in January 2021, instructing a journalist to read Pierce's book.

Extremists preparing for a civil war call for the penetration of law enforcement by members of the far right, a process that has been ongoing for decades. A 2019 article by law professor Vida Johnson described "an epidemic of white supremacists in police departments", with scandals in over 100 police departments in over forty different states.[14] A 2021 Reuters analysis backed up these figures, finding a number of active and retired law-enforcement trainers on a membership database of the extremist Oath Keepers organization.[15] There is also circumstantial evidence of members of law enforcement moving aside to allow rioters to storm the Capitol building, a defence being used by many of those rioters who were arrested and charged.[16] Without firm evidence it is only conjecture to suggest that some officers were ideologically motivated to allow insurrectionists to enter the Capitol, as a failure of leadership and lack of manpower is more likely to explain the events of the day, but even the possibility of this level of law-enforcement penetration must be taken seriously.

A second civil war would be likely to take the form of guerrilla warfare. It would be fought by multiple militias around the country, targeting infrastructure, civilians, minorities, politicians, judges and federal employees. The goal of such actions would be to destabilize the country and undermine the authority of the federal government, demonstrating that it could no longer keep citizens safe or provide basic necessities. This would, extremists hope, lead to greater distrust of the state and growing support for violent measures.

The insurrection attempt of January 2021 could easily have been the first stage in a sustained series of attacks. These attacks have continued. In the first eight months of 2022, there were more than 100 reported incidents (attacks or suspicious activity) at US power stations – a decade-long high.[17] While Republican politicians seem happy to ignore the extremist threat illustrated by the storming of the Capitol, the FBI does not seem willing to let it go. Now cognizant of the threat posed by right-wing terrorists in the US, after years of focusing primarily on Islamic extremism, the FBI has arrested over 1,000 people in relation to the riot at the Capitol.

This is not the end of the threat. Dangerous ideas of "white replacement", trumpeted by media and political figures, will continue to fuel this movement as the nation moves closer to the reality of white Americans no longer being the ethnic majority by the mid-2040s. This is not a purely American issue, with support growing across Europe for far-right, anti-immigrant movements citing the same white-replacement theory. .

Christopher Sebastian Parker, a professor of political science at the University of California, argues that a civil war in America is a question of "when, not if". He suggests that this will occur after the 2024 election, as both Republicans and Democrats view an opposition victory as an "existential threat" to their way of life. Parker explains how similar conditions created the first civil war: "Democrats viewed the newly established Republican party as a threat to their way of life. Republicans, for their part, saw southern intransigence on the issue of slavery as a threat to the union." He goes on to explain the modern parallels that would lead to a second civil war: "Today, Republicans, driven by the existential threat of losing 'their' (white) country, will continue their attack on democracy as a means towards preserving America for 'real' Americans. Democrats, on the other hand, see the 'Magafication' of the GOP as an existential threat to liberal democracy."[18] Like Barbara Walter, Parker believes that this will lead to a civil war featuring "terrorism, guerrilla war and ethnic cleansing …

waged from sea to shining sea" and that "race and racism will lead to another very American conflagration".[19]

Most of those who see civil war in the future warn of the perilous state of US institutions, primarily the weakening of democracy and the slide toward authoritarianism. This is another internal threat we should take a look at.

A move from democracy to authoritarianism

Predictions of civil war and secession are intrinsically linked to the ongoing legitimacy crisis of the US democratic system. Through analysis of previous empires, it is clear that disputed succession legitimacy is one of the primary causes of civil unrest leading to imperial collapse, and the American Empire is equally exposed to this risk. Democracy is vital to the continued survival of the American Empire, as the United States was built upon this foundation, and the peaceful transfer of power is its cornerstone. It is difficult to imagine how the US could even continue as an authoritarian or autocratic state. That being said, the attitude of "it could never happen here" is a dangerous one, leading to complacency and unintended consequences.

It should be noted with interest that many nations that are now transitioning to a post-democratic system of government began their democratic lives in reaction to imperial autocratic rule, but these historical instances have mostly disappeared from living memory or are not well known. In most of these nations the transition is not sudden but a gradual one, with constitutions being altered, terms limits lengthened and democratic norms eroded. In Turkey, for instance, democracy emerged after the Second World War, but President Erdoğan is now seemingly intent on suppressing democracy and maintaining his personal rule.

In Russia, the October Revolution of 1917 was meant to create a fairer society for all after centuries of tsarism, but instead it just replaced one autocratic ruler with a succession of others draped in a communist flag. The nation flirted briefly with liberal democracy following the abdication of Nicholas II, but the Bolsheviks seized power and Lenin called the shots thereafter. The post-Soviet experiment with democracy was always unlikely to take root, and now the country is led again by an autocrat eliminating anyone who threatens his power.

Elsewhere, Hungary was not a democracy during the Habsburg Empire, nor under the conservative authoritarian rule of Miklós Horthy between 1920 and 1944. After the Second World War, the Soviets held sway and crushed the attempted uprising of 1956. A peaceful transition to democracy eventually occurred in 1989 as the Cold War ended, but this has not stopped the country from a gradual backsliding into an "electoral autocracy" under Viktor Orbán – it's a democracy in name only.

The point is this: these countries have all experienced authoritarianism or autocracy in their recent past and they have all seen glimpses of democracy before it was taken away from them. The US is not immune to the risk of losing its democracy, even with its longer democratic tradition – it can happen anywhere. Democracies need to be constantly maintained and protected to survive. It is dangerous to think otherwise, and an understanding of this point is required to bring recent events more fully into focus.

The integrity of the US democratic process and its succession legitimacy have been under threat since the events in Florida during the presidential election in 2000. The outcome of the election and the identity of the next occupant of the Oval Office hinged on the Florida result, but it was too close to call. Many networks called the race for Al Gore based on exit poll data, but he did not claim victory. Legitimate Republican protests were lodged and the networks soon reversed course and began to declare George W. Bush as the winner. This was followed by an official announcement from Florida secretary of state Katherine Harris, the official charged with certifying the winner of the vote. Harris was also a close ally of the Republican candidate's brother, Governor Jeb Bush, and had also been co-chair of George W. Bush's statewide campaign. These facts clearly represented a conflict of interest for Harris and should have led to a recusal from the responsibility of certifying the vote, but this did not happen. Gore called Bush twice, once to congratulate him and once to rescind the congratulations as a recount was clearly in order due to the razor-thin margins at play. Republicans disagreed, insisting that the race had been called and would be accepted by the US Senate, where they held control.

A five-week legal battle ensued, with the Democrats suing for a recount in certain counties where they thought it would help overcome the narrow margin. This request was rebuffed by the state's circuit court but upheld by the Florida Supreme Court. Republicans appealed to the conservative-controlled US Supreme Court, which voted 7–2 to end the recount. In addition, the Supreme Court voted 5–4 that no alternative method of recounting could be established in a timely manner, thus handing the presidency to George W. Bush.[20] This decision exposed the first crack in the integrity of the US democratic system in living memory. Surely a delayed but accurate answer is preferable to a rushed and controversial one? If Belgium was able to function for 541 days without a government, surely the US could have endured a few more weeks of uncertainty to ensure the correct result was reached and the legitimacy of succession was maintained?

The Obama "birther" conspiracy was the next attack on US succession legitimacy, and it was an ideological precursor to the theory of "white replacement". For certain sections of society, the idea of a black president with Kenyan roots and a Muslim middle name (Hussein) was unacceptable. The baseless conspiracy theory that Obama was not born on US soil and was therefore ineligible for the presidency actually surfaced during the 2008 Democratic primaries and was circulated by supporters of Hillary Clinton before taking root and flowering within the Republican Party. By 2011, as many as half of Republican voters believed that Obama was born overseas and was therefore an illegitimate president. This falsehood would then be given as "evidence" in support of all manner of accusations. Obama was supposedly "more African than American in his roots" (Rush Limbaugh); he apparently viewed America as "a force for global domination and destruction" (Dinesh D'Souza) and he was said to be part of an international alliance between the American left and political Islam to impose Sharia law on the West (Andrew McCarthy).[21]

In a similar fashion to the responses to Trump's efforts to sow the seeds for his baseless claims of election fraud in 2020, prominent Republicans issued non-disavowals and made jokes regarding the birther conspiracy theory and the accusations it prompted. John Boehner and Mitch McConnell said they accepted Obama "at his word", leaving enough space for doubt in the minds of their supporters. This desire to "keep the base onside" is a key feature of what would become the Republican response to Trump's actions in the future. Mitt Romney joked in 2012 that nobody had "ever asked to see my birth certificate; they know that this is the place that we were born and raised". The inference being that, as a white American, Romney did not have to prove his roots but, as a black American, Obama did. Romney probably came to regret this joke, as he later became one of the most vocal critics of the damage done to US legitimacy by the loudest proponent of the birther conspiracy: reality-show celebrity and property magnate Donald J. Trump.

What the journalist Adam Serwer labels as Trump's "trademark innu- endos and falsehoods", coupled with a willing accomplice in the shape of Fox News, spread the conspiracy as far and wide as possible – hours and hours were dedicated to the subject.[22] Romney, in a manner similar to that of many Republicans to follow, was happy to ignore the malignant undertones of Trump's birther crusade, happily accepting Trump's endorsement for the 2012 election and the support of his growing base: "It means a great deal to me to have the endorsement of Mr. Trump."[23]

All in all, these refusals to disavow baseless attacks on succession legitimacy and the integrity of the democratic process prepared the political landscape for Trump to exploit – and exploit it he did. During the 2016 election, Trump and his team appealed to foreign power and adversary Russia to help sway the election in his favour. To dismiss this as "Russiagate" is to ignore the facts, as these attempts were made at Trump's behest. Undoubtedly, Hillary Clinton was an unpopular candidate and the Democrats needed to examine their own failings rather than *only* blaming Russian interference, but that interference should not be ignored altogether. The Mueller Report in 2019 laid out a clear road map that could be followed for obstruction of justice charges to be filed.[24] The fact that these charges did not follow, and the fact that he survived the first attempt to impeach him, is likely to have emboldened Trump and convinced him that the integrity of the 2020 election could be questioned and overturned.

Trump spent the weeks and months leading up to the 2020 election casting doubt on every aspect of the democratic process, questioning the legitimacy of postal votes, doubting the accuracy of voting machines and even conjuring conspiracies involving Chinese and Venezuelan influence. Most pointedly, Trump repeatedly refused to commit to the peaceful transfer of power – the cornerstone of the democratic process – in the event of losing the election. His jokes and comments implied that the only legitimate result would be his winning and therefore he had no need to commit to any transfer of power.[25]

Trump adviser Steve Bannon's playbook of "flooding the zone with shit" was followed to the letter. This could only lead to confusion, as planned. Too many falsehoods to be successfully countered were propagated, making it impossible for a weary public to discern fact from fiction. As historian Anne Applebaum later noted, this was the same tactic used by the Russians to sow confusion over the shooting down of Malaysia Airlines Flight MH17 in 2014. This has led to the truth of the incident being seen in Russia as "unknowable", but widely known outside of Russia.[26]

Trump's premature declaration of victory in the early hours of 4 November 2020 and his calls to "stop the count" were all designed to attack the legitimacy of the electoral process and damage the succession legitimacy of Joe Biden. This tactic was even divulged to aides on 1 November, days before the election, and reported by some media outlets at the time.[27] Trump probably did not expect, or even intend, his premature victory declaration to be sufficient to stop the count or overturn the result. He seemed to be aiming to use the subsequent confusion to create a delay, and during this time he would apply pressure to election officials who he hoped would be compliant enough to assist with his plan to subvert democracy. In a recorded call on 2 January 2021, he pressured Georgia's Republican secretary of state Brad Raffensperger to collude with him and overturn the 11,779-vote deficit:

> All I want to do is this: I just want to find 11,780 votes, which is one more than we have … There's nothing wrong with saying, you know, that you've recalculated.[28]

This attempt only failed because of the integrity of the Georgia officials tasked with certifying the votes. As we shall see with regard to upcoming elections, this kind of integrity might not be in evidence next time round.

The Capitol insurrection of January 2021

The insurrection attempt on 6 January 2021 was a near miss, an international embarrassment and a reminder of the precariousness of democratic institutions weakened by years of attacks. In the lead-up to this now infamous date, Trump had applied pressure to anyone he believed could overturn the election result. Attorney General William Barr, the Supreme Court and Vice President Mike Pence would all feel his ire after refusing his requests. On 19 December, Trump tweeted that it was "statistically impossible" for him to have lost the election and he instructed his supporters to attend a "big protest in DC" on 6 January: "Be there, will be wild!"

Prominent Republican supporters would also feed the dangerous false-hood of a stolen election. On 1 January, Texas congressman Louie Gohmert responded to the failure of his attempted lawsuit to force Vice President Pence to block certification of the Biden victory. He told Newsmax that "in effect, the ruling would be that you got to go to the streets and be as violent as Antifa".[29] Senator Ted Cruz, also of Texas, addressed a Georgia rally on 3 January and promised: "We will not go quietly into the night. We will defend liberty. And we are going to win." On 5 January, Eric Trump, the president's son, directly threatened non-compliant Republican members of Congress that they "will be primaried in their next election and they will lose".

On 6 January, certification day, Trump proxies addressed the crowd at the "Save America Rally", leveraging their existential fears, misplaced sense of patriotism and belief in falsehoods of widespread electoral fraud. Donald Trump Jr warned: "The people who did nothing to stop the steal … this isn't their Republican Party any more. This is Donald Trump's … We're coming for you and we're going to have a good time doing it." One of the more bizarre outbursts came from Trump's personal lawyer, Rudy Giuliani, a key architect of Trump's strategy to retain power. He declared: "If we're wrong, we will be made fools of … But if we're right, a lot of them will go to jail. So let's have trial by combat."

Donald Trump himself then addressed the crowd for over an hour, urging them to march on the Capitol building:

> We will not take it any more … You'll never take back our country with weakness. You have to show strength, and you have to be strong … I know that everyone here will soon be marching over to the Capitol building to peacefully and patriotically make your voices heard.

He continued his unfounded entreaties to Vice President Pence: "Because if Mike Pence does the right thing, we win the election … He has the absolute right to do it."[30]

Not only was this factually inaccurate but it was also wildly dangerous to Mr Pence himself, implying he might be a traitor to patriotic Americans by certifying the election of Joe Biden as president. These claims clearly had an effect, as a makeshift noose would later be erected outside the Capitol, with crowds chanting "Hang Mike Pence!" as they stormed the building in search of him. Trump watched TV coverage as the mayhem unfolded, unhappy that he had been talked out of leading the assault himself. As the crowd grew violent, he repeatedly ignored overtures that he should address his supporters and calm the situation, until finally he issued a statement saying "we have to have peace" and calling for the rioters to "go home now". He immediately undercut this by calling the rioters "very special" and sympathizing that he knew "how you feel", and that "this was a fraudulent election".[31]

In December 2020, 126 House Republicans had signed onto a Texas lawsuit to overturn the election results in Pennsylvania, Michigan, Wisconsin and Georgia. It was rejected by the Supreme Court, but this would not be the last attempt made by these individuals to subvert democracy.[32] On 6 January 2021, hours after running for their lives and hiding behind locked doors, 139 House Republicans and eight Senate Republicans complied with Trump's request and refused to certify the election results, another partisan blow dealt to succession legitimacy.[33]

Groundwork for a 2024 electoral coup

Trump's efforts to undermine confidence in the 2020 election did not stop when he finally left office. What is more, Republican Party machinery has also carried out a number of different anti-democratic actions to prevent a Democrat victory in 2024. Between 1 January and 14 May 2021, at least 14 states enacted 22 new laws that restrict access to the vote, supposedly to combat voter fraud (which is not a significant problem). The real goal is to make it more difficult for certain groups (who traditionally lean Democrat) to vote.

These actions include a Georgia bill forbidding the use of mobile voting stations – unless during governor-declared emergencies – and banning the use of provisional ballots for those who attend the wrong voting station. Both of these practices accounted for a combined total of nearly double the margin by which Joe Biden won the state of Georgia.[34] The Georgia law also gives the Republican-controlled state legislature the right to suspend election officials and name the chair of the State Election Board.

Efforts have also been made to install "election deniers" in every part of the electoral process, many in roles so inconspicuous that they would not ordinarily warrant any attention, including ordinary poll workers.[35] Given the potential power of secretaries of state to change election results, a concerted Republican effort to secure allies in these positions has also been under way. Groups such as the America First Secretary of State Coalition have been created. According to its website, it seeks to "promote and establish messaging that Secretary of State elections all across the country are a priority ... because they are predominantly responsible for the election process in each state".[36] Founder Jim Marchant even explicitly admitted in 2022 that the goal was to "fix 2020 like President Trump said".[37]

These efforts were roundly defeated at the 2022 midterm elections, and Trump was blamed by Republicans for costing them a Senate majority. This offered some hope that a majority of Americans still value the integrity of their democracy, but these attempts will not stop. Trump himself shows no sign of giving up on his desire to be president again.[38]

Where the unimpeachable nature of certain officials' characters narrowly prevented an electoral coup in 2020, the same outcome cannot be expected in 2024. The mere fact that the entire system of American democracy relies to a significant degree on the integrity and good character of its officials shows how vulnerable the system is, and how desperately reform is needed to defend it and preserve any legitimacy it retains.

The Democrats are not without fault, although their transgressions against democracy are not on the same level as those outlined above. The successful attempt by the Democratic National Committee to prevent Senator Bernie Sanders from gaining the 2016 nomination was shameful, self-defeating and deeply anti-democratic. The revelation that Joe Biden's team attempted to exercise censor control over Twitter and certain traditional media outlets in the run-up to the 2020 election was another damaging blow to the succession legitimacy of US democracy.[39] It also feeds into the narrative of a "stolen" election enabled by "a radical left media" and "deep-state establishment".

A final statistic on this subject: 40 per cent of the respondents in the Wintemute poll discussed earlier believed that "having a strong leader for America is more important than having a democracy".[40] Even with the usual caveats regarding polling, this is truly frightening.

Compassionate Change

There is a much-quoted maxim: "Take the world as it is, not as you think it ought to be". I disagree. This is defeatist and only serves to limit our thinking as a species. I prefer to be clear-eyed about the realities of the current global situation, while also striving to think better and dream bigger.

At the heart of that maxim is an assumption that *realism* is the dominant force shaping international relations and, ultimately, human interactions on a global scale. Realism is the theory in international relations that the world is a chaotic and dangerous place, with nation states engaged in constant competition with one another to obtain and wield power. While I believe that this state of affairs is evident through much of human history, I do not believe that realism represents the pinnacle of where we should be aiming as a species. It stresses contest over collaboration and power over compassion.

The very nature of this mindset fosters a zero-sum ideology – my gain can only come at your loss – which I see as fundamentally destructive for humanity as a whole. I believe that realism does not represent the inevitable state of human interactions, but it has been the default setting, and the easy option, for much of human history. When alternative models of collaboration are explored but do not immediately seem to succeed, the reflex response is a return to the realist mindset. We might be tempted to view this as "human nature", but the realist mindset simply ensures that, whatever its origins, we will never escape this destructive world view.

This brings me to a crucial question that many readers may still be asking: why do I argue for the continuation of the American Empire, and warn of the dangers of its collapse? Surely the world is better off without an empire like this. An empire that has been responsible for so much harm, destruction and misery for so many people around the world. An empire that is ruled by a reverence for a broken capitalist model that perpetuates selfishness and inequality and spreads this ideology across the globe. An empire with a ruling class mired in corruption and supported by a meek and complicit media class. An empire that regularly employs staggering double standards to justify inhumane actions by itself and its allies while simultaneously condemning the same actions by those it opposes. Is any empire, or hegemon, by its very nature antagonistic to global collaboration? Would a more multipolar world not be better for all, with many states of similar strength jostling for influence?

No, I do not believe so. My reasoning is simple: I am taking the world as it is, but also how I think it ought to be. The reality is that the most likely alternative to the current state of affairs is not democratic and collaborative – it is authoritarian and intolerant.

The reflexive resort to realism still exists, and for a new paradigm to take hold it will require leadership by example: genuine, unhypocritical leadership that shows the world the benefits of an equitable reality for all, where people are treated with respect and dignity. America has all the attributes required to be this leader, to evolve into a *compassionate empire* that serves to help all mankind.

This type of leadership could bring about an aspirational multipolar reality, one of collaboration not competition. America's size, language, natural resources, position of security, influence, and stable demographic outlook, make it the only possible candidate for this role today. Above all, it has also demonstrated an ability to reflect on past mistakes and make efforts to avoid repeating the same errors in future. The words of two American presidents illustrate this best. President Obama's acknowledgement in 2016 of the toll inflicted by US bombings of Laos during the Vietnam War was a crucial first step. President Biden's warning to Israel after the Hamas atrocities of October 2023 built upon this, urging Prime Minister Netanyahu to not follow American example in reacting to 9/11 and be "consumed" by rage. Biden conceded that America had "sought justice and got justice" but also that it had "made mistakes".[1]

It is easy to dismiss the words of both presidents as empty rhetoric, but I believe they represent more. A nation that is willing to reflect on and apologize for even some its mistakes is rarer than you might think. For a hegemon or empire to do so, while still in a position of global dominance, is unheard of. Can you picture Putin apologizing for the massacre at Grozny or Xi Jinping apologizing for Tiananmen Square, even in their current geopolitical position, let alone if they enjoyed America's superiority?

America is an empire in its relative infancy; it can and must evolve in the interest of its own survival but also to help bring about a fairer future for the world. One thing is for certain: the status quo will not lead to the achievement of these goals. As access to information continues to expand, widening inequality and the hypocrisy of America's oligarchical class are becoming harder to conceal and therefore harder to ignore. Advances in technology will only exacerbate this situation in the future. The leadership of both the major political parties should consider the words of President Franklin Delano Roosevelt and take a look at themselves:

> I should like to have it said of my first administration that the forces of selfishness and of lust for power met their match. I should like to have it said of my second administration that in it these forces met their master.[2]

As we have seen, there is much that needs to change, and there will be much opposition from an entrenched oligarchical class, but a better future is possible for those brave enough to strive for it. I will end this book as I began it, with optimism and a clarion call for change.

Steps Toward Compassionate Change

Capitalism 2.0

Capitalism is broken – it has been for some time, and it will only get worse unless action is taken. Runaway inequality is now the defining feature of a broken capitalist model, with the gap between rich and poor widening by the day. We must stop companies from profiting from human suffering, put people before profit, and value human lives over share price. This involves aggressive regulation on industries that are embedded deep within the American oligarchy: armaments, fossil fuels, Big Healthcare, Big Pharma, Big Tobacco, Big Food, Big Media. For companies whose profits are derived from contracts from the American government, this regulation would be simple to achieve if the political will existed.

Higher levels of taxation for the super-rich are also both logical and ethical. We must evolve into a society that can legitimately ask itself: how much is too much? The myth of scarcity must also be exposed as a creation of the selfish and unscrupulous. Scarcity is not the issue; overconsumption and greed are the problem. The irony of the current situation is that not even those who are "winning" are happy. The richest in society are often dissatisfied because their lives lack meaning, and the accumulation of material possessions is simply a never-ending cycle of diminishing gratification. Those at the bottom are unhappy for more obvious reasons, as they struggle to survive on a daily basis. We know that malnourishment is among the leading causes of early death on our planet, but diseases linked to overconsumption are also on that list. Tax reform to redistribute wealth to the less fortunate is part of the solution in the short term, but deeper, longer-term thinking about human wellbeing and flourishing will also be required.

As advances in AI lead to a future without the apparent need for employment, the time to make changes is now. We need to stop defining the value of a human being by their labour output, and begin to value how a human being can contribute to society. If AI developments are controlled and owned by the few and not the many, then a dystopian future looks unavoidable. To prevent this, an argument for a techno-logical post-capitalist future must be made, and the idea of American socialism must be reclaimed. The weaponization of this single word has given critics the ability to shut down all conversations regarding equality and progress. Americans should heed the warning of President Harry Truman in 1952:

> Socialism is a scare word they've hurled at every advance the people have made. Socialism is what they called public power, social secu-rity, deposit insurance, and independent labour organizations. Socialism is their name for anything that helps all people.[3]

The current system of government bailouts, share buybacks and a diminishing social-security safety net is not the "free market" at work. The free market is a myth perpetuated by those it enriches at the expense of those it punishes. It is socialism for the rich – and the cruellest capitalism possible for the rest. American workers must unionize and quickly: there is strength in numbers. This is one of the only tools at their disposal if they have any hope of winning in this rigged game.

Modern capitalism is rigged and manipulated in many other ways, but it's worth touching briefly on one more, which is encapsulated in the concept of resource scarcity. Resource scarcity has been exaggerated in some cases, invented in others and exploited by some industries and governments to ensure we remain trapped, as consumers and citizens, by our primal animal instincts and fears. We have the resources to feed, clothe and shelter every human being on the planet, but we choose not to. We have the capacity to provide unlimited clean energy for every human being on the planet, but we decide instead to burn fossil fuels, destroying our delicate ecosystem in the process. We are told we don't have enough of certain resources, but we are also encouraged by capitalism to consume more. The cognitive dissonance within the current capitalist worldview stifles our capacity for basic human decency. It's a world view that is so powerful, so pervasive, that we struggle to see an alternative, and we wilfully ignore the suffering of those who are on the losing side of modern capitalism. We can do better. We must do better.

Democracy reimagined

American democracy is rotten to its core, with politicians serving themselves first and the people second. This is inevitable in a society dominated by unchecked capitalism, and it will not improve unless the relationship between money and politics is eradicated root and branch. The links between Big Industry and politics must be severed, as the entire notion of political lobbying is the antithesis of a fair and transparent society. The revolving door between politics and Big Industry must also be slammed shut; those who enter politics must do so to help their fellow citizens, not enrich themselves.

The institutions of democracy must be respected and renewed as the faith and trust placed in them by the people is eroded to the point of breaking. Democracy and the institutions that ensure its smooth running are fragile, man-made constructs, and they involve tacit agreement between the rulers and the ruled. If legitimate election results are labelled fraudulent by the losers, democracy itself is at risk. If a supposedly apolitical Supreme Court acts with clearly political motivation, and its members accept favours from external actors pushing their own agenda, democracy itself is at risk. If members of Congress and their families profit from the decisions they themselves make, democracy itself is at risk. You can fool some of the people some of the time, but you can't fool all of the people all of the time. Eventually the people will demand an end to these corrupt practices, and not a moment too soon.

What does a possible alternative look like? Inspiration can often be found where we least expect it. Rather than obsess about the political structures and cultures of other nations, we could look at democracy within a religion. The Bahá'í Faith is worth considering, without any need to subscribe to its spiritual beliefs; it possesses a model of democracy that ensures its leaders act only for the good of the community, not the good of themselves. Processes of consultation and collaboration are followed rather than the adversarial theatrics favoured by American democracy. Politicking and electioneering are banned, and to be elected to serve is a responsibility, not a reward. Decentralized ways of communicating and making decisions ensure that the views of all are respected, and the needs of the collective are met. I am not a member of an organized religion myself, but a good idea is a good idea, regardless of the source.

Can changes like these be implemented on a national, and eventually global, scale for the good of humanity? It is not impossible given time, despite the current dominance of the hyper-capitalist worldview. To begin the process of reimagining democracy, to seek out different ways of understanding the problems, to keep an open mind – these are the necessary first steps.

Compassionate international relations

A fundamental shift in how the US engages with the world is required so that it can lead the world into peaceful multipolarity by treating others as it wishes to be treated. America can set a positive example, and then other nations and their peoples are much more likely to follow its lead – people everywhere yearn to be free, valued and respected. America and its allies must hold themselves to a higher ethical standard, as currently there are many who view the US as hypocritical and self-serving. The global challenges that exist today, and that will increase in future, require global solutions; the American Empire is uniquely positioned to lead that effort. It must match the lofty rhetoric of its founding ideals to corresponding actions and thereby prove that its veneration and celebration of life, liberty and the pursuit of happiness are more than just empty words. Put simply, it must become a *compassionate* empire, guided by empathy rather than self-interest.

It might be tempting to dismiss this vision as naive, weak or unrealistic, and simply declare that the world is a dangerous place where suffering is inevitable. This would be the easy way out. Thinking differently, and pursuing a new approach, might feel unusual or uncomfortable at first, but inspiration exists for those willing to seek it – and the rewards would be worth it. Back in 1978, systems theorist Ervin Laszlo rightly stated that a change in the nature of human interaction was required, from adversarial "negative-sum" and "zero-sum" relations toward cooperative "positive-sum" relations. Laszlo identified numerous societal dysfunctions such as idealized norms of aggression, competitive acquisition and unregulated competition that needed to be understood and addressed. His words are no less true today than they were almost fifty years ago:

> The remarkable feature of international relations in an age of interdependence is that the basic long-term processes present potentials for positive-sum games. Regrettably, national leaders intent on gaining short-term advantages for their own countries in an atmosphere of mutual distrust, if not hostility, are not playing such games. For example, the international balance of power gives rise to a game which is at best a zero-sum; the gains of one side balance with the losses of others. This can degenerate into a negative-sum game with the outbreak of large-scale war … Yet the situation could be transformed into a positive-sum game with the establishment of a system of world security through disarmament and mutually agreed peacekeeping. No nation would risk being damaged or wiped out, and all could spend the major part of the huge sums which now go to defence and the military on projects of concrete human benefit.[4]

Merciless Darwinian competition is not the unalterable condition or the default mode of human beings. Although aggression is real, dangerous and all too common across human history, we are also hardwired for compassion and altruism, beyond simple or even enlightened self-interest.[5] Compassion and altruism, I would argue, are the truest and noblest aspects of human nature. It is when we are driven by fear that we revert to realism, guided by our most selfish and destructive urges – fear of scarcity, fear of harm, fear of imprisonment and, most crucially, fear of the "other". Paradoxically, this is best illustrated by nationalism. Nationalism shows that we clearly possess this inherent drive toward affiliation and cooperation, but the artificial creation of the concept of the "other" has hijacked this drive, applying it for harm rather than good. Overcoming such pitfalls and channelling our nobler instincts is by no means easy in troubled times, but we are not a lost cause.

How, then, does America begin to pursue a more compassionate, ethical foreign policy in a world with more than a few ruthless adversaries? It won't be straightforward, but America needs to get its own house in order first. As mentioned above, domestic democratic reform is essential. The quality and probity of its leaders needs to improve – fast. Then, on the international stage, difficult but ethical stances can increasingly be taken by better leaders. Aided by committed diplomats, confirmed by an improved and more efficient Congress, better leaders can make better agreements and alliances. Engagement in and leadership of international institutions, guided by altruism and cooperation rather than individual or national self-interest, is also vital. If current institutions are not fit for purpose, new ones must be created with these guiding principles firmly at their heart. Leading by example means exactly that. Compassion can be contagious, but it must be genuine, as hypocrisy is easy to spot and leads inexorably to cynicism.

A virtuous circle needs to start somewhere. Pressure from below, from normal citizens who want their country and their planet to succeed and survive, is crucial. Compassion begins with individuals, and extends upwards and outwards, until governments have no choice but to alter their direction. Ordinary citizens can make a difference, and organized collective actions can exert outsized pressure, far greater than the sum of their parts. Grassroots campaigns, charities and aid organizations can all work in tandem to create irresistible conditions for change.

Our interconnected world of instant communication and social media offers an incredible opportunity to connect with similarly minded people all over the world, in previously unimaginable numbers. Cat videos are indeed fantastic, but there also exists a huge potential to harness digital tools not just for frivolity, but for the betterment of humanity. Other technologies also offer hope for the spread of empathy and compassion. Advances in AI and VR technology could allow us to almost literally walk a mile in another's shoes, share their suffering, even see it as our own. In such a future, ignoring the plight of others would simply not be an option.

One final and important consideration should be that compassion comes at a cost. It is the hard choice, not the easy option. For the American Empire, acting altruistically will not be cheap and the benefits will not always be immediately recognizable. The US is uniquely placed, however, with an economy that allows it to generate far more than it needs. It does not need to spend quite as much as it does on weapons of war to maintain its military supremacy. Moreover, many future problems would be prevented by acting with altruism today, rather than allowing problem-generating conditions to arise or worsen in the first place. Funds from seemingly ever-expanding military budgets can and should be diverted to assist in creating the conditions for peace and prosperity at home and abroad. This logic may seem counter-intuitive, but it would ultimately cost the US far less in terms of dollars and human suffering – and it would be the right thing to do.

To those who remain unconvinced, I ask a simple question: what is the alternative? The status quo is not working, and without radical changes to many aspects of our societies and our mentalities we are doomed to keep on repeating the mistakes of the past.

New media
The American media no longer represents the people, and only speaks truth to power when it is in the interests of its shareholders and the political tribe it has chosen to follow. A free media is a vital ingredient

for a healthy democracy, but the American media is not free – it is bought and paid for, its members now a part of the oligarchical system they should be exposing. Americans have awakened to this fact and their trust in traditional media is at an all-time low, with viewers and listeners deserting in their thousands.

New media sources are springing up daily and can provide an alternative to the corporate-owned traditional outlets. Americans must proceed with caution, however, as new media is not immune to bias and pursuing the goals and agendas of special interests. There are also fewer mechanisms and regulations in place to ensure truth and objectivity, so Americans must exercise their own diligence, must question the motives of those sharing the information. Misinformation and propaganda are exploding with the spread of social media, and the big platforms are doing little to address this situation. Think before you post or repost anything. Treat others online the same way you would like to be treated in real life – peaceful discourse and non-violent disagreement are crucial for a society to function.

Ronald Reagan once speculated that it would require the existence of a threat from a non-human civilization to unite humankind against this new foe.[6] Within our current paradigm this is still accurate, as the tribalist instincts of humans seemingly require the "other" as a foe to unite against. It is my hope that an alien invasion would not be required for humanity to understand and appreciate our shared heritage and the potential for a bright and peaceful future as one human race – with empathy and global collaboration at the heart. It is my hope that enough Americans share this desire and can take the steps needed to lead the world in this direction. It needn't be a Hollywood fantasy that good people can join together and change things for the better – it can happen for real.

A better future

If there is one message to take away from this book, it is this: the American people deserve better and must demand better. The oligarchical class must recognize the dangerous ground on which they tread, as rampant inequality, disputes over succession legitimacy, military misadventure, economic oppression and environmental degradation have all led to the fall of many empires in the past. Hopefully, new generations with less susceptibility to groupthink, fewer entrenched views, and greater faith in what can and should be achieved, will be able to take the American Empire forward, for the good of the country and the benefit of the world.

A Final Thought

For all of you who have reached the end of this journey, I ask you to indulge me for a few moments longer and join me in a quick thought experiment.

Close your eyes and imagine that tomorrow it was scientifically proven, beyond any doubt, that reincarnation was a reality. Not only this, but the reality you are born into in your next life is shaped entirely by the goodness of your actions in this one. Compassion, empathy and kindness would be rewarded with an easier, happier, more fulfilling existence the next time around. How would you behave? If anyone can honestly say they would make the exact same decisions, then they are either lying or they represent the needle in the metaphysical haystack.

What does this prove? As much as we claim to act with future generations in mind, this is simply not the case for the majority of decisions made by humans every day. This does not make us evil; it simply makes us human. Our limited lifespan ensures we only focus on a miniscule period of human history and our actions reflect this, limiting our scope and preventing humanity from realizing its true potential.

Think big ... dream bigger.

Acknowledgements

There have been many writers and thinkers whose work has inspired me to write this book, and many whose ideas have also informed my own. The example set by Senator Bernie Sanders – in not just his words but also his actions – is an ongoing inspiration. I am an eternal optimist and writers such as Yuval Noah Harari and Steven Pinker have helped me retain this optimism for humanity even in the face of often tragic global circumstances and seemingly endless suffering. Michael Karlberg's *Beyond the Culture of Contest* served as an ethical compass during the writing of this book, and his vision of a mutualist alternative to adversarialism is a future worth striving for. *Confessions of an Economic Hitman* by John Perkins, served as an invitation to fully investigate the realities of the American Empire. Harari's book *Sapiens* remains my favourite work of non-fiction, and the ability to turn potentially complicated topics into books that are both accessible and digestible is a skill I greatly admire and one I aim to emulate. Tim Marshall's *Prisoners of Geography* is another excellent example in this regard. Matt Taibbi's many books exploring the issues present in the modern US have also been an inspiration, as have Robert Reich's. Where these individuals have led, I am keen to follow, asking difficult questions, illustrating uncomfortable truths and speaking truth to power wherever possible.

I would like to thank Stella for organizing me and working tirelessly to make sure as many people as possible are able to read this book. Thank you, Rachael, for the support, Robert, for your guidance during the editing process and Mickey for your assistance recording the audiobook. Finally, Guy and Lauren are the creative geniuses responsible for the artwork that has brought my ideas to life with such a visual flourish. Thank you all.

About the Author

Patrick Watts obtained his bachelor's degree in History at Birmingham University in England. While working as a chartered financial adviser, he completed his master's degree in International Relations and Contemporary Warfare at King's College London within the Department of War Studies. His dissertation, "Method not madness: discourse analysis to examine how President Trump has attempted to alter NATO principles, identity and culture", laid the groundwork for his first book, The End of the American Empire.

Patrick is currently studying to complete his MSc degree with the Alef Trust, in Consciousness, Spirituality and Transpersonal Psychology. Based in London, he has travelled widely across the United States, developing a deep and non-partisan understanding of American politics, culture and society.

Don't be a stranger!

Join us at www.patrickwattsbooks.com to stay informed on all things *The End of the American Empire* and be the first to hear about news on the upcoming sequel!

∞ Newsletter ∞ Media Appearances ∞ Compassionate Change Initiative ∞ Essays ∞ Podcasts ∞

Pass it on: The Power of Three

If you enjoyed this book and the message of compassionate change resonated with you, please do not keep it to yourself! Think of three people who would also find it interesting, give them a call and ask them to do the same in turn if they also enjoy the book.

Lasting change can develop from a ripple into a wave.

Help us make it happen.

Notes

CHAPTER I – THE HISTORY OF THE AMERICAN EMPIRE

1 George Santayana, writer and philosopher, made this statement in his multivolume work *The Life of Reason* (1905–6). It has subsequently been regurgitated by many political figures, including most notably Winston Churchill in 1948.

2 From 1803 to 1867, the mainland territory of the United States was altered through various land purchases, annexations and cessions, beginning with the most well known (Louisiana Purchase, 1803) and ending with the acquisition of the northernmost part of the modern Unites States (Alaska, 1867).

3 "Seigniorage" allows the US to trade a $100 bill, which costs cents to produce, for the equivalent $100 value of tangible goods and services. It is estimated that the equivalent of $7.5 trillion of goods and services have been obtained using this effective "discount" (see David Z. Morris, "The end of exorbitant privilege: inflation, the global dollar and what comes next", *CoinDesk*, 5 August 2021, https://www.coindesk.com/markets/2021/08/05/the-end-of-exorbitant-privilege-inflation-the-global-dollar-and-what-comes-next/).

4 https://knoema.com/mhrzolg/historical-gdp-by-country-statistics-from-the-world-bank-1960-2019

5 Carmen Ang, "The top 100 most valuable brands in 2022", Visual Capitalist, 27 October 2022, https://www.visualcapitalist.com/top-100-most-valuable-brands-in-2022/

6 Tanner Mirrlees, *Hearts and Mines: The U.S. Empire's Culture Industry* (2016), p.5

7 Victoria de Grazia, *Irresistible Empire: America's Advance through Twentieth-Century Europe* (2005)

8 Nicholas Schou, "How the CIA hoodwinked Hollywood", *The Atlantic*, 14 July 2016, https://www.theatlantic.com/entertainment/archive/2016/07/operation-tinseltown-how-the-cia-manipulates-

hollywood/491138/

9   Paul Moody, "U.S. embassy support for Hollywood's global
    dominance: Cultural Imperialism Redux", *International
    Journal of Communication*, 11(2017), https://bura.brunel.ac.uk/
    bitstream/2438/14791/4/FullText.pdf

10 "U.S. defense spending compared to other countries", Peter G.
    Peterson Foundation, 24 April 2023, https://www.pgpf.org/chart-
    archive/0053_defense-comparison

11 https://education.nationalgeographic.org/resource/big-stick-diplomacy

12 Max Roser, Esteban Ortiz-Ospina, Hannah Ritchie, Edouard
    Mathieu and Bastian Herre, "Military personnel and spending",
    2013, https://ourworldindata.org/military-personnel-spending

13 Amrita Jash, "China's 2022 defense budget: behind the numbers",
    China Brief, 2/18 (2022), https://jamestown.org/program/chinas-
    2022-defense-budget-behind-the-numbers/

14 Stockholm International Peace Research Institute, *SIPRI Yearbook
    2022* (2022), 342, https://sipri.org/sites/default/files/YB22%2010%20
    World%20Nuclear%20Forces.pdf

15 J. M. Pearce and D. C. Denkenberger, "A national pragmatic safety
    limit for nuclear weapon quantities", *Safety*, 4/25 (2018), https://doi.
    org/10.3390/safety4020025

16 https://worldpopulationreview.com/country-rankings/military-
    size-by-country; https://www.statista.com/statistics/1293365/
    nato-overall-military-personnel/

17 David Axe, "The Ukrainian army has more tanks now than
    when the war began – because it keeps capturing them from
    Russia", *Forbes*, 24 March 2022, https://www.forbes.com/sites/
    davidaxe/2022/03/24/the-ukrainian-army-has-captured-enough-
    russian-tanks-to-make-good-all-its-own-losses-and-then-some/

18 https://worldpopulationreview.com/country-rankings/largest-navies-in-
    the-world

19 David Axe, "Yes, the Chinese navy has more ships than the U.S.
    navy. But it's got far fewer missiles", *Forbes*, 10 November 2021,
    https://www.forbes.com/sites/davidaxe/2021/11/10/yes-the-chinese-
    navy-has-more-ships-than-the-us-navy-but-its-got-far-fewer-missiles/

20 https://www.globalfirepower.com/navy-aircraft-carriers.php

21 Gerrard Kaonga, "How China's 003 aircraft carrier Fujian compares
    with U.S. navy", *Newsweek*, 17 June 2022, https://www.newsweek.

com/china-type-003-aircraft-carrier-fujian-comparison-u-s-navy-plan-pla-1716762

22 David Axe, "How many stealth warplanes are there in the world – and who has them?", *Forbes*, 1 July 2020, https://www.forbes.com/sites/davidaxe/2020/07/01/how-many-stealth-warplanes-are-there-in-the-world-and-who-has-them/

23 Valerie Insinna, "Watchdog group finds F-35 sustainment costs could be headed off affordability cliff", *Defense News*, 7 July 2021, https://www.defensenews.com/air/2021/07/07/watchdog-group-finds-f-35-sustainment-costs-could-be-headed-off-affordability-cliff/

24 https://armedforces.eu/air_forces/ranking_drones

25 Ruqaiyah Zarook, "Map of the week: mapping the global U.S. military bootprint", Ubique, 5 November 2021, https://ubique.americangeo.org/map-of-the-week/map-of-the-week-mapping-the-global-u-s-military-bootprint/

26 https://www.statista.com/statistics/269729/documented-civilian-deaths-in-iraq-war-since-2003/

27 BBC News, "Iraq study estimates war-related deaths at 461,000", 16 October 2013, https://www.bbc.co.uk/news/world-middle-east-24547256

28 https://www.statista.com/statistics/263798/american-soldiers-killed-in-iraq/; Tim Bullman and Aaron Schneiderman, "Risk of suicide among U.S. veterans who deployed as part of Operation Enduring Freedom, Operation Iraqi Freedom, and Operation New Dawn", *Injury Epidemiology*, 8(40) (2021), https://injepijournal.biomedcentral.com/articles/10.1186/s40621-021-00332-y

29 https://www.aclu.org/issues/human-rights/treaty-ratification

30 John B. Bellinger III, "Obama, Bush, and the Geneva conventions", *Foreign Policy*, 11 August 2010, https://foreignpolicy.com/2010/08/11/obama-bush-and-the-geneva-conventions/

31 BBC News, "Huawei arrest: Justin Trudeau denies political motivation", 7 December 2018, https://www.bbc.co.uk/news/world-us-canada-46471904

32 BBC News, "Harry Dunn crash: Biden team says Anne Sacoolas extradition refusal 'final'", 28 January 2021, https://www.bbc.co.uk/news/uk-england-northamptonshire-55849608

33 Steven Mintz, "Historical context: facts about the slave trade and slavery", n.d., https://www.gilderlehrman.org/history-resources/

teacher-resources/historical-context-facts-about-slave-trade-and-slavery; Henry Louis Gates Jr, "How many slaves landed in the US?", *The Root*, 6 January 2014, https://www.theroot.com/how-many-slaves-landed-in-the-us-1790873989

34 Nada Hassanein, "Native Americans die younger, CDC study shows", *USA Today*, 23 November 2021, https://eu.usatoday.com/story/news/health/2021/11/23/native-americans-life-expectancy-cdc/6360395001/

35 Katherine E. McKinney, Scott D. Sagan & Allen S. Weiner, "Why the atomic bombing of Hiroshima would be illegal today", *Bulletin of the Atomic Scientists*, 76:4 (2020), 157–165, https://doi.org/10.1080/00963402.2020.1778344

36 Bill Chappell, "U.N. treaty banning nuclear weapons takes effect, without the U.S. and other powers", NPR, 22 January 2021, https://www.npr.org/2021/01/22/959583731/u-n-treaty-banning-nuclear-weapons-takes-effect-without-the-u-s-and-others

37 https://en.wikipedia.org/wiki/Vietnam_War_casualties

38 https://www.history.com/news/laos-most-bombed-country-vietnam-war

39 John Pilger, "The long secret alliance: Uncle Sam and Pol Pot", *CovertAction Quarterly*, 62 (1997), https://msuweb.montclair.edu/~furrg/pol/pilgerpolpotnus.pdf

40 Meg Sullivan, "UCLA demographer produces best estimate yet of Cambodia's death toll under Pol Pot", 16 April 2015, https://newsroom.ucla.edu/releases/ucla-demographer-produces-best-estimate-yet-of-cambodias-death-toll-under-pol-pot

41 Bethany Allen-Ebrahimian, "64 years later, CIA finally releases details of Iranian coup", *Foreign Policy*, 20 June 2017, https://foreignpolicy.com/2017/06/20/64-years-later-cia-finally-releases-details-of-iranian-coup-iran-tehran-oil/

42 Seymour M. Hersh, "Torture at Abu Ghraib", *New Yorker*, 30 April 2004, https://www.newyorker.com/magazine/2004/05/10/torture-at-abu-ghraib

43 Ali Harb, "Guantanamo 20 years on: a legacy of 'injustice' and 'abuse'", Al Jazeera, 11 January 2022, https://www.aljazeera.com/news/2022/1/11/guantanamo-20-years-on-a-legacy-of-injustice-and-abuse

44 https://www.aclu.org/issues/national-security/torture/extraordinary-rendition

45 Conor Friedersdorf, "America's shadow death row", *The Atlantic*, 22 January 2021, https://www.theatlantic.com/ideas/archive/2021/01/americas-shadow-death-row/617757/

CHAPTER 2 – THE END OF EMPIRES

1 All the statistics in this chapter are necessarily rough estimates. Unless otherwise indicated, the statistics regarding the peak geographical extent of an empire are based on figures collected in Rein Taagepera, "Expansion and contraction patterns of large polities: context for Russia", *International Studies Quarterly*, 41:3 (1997), https://doi.org/10.1111/0020-8833.00053 or in Peter Turchin et al., "East–West orientation of historical empires and modern states", *Journal of World Systems Research*, 12:2 (2006), https://doi.org/10.5195/jwsr.2006.369. The peak population of each empire is not easy to establish. Sources are given where possible, but all the figures should be treated as provisional and inevitably imprecise. For maps of the empires, the website of the World History Encyclopedia is a useful resource: https://www.worldhistory.org/

2 See Josef Wiesehöfer, "The Achaemenid Empire", in Ian Morris and Walter Scheidel (eds), *The Dynamics of Ancient Empires: State Power from Assyria to Byzantium* (2009), pp.66–98 (table 3.1)

3 Walter Scheidel, "The Scale of Empire", in P. F. Bang, C. A. Bayly and Walter Scheidel (eds), *The Oxford World History of Empire: Volume One: The Imperial Experience* (2021), p.103

4 Josep M. Colomer, *Great Empires, Small Nations: The Uncertain Future of the Sovereign State* (2007), p.7

5 Based on the 2 CE census, but see also Kent G. Deng, "Fact or fiction? Re-examination of Chinese premodern population statistics", London School of Economics working paper 76/03 (2003), https://eprints.lse.ac.uk/22353/1/wp76.pdf

6 Walter Scheidel, "Demography", in W. Scheidel, I. Morris and R. Saller (eds), *The Cambridge Economic History of the Greco-Roman World* (2007)

7 Alexander Demandt, *Der Fall Roms* (1984),p.695; https://courses.washington.edu/rome250/gallery/ROME%20250/210%20Reasons.htm

8 Warren T. Treadgold, *A History of the Byzantine State and Society* (1997), p.278

9 Colomer, *Great Empires*, p.7; https://en.wikipedia.org/wiki/Demographics_of_the_Ottoman_Empire

10 Based on Colomer, Great Empires, p.7 and Thomas J. Barfield, *Shadow Empires: An Alternative Imperial History* (2023), p.201

11 Based on Colomer, *Great Empires*, p.7 and Scheidel, "The Scale of Empire", p.103

12 Scheidel, "The Scale of Empire", p.92

13 David Carrasco, *The Aztecs: A Very Short Introduction* (2012), p.3

14 Ibid.

15 The figure regarding geographical area is based on the estimate for 1520 in Taagepera (1997), p.497, while the population estimate is based on figures for 1520 which are discussed in Linda A. Newsom, "Indian population patterns in colonial Spanish America", *Latin American Research Review*, 20:3 (1985), p.43

16 See Colomer, *Great Empires*, p.7, which gives this figure in relation to the empire's peak period of 1780–1830.

17 Based on the 1897 census: https://en.wikipedia.org/wiki/Russian_Empire_census

18 Based on the 1910 census: https://en.wikipedia.org/wiki/Ethnic_and_religious_composition_of_Austria-Hungary

19 Based on the 1940 census: https://en.wikipedia.org/wiki/Demography_of_the_Empire_of_Japan

20 Based on the 1901 census and estimates of increasing population into the 1920s as the empire reached its greatest geographical extent: https://en.wikipedia.org/wiki/Demographics_of_the_British_Empire

21 Scheidel, "The Scale of Empire", p.103

22 FinTech Global, "How the Queen's passing will change currency in the Commonwealth", 20 September 2022, https://fintech.global/2022/09/20/how-the-queens-passing-will-change-currency-commonwealth

CHAPTER 3 – SOCIETY: DECAY FROM WITHIN

1 Shirin Ali, "Here are the states with the largest declines in life expectancy", *The Hill*, 23 August 2022, https://thehill.com/changing-america/well-being/longevity/3612531-here-are-the-states-with-the-largest-declines-in-life-expectancy/

2 A.S. Venkataramani, R. O'Brien R and A.C. Tsai, "Declining life expectancy in the United States: the need for social policy as

health policy", *JAMA*, 325(7) (2021), https://doi.org/10.1001/jama.2020.26339

3 Jane Greenhalgh, "U.S. life expectancy fell by 1.5 years in 2020, the biggest drop since WWII", NPR, 21 July 2021, https://www.npr.org/sections/coronavirus-live-updates/2021/07/21/1018590263/u-s-life-expectancy-fell-1-5-years-2020-biggest-drop-since-ww-ii-covid

4 https://covid.cdc.gov/covid-data-tracker/#datatracker-home

5 https://worldpopulationreview.com/country-rankings/murder-rate-by-country

6 https://health.ucdavis.edu/what-you-can-do/facts.html

7 https://worldpopulationreview.com/country-rankings/gun-deaths-by-country

8 https://watson.brown.edu/costsofwar/costs/human/military/killed

9 https://worldpopulationreview.com/country-rankings/gun-ownership-by-country

10 https://health.ucdavis.edu/what-you-can-do/facts.html

11 Madeline Drexler, "Guns and suicide: the hidden toll", *Harvard Public Health*, Winter 2013, https://www.hsph.harvard.edu/magazine/magazine_article/guns-suicide/

12 https://www.opensecrets.org/federal-lobbying/industries/summary?cycle=2022&id=q13; https://www.opensecrets.org/industries/lobbying.php?ind=Q12++

13 https://www.singlecare.com/blog/news/prescription-drug-statistics/

14 https://drugabusestatistics.org/drug-overdose-deaths/

15 Ibid; https://nida.nih.gov/drug-topics/trends-statistics/overdose-death-rates

16 Brett Kelman, "These Nashville doctors were running pill mills. Purdue Pharma sold to them anyway", *The Tennessean*, 11 July 2018, https://www.tennessean.com/story/news/2018/07/11/oxycontin-lawsuit-purdue-pharma-encouraged-pill-mills-sell-opioids/768322002/

17 Fred Schulte, "How America got hooked on a deadly drug", KFF Health News, 13 June 2018, https://khn.org/news/how-america-got-hooked-on-a-deadly-drug/

18 Martin Wall, "The Sackler family will still be rich after the opioid epidemic payout", *Irish Times*, 5 June 2023, https://www.irishtimes.com/world/us/2023/06/05/sackler-family-to-pay-billions-as-part-of-opioid-epidemic-deal-but-will-remain-rich/; https://www.forbes.com/profile/sackler/

19 Jan Hoffman, "Purdue Pharma is dissolved and Sacklers pay $4.5 billion to settle opioid claims", *New York Times*, 1 September 2021, https://www.nytimes.com/2021/09/01/health/purdue-sacklers-opioids-settlement.html

20 Jan Hoffman, "Sacklers and Purdue Pharma reach new deal with states over opioids", *New York Times*, 3 March 2022, https://www.nytimes.com/2022/03/03/health/sacklers-purdue-oxycontin-settlement.html

21 https://www.opensecrets.org/industries/indus.php?ind=N01

22 Lawrence O. Gostin, "'Big Food' is making America sick", *The Milbank Quarterly*, 94(3) (2016), https://www.ncbi.nlm.nih.gov/pmc/articles/PMC5020160/

23 Christopher Doering, "Where the dollars go: lobbying a big business for large food and beverage CPGs", *Food Dive*, 6 December 2021, https://www.fooddive.com/news/where-the-dollars-go-lobbying-a-big-business-for-large-food-and-beverage-c/607982/

24 David B. Allison et al., "Annual deaths attributable to obesity in the United States", *JAMA*, 282(16) (1999), https://jamanetwork.com/journals/jama/fullarticle/192032

25 https://endocrinenews.endocrine.org/u-s-leads-developed-nations-in-diabetes-prevalence

26 https://www.tfah.org/report-details/state-of-obesity-2020/

27 https://www.cdc.gov/heartdisease/facts.htm

28 https://www.feedingamerica.org/hunger-in-america; https://www.ers.usda.gov/topics/food-nutrition-assistance/food-security-in-the-u-s/

29 https://ourworldindata.org/food-insecurity

30 https://www.worlddata.info/average-income.php

31 Eric Berger, "Why is there a baby formula shortage in the US, and what can parents do?", *Guardian*, 18 May 2022, https://www.theguardian.com/us-news/2022/may/18/baby-formula-shortage-why-is-there-none-what-to-do-causes-explained

32 Annalisa Merelli, "The US has a lot of money, but it does not look like a developed country", *Quartz*, 10 March 2017, https://qz.com/879092/the-us-doesnt-look-like-a-developed-country/

33 https://data.oecd.org/healtheqt/hospital-beds.htm

34 https://www.drugwatch.com/featured/us-drug-prices-higher-vs-world/

35 Allie Nawrat, "Comparing the US's ten most expensive drugs with prices in the UK", 22 August 2018, Pharmaceutical Technology,

https://www.pharmaceutical-technology.com/features/us-most-expensive-drugs-uk-prices/

36 Fraiser Kansteiner et al., "The 15 highest paid pharma CEOs of 2021", *Fierce Pharma*, 27 June 2022, https://www.fiercepharma.com/special-reports/15-highest-paid-biopharma-ceos-2021

37 Ken Berman, "Big Pharma, big dividends", *Forbes*, 18 January 2018, https://www.forbes.com/sites/kenberman/2018/01/18/big-pharma-big-dividends/

38 Julia Kollewe and Mark Sweney, "AstraZeneca signs new Covid contracts in shift away from not-for-profit", *Guardian*, 12 November 2021, https://www.theguardian.com/business/2021/nov/12/astrazeneca-sells-22bn-of-covid-vaccine-in-first-nine-months

39 ActionAid, "Pharmaceutical companies reaping immoral profits from Covid vaccines yet paying low tax rates", 15 September 2021, https://actionaid.org/news/2021/pharmaceutical-companies-reaping-immoral-profits-covid-vaccines-yet-paying-low-tax-rates

40 Spencer Kimball, "Moderna CEO Bancel's golden parachute soared by hundreds of millions over the pandemic", CNBC, 10 March 2022, https://www.cnbc.com/2022/03/10/moderna-ceos-golden-parachute-soared-by-hundreds-of-millions-over-the-pandemic.html

41 Charles Boustany, "No, pharmaceutical companies are not 'war profiteers'", RealClearPolicy, 22 November 2021, https://www.realclearpolicy.com/articles/2021/11/22/no_pharmaceutical_companies_are_not_war_profiteers_804611.html

42 ActionAid, "Pharmaceutical companies reaping immoral profits"

43 Camila DeChalus et al., "As the pandemic raged, at least 75 lawmakers bought and sold stock in companies that make COVID-19 vaccines, treatments, and tests", *Business Insider*, 13 December 2021, https://www.businessinsider.com/lawmakers-bought-sold-covid-19-related-stocks-during-pandemic-2021-12?r=US&IR=T

44 Slavek Roller, "Pension and state funds dominating biomedical R&D investment: fiduciary duty and public health", *Global Health*, 15, 55 (2019), https://doi.org/10.1186/s12992-019-0490-x

45 Nisha Kurani and Cynthia Cox, "What drives health spending in the U.S. compared to other countries", Peterson-Kaiser Health System Tracker, 25 September 2020, https://www.healthsystemtracker.org/brief/what-drives-health-spending-in-the-u-s-compared-to-other-countries/

46 Ibid.

47 Ibid.

48 Bob Herman, "Health care executive pay soars during pandemic", *Axios*, 14 June 2021, https://www.axios.com/2021/06/14/health-care-ceo-pay-2020-pandemic

49 Bob Herman, "Health care CEO pay outstrips infectious disease research", *Axios*, 1 June 2020, https://www.axios.com/2020/06/01/health-care-ceo-pay-2019

50 Jack Clover and Nicola Small, "NHS bosses raking in £300,000-a-year plus bonuses in 'slap in the face' to nurses", *Daily Mirror*, 1 May 2021, https://www.mirror.co.uk/news/politics/nhs-bosses-raking-300000-year-24021086

51 Jennifer Tolbert, Patrick Drake and Anthony Damico, "Key facts about the uninsured population", KFF, 19 December 2022, https://www.kff.org/uninsured/issue-brief/key-facts-about-the-uninsured-population/

52 Vaughn Himber, "Employer-sponsored health insurance statistics: what the data tells us", eHealth, 20 October 2022, https://www.ehealthinsurance.com/resources/small-business/how-many-americans-get-health-insurance-from-their-employer

53 Dana Miller Ervin, "Here's why hospital bills are so high in the U.S. health care system", WFAE, 7 September 2021, https://www.wfae.org/health/2021-09-07/heres-why-hospital-bills-are-so-high-in-the-u-s-health-care-system

54 Chris Osman, "An ocean apart: US and EU employment law compared", Practical Law, 23 January 2001, https://content.next.westlaw.com/7-101-3606

55 Ervin, "Here's why hospital bills are so high"

56 Ibid.

57 Irene Papanicolas, "Health care spending in the United States and other high-income countries", *JAMA*, 319(10) (2018), https://jamanetwork.com/journals/jama/article-abstract/2674671

58 Ervin, "Here's why hospital bills are so high"

59 Oliver J. Wouters, "lobbying expenditures and campaign contributions by the pharmaceutical and health product industry in the United States, 1999–2018", *JAMA Internal Medicine*, 180(5) (2020), https://jamanetwork.com/journals/jamainternalmedicine/fullarticle/2762509

60 https://www.opensecrets.org/federal-lobbying/industries/ summary?id=F09

61 Wouters, "Lobbying expenditures"

62 https://www.opensecrets.org/industries/indus.php?Ind=H

63 https://www.opensecrets.org/industries/recips.php?cycle=2022&ind=H

64 Matthew S. McCoy et al., "Historical trends in health care-related financial holdings among members of Congress", *PLOS One* 16(7) (2021), https://doi.org/10.1371/journal.pone.0253624

65 David Jagielski, "Here's how healthcare stocks have historically performed after a down January", The Motley Fool, 12 February 2022, https://www.fool.com/investing/2022/02/12/heres-how-healthcare-stocks-have-historically-perf/; https://ycharts.com/indicators/sp_500_5_year_return

66 Chris Flood, "US pension plans dodge queries on healthcare holdings", *Financial Times*, 2 November 2019, https://www.ft.com/content/9f09fba3-39ad-4cfb-a011-0fc59fec26e5

67 Texas A&M University, "Why American infant mortality rates are so high", *ScienceDaily*, 13 October 2016, https://www.sciencedaily.com/releases/2016/10/161013103132.htm

68 https://www.gov.uk/employers-maternity-pay-leave

69 Miranda Bryant, "Maternity leave: US policy is worst on list of the world's richest countries", *Guardian*, 27 January 2020, https://www.theguardian.com/us-news/2020/jan/27/maternity-leave-us-policy-worst-worlds-richest-countries

70 Drew DeSilver, "U.S. students' academic achievement still lags that of their peers in many other countries", Pew Research Center, 15 February 2017, https://www.pewresearch.org/fact-tank/2017/02/15/u-s-students-internationally-math-science/

71 Ibid.

72 Kate Barrington, "The 15 biggest failures of the American public education system", Public School Review, 14 February 2023, https://www.publicschoolreview.com/blog/the-15-biggest-failures-of-the-american-public-education-system

73 Marc Tucker, "Why other countries keep outperforming us in education (and how to catch up)", *Education Week*, 2 June 2021, https://www.edweek.org/policy-politics/opinion-why-other-countries-keep-outperforming-us-in-education-and-how-to-catch-up/2021/05

74 Dave Dentel, "Census data shows phenomenal homeschool growth",

1 April 2021, https://hslda.org/post/census-data-shows-phenomenal-homeschool-growth

75 https://www.theschoolrun.com/home-education-around-world

76 Sally Weale, "Councils in England report 34% rise in elective home education", *Guardian*, 24 November 2021, https://www.theguardian.com/education/2021/nov/24/councils-england-report-34-rise-elective-home-education-children

77 OECD, "Survey of Adult Skills: Country Note – United States" (2013), https://www.oecd.org/skills/piaac/Country%20note%20-%20United%20States.pdf

78 OECD, "Education at a Glance 2014: OECD Indicators: Country Note – United States" (2014), https://www.oecd.org/unitedstates/United%20States-EAG2014-Country-Note.pdf

79 Ibid.

80 Zack Friedman, "Student loan forgiveness: Bernie Sanders says Biden should cancel all $1.8 trillion of student loans", *Forbes*, 23 February 2023, https://www.forbes.com/sites/zackfriedman/2022/02/23/bernie-sanders-wants-biden-to-cancel-all-18-trillion-of-student-loans/?sh=44a041cc535f

81 Daniel Rivero, "The debt trap: how the student loan industry betrays young Americans", *Guardian*, 6 September 2017, https://www.theguardian.com/money/2017/sep/06/us-student-debt-loans-navient-sallie-mae

82 Hannah Ritchie, Max Roser and Pablo Rosado, "Renewable energy", 2022, https://ourworldindata.org/renewable-energy

83 Cary Funk and Meg Hefferon, "U.S. public views on climate and energy", Pew Research Center, 25 November 2019, https://www.pewresearch.org/science/2019/11/25/u-s-public-views-on-climate-and-energy/

84 https://ccpi.org/ccpi-philosophy-team/

85 https://ccpi.org/ranking/

86 https://ccpi.org/country/usa/

87 Inci Sayki and Jimmy Cloutier, "Oil and gas industry spent $124.4 million on federal lobbying amid record profits in 2022", OpenSecrets, 22 February 2023, https://www.opensecrets.org/news/2023/02/oil-and-gas-industry-spent-124-4-million-on-federal-lobbying-amid-record-profits-in-2022/

88 Alan Zibel, "Big Oil's Capitol Hill allies", Public Citizen, 10

February 2021, https://www.citizen.org/article/big-oils-capitol-hill-allies/

89 Scott Waldman, "How Manchin used politics to protect his family coal company", *Politico*, 8 February 2022, https://www.politico.com/news/2022/02/08/manchin-family-coal-company-00003218

90 Andy Hirschfeld, "Joe Manchin has made $5.2M from his coal company – and gets big donations from fossil-fuel industry", *Salon*, 2 October 2021, https://www.salon.com/2021/10/02/joe-manchin-has-made-52m-from-his-coal-company--and-gets-big-donations-from-fossil-fuel-industry_partner/

91 David Moore, "At least 100 House members are invested in fossil fuels", *Sludge*, 29 December 2021, https://readsludge.com/2021/12/29/at-least-100-house-members-are-invested-in-fossil-fuels/

92 Andrew Chung, "US Supreme Court rulings darken forecast for EPA powers", Reuters, 31 May 2023, https://www.reuters.com/world/us/us-supreme-court-rulings-darken-forecast-epa-powers-2023-05-31/

93 Robert Rapier, "Surprise! The U.S. is still energy independent", *Forbes*, 8 March 2022, https://www.forbes.com/sites/rrapier/2022/03/08/surprise-the-us-is-still-energy-independent/

94 https://data.oecd.org/gdp/gross-domestic-product-gdp.htm#indicator-chart

95 https://data.oecd.org/gdp/investment-gfcf.htm#indicator-chart

96 https://data.oecd.org/gdp/investment-by-asset.htm

97 World Economic Forum, *The Global Competitiveness Report* (2019),https://www3.weforum.org/docs/WEF_TheGlobalCompetitivenessReport2019.pdf

98 David Schaper, "Potholes, grid failures, aging tunnels and bridges: infrastructure gets a c-minus", NPR, 3 March 2021, https://www.npr.org/2021/03/03/973054080/potholes-grid-failures-aging-tunnels-and-bridges-nations-infrastructure-gets-a-c?t=1653643170005

99 World Health Organization, *Global Status Report on Road Safety* (2018), https://www.who.int/publications/i/item/9789241565684

100 Angie Schmitt, "Why the U.S. leads the developed world on traffic deaths", Streetsblog USA, 13 December 2018, https://usa.streetsblog.org/2018/12/13/why-the-u-s-trails-the-developed-world-on-traffic-deaths

101 Schaper, "Potholes", 2021

102 https://www.oecdbetterlifeindex.org/topics/housing/

103 https://www.oecd.org/els/family/HC3-1-Homeless-population.pdf

104 Smiljanic Stasha, "The state of homelessness in the US – 2023", Policy Advice, 23 March 2023, https://policyadvice.net/insurance/insights/homelessness-statistics/

105 John Creamer, "Inequalities persist despite decline in poverty for all major race and Hispanic origin groups", United States Census Bureau, 15 September 2020, https://www.census.gov/library/stories/2020/09/poverty-rates-for-blacks-and-hispanics-reached-historic-lows-in-2019.html

106 Terry Gross, "A 'forgotten history' of how the U.S. government segregated America", NPR, 3 May 2017, https://www.npr.org/2017/05/03/526655831/a-forgotten-history-of-how-the-u-s-government-segregated-america

107 Elisabeth Jacobs and Kate Bahn, "Women's History Month: U.S. women's labor force participation", Washington Center for Equitable Growth, 22 March 2019, https://equitablegrowth.org/womens-history-month-u-s-womens-labor-force-participation/

108 Ibid.

109 Ibid.

110 OECD, *Enabling Women's Economic Empowerment* (2019), https://www.oecd-ilibrary.org/sites/4d0229cd-en/index.html?itemId=/content/component/4d0229cd-en

111 OECD, "Gender wage gap (indicator), 2023, https://data.oecd.org/earnwage/gender-wage-gap.htm

112 Rakesh Kochhar, "The enduring grip of the gender pay gap", Pew Research Center, 1 March 2023, https://www.pewresearch.org/social-trends/2023/03/01/the-enduring-grip-of-the-gender-pay-gap/

113 Carolina Aragão, "Gender pay gap in U.S. hasn't changed much in two decades", Pew Research Center, 1 March 2023, https://www.pewresearch.org/fact-tank/2021/05/25/gender-pay-gap-facts/

114 *U.S. Spencer Stuart Board Index* (2022), p.7, https://www.spencerstuart.com/-/media/2022/october/ssbi2022/2022_us_spencerstuart_board_index_final.pdf

115 Alliance for Board Diversity and Deloitte, *Missing Pieces Report: A Board Diversity Census of Women and Underrepresented Racial and Ethnic Groups on Fortune 500 Boards, 7th edition* (2023),

pp.18–19, https://www2.deloitte.com/content/dam/Deloitte/us/
Documents/US-Missing-Pieces-7th-Edition-final.pdf

116 OECD, "Women in politics (indicator)", 2023, https://data.oecd.org/
inequality/women-in-politics.htm

117 Ibid.

118 OECD, "Violence against women (indicator)", 2023, https://data.
oecd.org/inequality/violence-against-women.htm#indicator-chart

119 Ibid.

120 Council on Foreign Relations, "Abortion Law: Global Comparisons",
24 June 2022, https://www.cfr.org/article/abortion-law-global-
comparisons

CHAPTER 4 – POLITICS: THE COLD CIVIL WAR

1 Mary Clare Jalonick, "What insurrection? Growing number in GOP
downplay Jan. 6", Associated Press, 14 May 2021, https://apnews.
com/article/politics-michael-pence-donald-trump-election-2020-
capitol-siege-549829098c84b9b8de3012673a104a4c

2 Sam Levine, "Republicans poised to rig the next election by
gerrymandering electoral maps", *Guardian*, 27 July 2021, https://
www.theguardian.com/us-news/2021/jul/27/gerrymandering-
republicans-electoral-maps-political-heist

3 Ed Pilkington, "Report shows the extent of Republican efforts to
sabotage democracy", *Guardian*, 24 December 2021, https://www.
theguardian.com/us-news/2021/dec/23/voter-suppression-election-
interference-republicans

4 Kate Reilly, "Read Hillary Clinton's 'basket of deplorables' remarks
about Donald Trump supporters", *Time*, 10 September 2016, https://
time.com/4486502/hillary-clinton-basket-of-deplorables-transcript/

5 Serena Marshall, "Obama has deported more people than any other
president", ABC News, 29 August 2016, https://abcnews.go.com/
Politics/obamas-deportation-policy-numbers/story?id=41715661;
"Deportations of undocumented immigrants are at a record
low", *The Economist*, 12 June 2021, https://www.economist.com/
united-states/2021/06/12/deportations-of-undocumented-immigrants-
are-at-a-record-low

6 Rashawn Ray and William A. Galston, "Did the 1994 crime bill
cause mass incarceration?", Brookings Institute, 28 August 2020,

https://www.brookings.edu/blog/fixgov/2020/08/28/did-the-1994-crime-bill-cause-mass-incarceration/

7 Darragh Roche, "Biden, Pelosi among Democrats who sent fundraising emails after Roe ruling", *Newsweek*, 25 June 2022, https://www.newsweek.com/biden-pelosi-democrats-fundraising-emails-roe-v-wade-ruling-1719159

8 Moira Donegan, "Biden's executive order on abortion is better than nothing. But not much better", *Guardian*, 10 July 2022, https://www.theguardian.com/commentisfree/2022/jul/10/biden-executive-order-abortion-white-house

9 https://www.washingtonpost.com/video/politics/trump-slams-obamas-executive-orders/2016/01/07/38afbaca-b5b4-11e5-8abc-d09392edc612_video.html

10 https://www.presidency.ucsb.edu/statistics/data/executive-orders

11 William G. Howell, *Power Without Persuasion: The Politics of Direct Presidential Action* (2003)

12 Lukas Leuzinger, "Coalitions in parliamentary democracies: can we find consensus in times of polarisation?", openDemocracy, 14 June 2017, https://www.opendemocracy.net/en/coalitions-in-parliamentary-democracies-can-we-find-consensus-in-times-of-polarisati/

13 Darrell M. West, "It's time to abolish the Electoral College", Brookings Institute, 15 October 2019, https://www.brookings.edu/articles/its-time-to-abolish-the-electoral-college/

14 Matt Taibbi, *The Great Derangement: A Terrifying True Story of War, Politics, and Religion at the Twilight of the American Empire* (2008)

15 Stevie Rosignol-Cortez, "Did Democrats make record use of the filibuster in the last Congress?", Gigafact, 27 June 2021, https://gigafact.org/fact-briefs/do-both-political-parties-have-a-history-of-using-filibusters

16 Molly E. Reynolds, "What is the Senate filibuster, and what would it take to eliminate it?", Brookings Institute, 9 September 2020, https://www.brookings.edu/policy2020/votervital/what-is-the-senate-filibuster-and-what-would-it-take-to-eliminate-it/

17 Jon Terbush, "The rise of the filibuster, in one maddening chart", *The Week*, 8 January 2015, https://theweek.com/speedreads/454162/rise-filibuster-maddening-chart; https://www.senate.gov/legislative/cloture/clotureCounts.htm

18 Darragh Roche, "Joe Manchin supported filibuster reform in 2011, opposes Democrats' plan now", *Newsweek*, 19 January 2022, https://www.newsweek.com/joe-manchin-supported-filibuster-reform-2011-opposes-democrats-plan-now-senate-1670670

19 Ibid.

20 Robert Reich, "What should we do about the debt ceiling, and why should you care?", 24 September 2021, https://robertreich.org/post/663219210384785408

21 Mihir Zaveri, Guilbert Gates and Karen Zraick, "The government shutdown was the longest ever. Here's the history", *New York Times*, 25 January 2019, https://www.nytimes.com/interactive/2019/01/09/us/politics/longest-government-shutdown.html

22 Ibid.

23 Ibid.

24 Ibid.

25 Andrew Restuccia, Burgess Everett and Heather Caygle, "Longest shutdown in history ends after Trump relents on wall", *Politico*, 25 January 2019, https://www.politico.com/story/2019/01/25/trump-shutdown-announcement-1125529

26 Ylan Mui, "The government shutdown cost the economy $11 billion, including a permanent $3 billion loss, Congressional Budget Office says", CNBC, 28 January 2019, https://www.cnbc.com/2019/01/28/government-shutdown-cost-the-economy-11-billion-cbo.html

27 https://fiscaldata.treasury.gov/americas-finance-guide/national-debt/

28 Drew DeSilver, "5 facts about the U.S. national debt", Pew Research Center, 14 February 2023, https://www.pewresearch.org/short-reads/2023/02/14/facts-about-the-us-national-debt/

29 https://www.statista.com/statistics/268177/countries-with-the-highest-public-debt

30 Leika Kihara, "Japan at 'inflection point' in 25-year battle with deflation, government says", Reuters, 29 August 2023, https://www.reuters.com/markets/asia/japan-inflection-point-25-year-battle-with-deflation-govt-2023-08-29/

31 DeSilver, "5 facts about the U.S. national debt"

32 Melanie Lockert, "What is Modern Monetary Theory? Understanding the alternative economic theory that's becoming more mainstream", *Business Insider*, 22 July 2022, https://www.businessinsider.com/personal-finance/modern-monetary-theory?r=US&IR=T

33 Drew DeSilver, "In the U.S. and around the world, inflation is high and getting higher", Pew Research Center, 15 June 2022, https://www.pewresearch.org/short-reads/2022/06/15/in-the-u-s-and-around-the-world-inflation-is-high-and-getting-higher/

34 Sarah Min, "Ray Dalio says the U.S. is going to have a debt crisis", CNBC News, 28 September 2023, https://www.cnbc.com/2023/09/28/ray-dalio-says-the-us-is-going-to-have-a-debt-crisis.html

35 "Is it a risk for America that China holds over $1 trillion in U.S. debt?", *China Power*, 26 August 2020, https://chinapower.csis.org/us-debt/

36 Tim Begany, "Ways the United States can get out of debt", Investopedia, 3 October 2023, https://www.investopedia.com/financial-edge/0611/june-20-5-ways-the-u.s.-can-get-out-of-debt.aspx

37 https://www.imf.org/external/np/exr/mdri/eng/index.htm

38 Zahra Tayeb, "Elon Musk suggests that anyone over the age of 70 should be barred from running for political office", *Business Insider*, 4 December 2021, https://www.businessinsider.in/politics/world/news/elon-musk-suggests-that-anyone-over-the-age-of-70-should-be-barred-from-running-for-political-office/articleshow/88091530.cms

39 Karl Evers-Hillstrom, "Most expensive ever: 2020 election cost $14.4 billion", OpenSecrets, 11 February 2021, https://www.opensecrets.org/news/2021/02/2020-cycle-cost-14p4-billion-doubling-16/

40 Maggie Koerth, "How money affects elections", *FiveThirtyEight*, 10 September 2018, https://fivethirtyeight.com/features/money-and-elections-a-complicated-love-story/

41 Ibid.

42 Ibid.

43 https://poliengine.com/blog/how-many-politicians-are-there-in-the-us; there are also five non-voting delegates and one non-voting resident commissioner for Puerto Rico.

44 https://www.fairvote.org/voter_turnout#voter_turnout_101

45 https://www.fvap.gov/info/about-absentee-voting/elections

46 https://poliengine.com/blog/how-many-politicians-are-there-in-the-us

47 Julian E. Zelizer, "How conservatives won the battle over the courts", *The Atlantic*, 7 July 2018, https://www.theatlantic.com/ideas/archive/2018/07/how-conservatives-won-the-battle-over-the-courts/564533/

48 Ibid.

49 Ibid.

50 Tucker Higgins, "Trump nominates Amy Coney Barrett to Supreme Court, setting up election year confirmation battle", CNBC, 27 September 2020, https://www.cnbc.com/2020/09/25/trump-is-expected-to-nominate-amy-coney-barrett-to-fill-ginsburg-supreme-court-vacancy-.html

51 BBC News, "Amy Coney Barrett confirmed to US Supreme Court", 27 October 2020, https://www.bbc.co.uk/news/election-us-2020-54700307

52 Snejana Farberov, "Pregnancy from rape an 'opportunity,' Ohio Rep. Jean Schmidt says", *New York Post*, 29 April 2022, https://nypost.com/2022/04/29/pregnancy-from-rape-an-opportunity-rep-jean-schmidt-says/

53 Paul Waldman, "Welcome to the Supreme Court, where corruption has no meaning", *Washington Post*, 22 June 2023, https://www.washingtonpost.com/opinions/2023/06/22/supreme-court-corruption-alito/

CHAPTER 5 – MEDIA: THE EROSION OF TRUST

1 Charlotte L. Riley, "When the British Empire waged war on free speech", *Tribune*, 20 April 2021, https://tribunemag.co.uk/2021/04/pernicious-messaging

2 Ibid.

3 Mary L. Dudziak, "The toxic legacy of the Korean War", *Washington Post*, 1 March 2019, https://www.washingtonpost.com/outlook/2019/03/01/toxic-legacy-korean-war/

4 Joel Achenbach, "Did the news media, led by Walter Cronkite, lose the war in Vietnam?", *Washington Post*, 25 May 2018, https://www.washingtonpost.com/national/did-the-news-media-led-by-walter-cronkite-lose-the-war-in-vietnam/2018/05/25/a5b3e098-495e-11e8-827e-190efaf1f1ee_story.html

5 https://www.history.com/this-day-in-history/seymour-hersh-breaks-my-lai-story

6 John Coatsworth, "United States interventions. What for?", ReVista, 15 May 2005, https://revista.drclas.harvard.edu/united-states-interventions/

7 Wolf Blitzer, "Search for the 'smoking gun'", CNN, 10 January 2003, https://edition.cnn.com/2003/US/01/10/wbr.smoking.gun/

8 Al Jazeera, "US 'plans to attack seven Muslim states'", 22 September 2003, https://www.aljazeera.com/news/2003/9/22/us-plans-to-attack-seven-muslim-states

9 Pat Paterson, "The truth about Tonkin", *Naval History*, 22/1, February 2008, https://www.usni.org/magazines/naval-history-magazine/2008/february/truth-about-tonkin

10 Counter Extremism Project, "New study confirms YouTube algorithm promotes misinformation, conspiracies, extremism", 8 July 2021, https://www.counterextremism.com/blog/new-study-confirms-youtube-algorithm-promotes-misinformation-conspiracies-extremism

11 Breaking Points, "Krystal and Saagar reveal why they switched sides!", YouTube video, 7 June 2021, https://www.youtube.com/watch?v=Wgltm0KPoa8

12 Joe Berkowitz, "Why 'Breaking Points with Krystal and Saagar' became the No. 1 political podcast in a week", *Fast Company*, 12 June 2021, https://www.fastcompany.com/90646413/why-breaking-points-with-krystal-and-saagar-became-the-number-one-political-podcast-in-a-week

13 Tim Alberta, "Inside the meltdown at CNN", *The Atlantic*, 2 June 2023, https://www.theatlantic.com/politics/archive/2023/06/cnn-ratings-chris-licht-trump/674255/

14 Jon Swaine, "Donald Trump's team defends 'alternative facts' after widespread protests", *Guardian*, 23 January 2017, https://www.theguardian.com/us-news/2017/jan/22/donald-trump-kellyanne-conway-inauguration-alternative-facts

15 James D. Walsh, "Mad Scientists: Nowhere is the lab-leak debate more personal than among the experts investigating the origins of COVID", *Intelligencer*, 3 March 2023, https://nymag.com/intelligencer/article/covid-lab-leak-theory-jeffrey-sachs-peter-daszak.html

16 Jeffrey Sachs, "A Mediator's Guide to Peace in Ukraine", Common Dreams, 5 December 2023, https://www.commondreams.org/views/2022/12/05/mediators-guide-peace-ukraine

CHAPTER 6 – THE CHANGING NATURE OF WAR

1 NBC News, "Putin: Soviet collapse a 'genuine tragedy'", 25 April 2005, https://www.nbcnews.com/id/wbna7632057

2 Gideon Rachman, "Year in a Word: Thucydides's trap", *Financial*

Times, 18 December 2018, https://www.ft.com/content/0e4ddcf4-fc78-11e8-aebf-99e208d3e521; Graham Allison, *Destined for War: Can America and China Escape Thucydides's Trap?* (2017)

3 Xiujian Peng, "China's population is about to shrink for the first time since the great famine struck 60 years ago. Here's what that means for the world", World Economic Forum, 26 July 2022, https://www.weforum.org/agenda/2022/07/china-population-shrink-60-years-world/; "How severe are China's demographic challenges?", *China Power*, 6 March 2023, https://chinapower.csis.org/china-demographics-challenges/

4 Tim Jackson, *Prosperity Without Growth* (2009)

5 David Vine, Patterson Deppen and Leah Bolger, "Drawdown: improving U.S. and global security through military base closures abroad", Quincy Institute for Responsible Statecraft, 20 September 2021, https://quincyinst.org/report/drawdown-improving-u-s-and-global-security-through-military-base-closures-abroad/

6 Statista Research Department, "Budget of the U.S. Navy and the U.S. Marine Corps from fiscal year 2001 to 2024", 23 April 2023, https://www.statista.com/statistics/239290/budget-of-the-us-navy-and-the-us-marine-corps/

7 Mark F. Cancian, "Aid to Ukraine: the administration requests more money and faces political battles ahead", Center for Strategic and International Studies, 15 August 2023, https://www.csis.org/analysis/aid-ukraine-administration-requests-more-money-and-faces-political-battles-ahead

8 Scott Pelley, "President Joe Biden: the 2022 *60 Minutes* interview", CBS, 18 September 2022, https://www.cbsnews.com/news/president-joe-biden-60-minutes-interview-transcript-2022-09-18/

9 Lamar Johnson, "Biden ends slog on semiconductor bill with signature", *Politico*, 9 August 2022, https://www.politico.com/news/2022/08/09/biden-ends-slog-on-semiconductor-bill-with-signature-00050530

10 Editorial, "The war in Ukraine is exposing gaps in the world's food-systems research", *Nature*, 12 April 2022, https://www.nature.com/articles/d41586-022-00994-8

11 Reuters, "Russia extends quotas for fertiliser exports to help domestic farmers", 31 May 2022, https://www.reuters.com/article/ukraine-crisis-russia-fertilisers-idUSKBN2NH1G4

12 Tobias Gehrke, "Putin's critical raw materials are a threat to EU economic security", Egmont Institute, 15 March 2022, https://www.egmontinstitute.be/putins-critical-raw-materials-are-a-threat-to-eu-economic-security/

13 "President Trump Address to U.N. General Assembly", 25 September 2018, https://www.c-span.org/video/?451988-1/president-trump-address-un-general-assembly

14 Statista Research Department, "Share of gas supply from Russia in Europe in 2021, by selected country", 1 August 2023, https://www.statista.com/statistics/1201743/russian-gas-dependence-in-europe-by-country/

15 John Perkins, *Confessions of an Economic Hit Man* (3rd edn, 2023)

16 Mark Weisbrot and Jeffrey Sachs, "Economic sanctions as collective punishment: the case of Venezuela", Center for Economic and Policy Research, 25 April 2019, https://cepr.net/report/economic-sanctions-as-collective-punishment-the-case-of-venezuela/

17 Arsalan Bilan, "Hybrid warfare – new threats, complexity, and 'trust' as the antidote", *NATO Review*, 30 November 2021, https://www.nato.int/docu/review/articles/2021/11/30/hybrid-warfare-new-threats-complexity-and-trust-as-the-antidote/index.html

18 Ibid.

19 Thomas Corbett and Peter W. Singer, "China may have just taken the lead in the quantum computing race", *Defense One*, 14 April 2022, https://www.defenseone.com/ideas/2022/04/china-may-have-just-taken-lead-quantum-computing-race/365707/

20 Julia Voo et al., "National cyber power index 2020: methodology and analytical considerations", Cyber China Policy Initiative Report, September 2020, https://dash.harvard.edu/handle/1/37372389

21 Ibid.

22 Elsa B. Kania and Wilson Vorndick, "Weaponizing biotech: how China's military is preparing for a 'new domain of warfare'", *Defense One*, 14 August 2019, https://www.defenseone.com/ideas/2019/08/chinas-military-pursuing-biotech/159167/

23 He Fuchu, "Biotechnology will become the new strategic commanding heights of the future military revolution", *People's Liberation Army Daily*, 6 October 2015, https://web.archive.org/web/20190813042422/http://www.81.cn/jwgz/2015-10/06/content_6709533.htm

24 Ibid.

25 Ibid.

26 Robert Beckhusen and Noah Shachtman, "See for yourself: the Pentagon's $51 billion 'black' budget", *Wired*, 15 February 2012,https://www.wired.com/2012/02/pentagons-black-budget/; Yuval Rosenberg, "Trump administration asks for $81.1 billion 'black budget', the largest ever", *The Fiscal Times*, 28 February 2018, https://www.thefiscaltimes.com/2018/02/28/Trump-Administration-Asks-811-Billion-Black-Budget-Largest-Ever

CHAPTER 7 – INTERNATIONAL RELATIONS

1 Tana Johnson and Andrew Heiss, "Liberal institutionalism – its threatened past, its threatened future", Brookings Institution, 18 July 2018, https://www.brookings.edu/blog/future-development/2018/07/18/liberal-institutionalism-its-threatened-past-its-threatened-future/

2 Lowy Institute, "Global Diplomacy Index 2021", https://globaldiplomacyindex.lowyinstitute.org/country_rank.html

3 Kishan Rana, "A diplomatic necessity: why embassies persist in the digital age", *The Interpreter*, 6 April 2016, https://www.lowyinstitute.org/the-interpreter/diplomatic-necessity-why-embassies-persist-digital-age

4 Al Jazeera, "Trump-appointed US envoys in Iceland, UK, seem undiplomatic", 4 August 2020, https://www.aljazeera.com/news/2020/8/4/trump-appointed-us-envoys-in-iceland-uk-seem-undiplomatic

5 Robbie Gramer, "At embassies abroad, Trump envoys are quietly pushing out career diplomats", *Foreign Policy*, 5 February 2020, https://foreignpolicy.com/2020/02/05/us-embassies-abroad-trump-envoys-pushing-out-career-diplomats-deputy-chiefs-mission-south-africa-diplomacy-pompeo-lana-marks/

6 Doyle McManus, "Almost half the top jobs in Trump's state department are still empty", *The Atlantic*, 4 November 2018, https://www.theatlantic.com/politics/archive/2018/11/state-department-empty-ambassador-to-australi/574831/

7 Ibid.

8 David Smith, "Ambassador shortage hampers Biden foreign policy as

nominees hit logjam", *Guardian*, 14 November 2021, https://www.
theguardian.com/us-news/2021/nov/14/ambassador-shortage-biden-
foreign-policy-senate; Robbie Gramer, "America's top diplomats and
generals are stuck in Senate purgatory", *Foreign Policy*, 30 June
2023, https://foreignpolicy.com/2023/06/30/congress-national-security-
blanket-holds-state-department-pentagon/

9 Ibid.

10 Address by Senator Jesse Helms, Chairman, U.S. Senate Committee
on Foreign Relations, before the United Nations Security Council,
20 January 2000, https://www.govinfo.gov/content/pkg/CHRG-
106shrg62154/html/CHRG-106shrg62154.htm

11 Ibid.

12 Ibid.

13 Lesley Wroughton and Michelle Nichols, "U.S. quits U.N. human
rights body, citing bias vs. Israel, alarming critics", Reuters,
19 June 2018, https://www.reuters.com/article/us-un-rights-usa-
idUSKBN1JF24X

14 Colum Lynch, "U.S. to join U.N. Human Rights Council,
reversing Bush policy", *Washington Post*, 31 March 2009, https://
www.washingtonpost.com/wp-dyn/content/article/2009/03/31/
AR2009033102782.html?noredirect=on

15 "Full text: Trump's 2017 U.N. speech transcript", *Politico*, 19
September 2017, https://www.politico.com/story/2017/09/19/trump-
un-speech-2017-full-text-transcript-242879

16 Philip Remler, "Russia at the United Nations: law, sovereignty,
and legitimacy", Carnegie Endowment for International Peace, 22
January 2020, https://carnegieendowment.org/2020/01/22/russia-at-
united-nations-law-sovereignty-and-legitimacy-pub-80753

17 Ibid.

18 Jon Henley, "Moscow confirms attack on Kyiv during UN chief's
visit", *Guardian*, 29 April 2022, https://www.theguardian.com/
world/2022/apr/29/russia-carries-out-airstrike-on-kyiv-during-un-
chief-visit-ukraine-antonio-guterres

19 Jeffrey Feltman, "China's expanding influence at the United
Nations – and how the United States should react", Brookings
Institution, September 2020, https://www.brookings.edu/wp-content/
uploads/2020/09/FP_20200914_china_united_nations_feltman.pdf

20 Al Jazeera, "Outrage as UN debate on China's alleged Xinjiang

abuses rejected", 7 October 2022, https://www.aljazeera.com/
news/2022/10/7/un-human-rights-council-rejects-debate-on-treatment-
of-uighurs

21 Stephanie Kirchgaessner, "Saudis used 'incentives and threats' to shut
down UN investigation in Yemen", Guardian, 1 December 2021,
https://www.theguardian.com/world/2021/dec/01/saudi-arabia-yemen-
un-human-rights-investigation-incentives-and-therats

22 Ibid.

23 Chandler Green, "The United Nations by the numbers", United
Nations Foundation, 24 October 2018, https://unfoundation.org/
blog/post/the-united-nations-by-the-numbers/

24 Katelyn Balakir, "Failures and Successes of the UN", The Alliance
for Citizen Engagement, 22 August 2021, https://ace-usa.org/blog/
research/research-foreignpolicy/failures-and-successes-of-the-un/

25 "Funding the United Nations: how much does the U.S. pay?",
Council on Foreign Relations, 13 March 2023, https://www.cfr.org/
article/funding-united-nations-what-impact-do-us-contributions-have-
un-agencies-and-programs

26 Paul Farhi and Jeremy Barr, "The media called the 'lab leak'
story a 'conspiracy theory'. Now it's prompted corrections
– and serious new reporting", Washington Post, 10 June
2021, https://www.washingtonpost.com/lifestyle/media/
the-media-called-the-lab-leak-story-a-conspiracy-theory-now-its-
prompted-corrections--and-serious-new-reporting/2021/06/10/
c93972e6-c7b2-11eb-a11b-6c6191ccd599_story.html

27 "The history of the G7", website of the German Federal
Government, no date, https://www.bundesregierung.de/breg-en/
service/the-history-of-the-g7-397438

28 G20 membership comprises Argentina, Australia, Brazil, Canada,
China, France, Germany, India, Indonesia, Italy, Japan, the Republic
of Korea, Mexico, Russia, Saudi Arabia, South Africa, the United
Kingdom, the USA, and the European Union. Spain is also invited as
a permanent guest.

29 Ian Bremmer has written many books on this subject and hosts
a regular podcast series produced by his digital media company
GZERO Media.

30 Edward S. Mason and Robert E. Asher, The World Bank Since
Bretton Woods (1973), p.29

31 Ashley Seager, "For the British Treasury, only today is the war over", *Guardian*, 29 December 2006, https://www.theguardian.com/business/2006/dec/29/politics.secondworldwar

32 John Perkins, *Confessions of an Economic Hit Man* (3rd edn, 2023)

33 Lucy Komisar, "Interview with Joseph Stiglitz", *The Progressive*, June 2011, https://archive.globalpolicy.org/social-and-economic-policy/the-three-sisters-and-other-institutions/internal-critics-of-the-world-bank-and-the-imf/50588-interview-with-joseph-stiglitz.html?itemid=id#942

34 "What is China's belt and road initiative?", *The Economist*, 15 May 2017, https://www.economist.com/the-economist-explains/2017/05/14/what-is-chinas-belt-and-road-initiative

35 Ammar A. Malik et al., "Banking on the belt and road: insights from a new global dataset of 13,427 Chinese development projects", AidData, September 2021, https://www.aiddata.org/publications/banking-on-the-belt-and-road

36 Saptarshi Basak, "China's belt and road initiative: benevolent lending or 'debt-trap diplomacy'?", *The Quint*, 24 March 2022, https://www.thequint.com/explainers/china-belt-and-road-initiative-benevolent-lending-or-debt-trap-diplomacy-aiddata-report#read-more

37 Richard Javad Heydarian, "Hide your strength, bide your time", Al Jazeera, 21 November 2014, https://www.aljazeera.com/opinions/2014/11/21/hide-your-strength-bide-your-time

38 "What is China's belt and road initiative?", *The Economist*, 15 May 2017

39 Yasheng Huang, "Can the Belt and Road become a trap for China?", Project Syndicate, 22 May 2019, https://www.project-syndicate.org/commentary/china-belt-road-initiative-trap-by-yasheng-huang-2019-05

40 Dimitri de Boer, Christoph Nedopil and Danting Fan, "China clarifies its vision for a green belt and road initiative", ClientEarth, 4 April 2022, https://www.clientearth.org/latest/latest-updates/news/china-clarifies-its-vision-for-a-green-belt-and-road-initiative/

41 Carol Bertaut, Bastian von Beschwitz and Stephanie Curcuru, "The international role of the U.S. dollar: post-COVID edition", FEDS Notes, 23 June 2023, https://www.federalreserve.gov/econres/notes/feds-notes/the-international-role-of-the-us-dollar-post-covid-edition-20230623.html

42 Selwyn M. Gishen, "Is there a world currency? If so, what is it?", *Investopedia*, 14 July 2022, https://www.investopedia.com/ask/answers/08/is-there-a-world-currency.asp

43 Eswar S. Prasad, "Enduring pre-eminence: the US dollar might slip, but it will continue to rule", *Finance & Development*, June 2022, https://www.imf.org/en/Publications/fandd/issues/2022/06/enduring-preeminence-eswar-prasad

44 Bertaut et al., "The international role of the U.S. dollar: post-COVID edition"

45 Ibid.

46 Todd Prince, "A common BRICS currency to challenge the U.S. dollar? 'A very far-fetched notion,' expert says", Radio Free Europe / Radio Liberty, 31 August 2023, https://www.rferl.org/a/brics-common-currency-challenge-russia-brazil/32571316.html

47 Alex Gatopoulos, "Desperately seeking relevance: NATO in the 21st century", Al Jazeera, 14 June 2021, https://www.aljazeera.com/features/2021/6/14/desperately-seeking-relevance-nato-in-the-21st-century

48 Ibid.

49 "Relations with Ukraine", NATO, 28 July 2023, https://www.nato.int/cps/en/natohq/topics_37750.htm?

50 Anastasia Tenisheva, "'Uneasy allies': Putin and Xi set to meet for first time since Ukraine war", *Moscow Times*, 15 September 2022, https://www.themoscowtimes.com/2022/09/15/uneasy-allies-putin-and-xi-set-to-meet-for-first-time-since-ukraine-war-a78794

51 Victoria Kim and Clifford Krauss, "Asia is buying discounted Russian oil, making up for Europe's cutbacks", *New York Times*, 21 June 2022, https://www.nytimes.com/2022/06/21/world/asia/asia-is-buying-discounted-russian-oil-making-up-for-europes-cutbacks.html

52 Miriam Burrell, "Putin admits China has 'questions and concerns' over Ukraine during key meeting with Xi", *London Evening Standard*, 15 September 2022, https://uk.news.yahoo.com/putin-admits-china-questions-concerns-180739150.html

53 Faezeh Foroutan, "Suspicious bind: Iran's relationship with Russia", European Council on Foreign Relations, 2 September 2022, https://ecfr.eu/article/suspicious-bind-irans-relationship-with-russia/

54 "Why Vladimir Putin and Recep Tayyip Erdogan need each other", *The Economist*, 12 October 2022, https://www.economist.com/

europe/2022/10/12/why-vladimir-putin-and-recep-tayyip-erdogan-need-each-other

55 Rich Outzen, Yevgeniya Gaber and Brenda Shaffer, "How long can Turkey play both sides in the Ukraine war?", Atlantic Council, 18 August 2022, https://www.atlanticcouncil.org/blogs/new-atlanticist/how-long-can-turkey-play-both-sides-in-the-ukraine-war/

56 Anastasia Tenisheva, "'Uneasy allies': Putin and Xi set to meet for first time since Ukraine war", *Moscow Times*, 15 September 2022

CHAPTER 8 − ENVIRONMENTAL THREATS

1 The states of Washington and Oregon lie in the active crustal region of the Pacific Northwest, and the New Madrid Seismic Zone comprises parts of Arkansas, Illinois, Kentucky, Tennessee, Missouri, Mississippi and Indiana.

2 Brad Plumer, "What would happen if the Yellowstone supervolcano actually erupted?", *Vox*, 15 December 2014, https://www.vox.com/2014/9/5/6108169/yellowstone-supervolcano-eruption

3 Ibid.

4 NASA press release, "NASA confirms DART mission impact changed asteroid's motion in space", 11 October 2022, https://www.nasa.gov/press-release/nasa-confirms-dart-mission-impact-changed-asteroid-s-motion-in-space

5 Daisy Dobrijevic and Andrew May, "The Carrington Event: history's greatest solar storm", space.com, 24 June 2022, https://www.space.com/the-carrington-event

6 Matthew I. Hutchings, Andrew W. Truman and Barrie Wilkinson, "Antibiotics: past, present and future", *Current Opinion in Microbiology*, 51 (2019), https://doi.org/10.1016/j.mib.2019.10.008

7 C. Lee Ventola, "The antibiotic resistance crisis: part 1: causes and threats", Pharmacy and Therapeutics, 40(4) (2015), https://www.ncbi.nlm.nih.gov/pmc/articles/PMC4378521/

8 Ibid.

9 World Health Organization, "New report calls for urgent action to avert antimicrobial resistance crisis", 29 April 2019, https://www.who.int/news/item/29-04-2019-new-report-calls-for-urgent-action-to-avert-antimicrobial-resistance-crisis

10 Wangxue Chen, "Will the mRNA vaccine platform be the panacea

for the development of vaccines against antimicrobial resistant (AMR) pathogens?", *Expert Review of Vaccines*, 21(2) (2022), https://www.tandfonline.com/doi/full/10.1080/14760584.2022.2011226

11 Tammana Begum, "Soil degradation: the problems and how to fix them", Natural History Museum, 16 April 2021, https://www.nhm.ac.uk/discover/soil-degradation.html

12 Food and Agriculture Organization of the United Nations, "Global Symposium on Soil Erosion: Key Messages", 2019, https://www.fao.org/about/meetings/soil-erosion-symposium/key-messages/en/

13 "Soil Erosion in the United States", soilerosion.com, 16 September 2019, https://soilerosion.com/soil-erosion-in-the-united-states/

14 Krishna Karra and Tim Wallace, "A vivid view of extreme weather: temperature records in the U.S. in 2021", *New York Times*, 11 January 2022, https://www.nytimes.com/interactive/2022/01/11/climate/record-temperatures-map-2021.html

CONCLUSIONS

1 Julian Borger, "Barack Obama: Russia is a regional power showing weakness over Ukraine", *Guardian*, 25 March 2014, https://www.theguardian.com/world/2014/mar/25/barack-obama-russia-regional-power-ukraine-weakness

2 Ian Williams, "China's demographic time-bomb is ticking faster", *The Spectator*, 24 April 2022, https://www.spectator.co.uk/article/china-s-demographic-time-bomb-is-ticking-faster/

3 Lionel Shriver, "Why are so few Americans willing to defend their country?", *The Spectator*, 19 March 2022, https://www.spectator.co.uk/article/why-are-so-few-americans-willing-to-defend-their-country/

4 Inae Oh, "These are the regions where Americans are most likely to favor secession", *Mother Jones*, 23 September 2014, https://www.motherjones.com/politics/2014/09/these-are-regions-where-americans-are-most-likely-favor-secession/; Scott Malone, "Angry with Washington, 1 in 4 Americans open to secession", Reuters, 19 September 2014, https://www.reuters.com/article/us-usa-secession-exclusive-idUSKBN0HE19U20140919

5 Margaret Talev, "Two Americas Index: 20% favor a 'national

divorce'", *Axios*, 16 March 2023, https://www.axios.
com/2023/03/16/two-americas-index-national-divorce

6 Barbara F. Walter, "'These are conditions ripe for political violence':
   how close is the US to civil war?", *Guardian*, 6 November 2022,
   https://www.theguardian.com/us-news/2022/nov/06/how-close-is-the-
   us-to-civil-war-barbara-f-walter-stephen-march-christopher-parker

7 U.S. Department of Health and Human Services: Office of
   Minority Health, "Profile: American Indian/Alaska Native", https://
   minorityhealth.hhs.gov/omh/browse.aspx?lvl=3&lvlid=62

8 https://www.history.com/topics/black-history/slavery

9 Mark Hugo Lopez, Jens Manuel Krogstad and Jeffrey S. Passel,
   "Who is Hispanic?", Pew Research Center, 5 September 2023,
   https://www.pewresearch.org/short-reads/2023/09/05/who-is-hispanic/

10 Drew Gilpin Faust, "Death and Dying", National Park Service, no
   date, https://www.nps.gov/nr/travel/national_cemeteries/death.html

11 Taylor Orth, "Two in five Americans say a civil war is at least
   somewhat likely in the next decade", YouGov, 26 August 2022,
   https://today.yougov.com/topics/politics/articles-reports/2022/08/26/
   two-in-five-americans-civil-war-somewhat-likely

12 Garen J. Wintemute et al., "Views of American democracy and
   society and support for political violence: first report from a
   nationwide population-representative survey", medRxiv pre-print,
   2022, https://www.medrxiv.org/content/10.1101/2022.07.15.22277
   693v1

13 Barbara F. Walter, "'These are conditions ripe for political violence':
   how close is the US to civil war?", *Guardian*, 6 November 2022,
   https://www.theguardian.com/us-news/2022/nov/06/how-close-is-the-
   us-to-civil-war-barbara-f-walter-stephen-march-christopher-parker

14 Vida B. Johnson, "KKK in the PD: white supremacist police and
   what to do about it", *Lewis & Clark Law Review*, 23 (2019),
   https://law.lclark.edu/live/files/28080-lcb231article2johnsonpdf

15 Hassan Kanu, "Prevalence of white supremacists in law enforcement
   demands drastic change", Reuters, 12 May 2022, https://www.
   reuters.com/legal/government/prevalence-white-supremacists-law-
   enforcement-demands-drastic-change-2022-05-12/

16 Alexander Mallin, Alex Hosenball and Olivia Rubin, "In new
   defense, dozens of Capitol rioters say law enforcement 'let us in' to
   building", ABC News, 19 February 2021, https://abcnews.go.com/

US/defense-dozens-capitol-rioters-law-enforcement-us-building/
story?id=75976466

17 Vera Bergengruen, "'Is there something more sinister going on?'
Authorities fear extremists are targeting U.S. power grid", *Time*,
9 January 2023, https://time.com/6244977/us-power-grid-attacks-
extremism/

18 Barbara F. Walter, "'These are conditions ripe for political violence':
how close is the US to civil war?", *Guardian*, 6 November 2022

19 Ibid.

20 Ron Elving, "The Florida recount of 2000: a nightmare that
goes on haunting", NPR, 12 November 2018, https://www.npr.
org/2018/11/12/666812854/the-florida-recount-of-2000-a-nightmare-
that-goes-on-haunting

21 Adam Serwer, "Birtherism of a nation", *The Atlantic*, 13 May 2020,
https://www.theatlantic.com/ideas/archive/2020/05/birtherism-and-
trump/610978/

22 Ibid.

23 Ibid.

24 Ramsey Touchberry, "Robert Mueller laid road map for potential
indictment against Trump when he leaves office: ex-Watergate
prosecutor", *Newsweek*, 19 April 2019, https://www.newsweek.com/
robert-mueller-donald-trump-indictment-obstruction-1401793

25 BBC News, "US election: Trump won't commit to peaceful transfer
of power", 24 September 2020, https://www.bbc.com/news/election-
us-2020-54274115

26 Excerpts from the *Making Sense* podcast with Sam Harris, Anne
Applebaum, David Frum, Barton Gellman and George Packer,
episode 274, "The Future of American Democracy", 11 February
2022

27 Jonathan Swan, "Scoop: Trump's plan to declare premature victory",
Axios, 1 November 2020, https://www.axios.com/2020/11/01/trump-
claim-election-victory-ballots

28 Andy Sullivan and Michael Martina, "In recorded call, Trump
pressures Georgia official to 'find' votes to overturn election",
Reuters, 3 January 2021, https://www.reuters.com/article/us-usa-
election-trump-idUSKBN2980MG

29 Ed Pilkington, "Incitement: a timeline of Trump's inflammatory
rhetoric before the Capitol riot", *Guardian*, 7 January 2021, https://

www.theguardian.com/us-news/2021/jan/07/trump-incitement-inflammatory-rhetoric-capitol-riot

30 Brian Naylor, "Read Trump's Jan. 6 speech, a key part of impeachment trial", NPR, 10 February 2021, https://www.npr.org/2021/02/10/966396848/read-trumps-jan-6-speech-a-key-part-of-impeachment-trial

31 The Telegraph, "Donald Trump tells supporters to 'go home' after they storm Capitol", YouTube video, 6 January 2021, https://www.youtube.com/watch?v=ZB8kjR4nYzk

32 Daniella Diaz, "READ: Brief from 126 Republicans supporting Texas lawsuit in Supreme Court", CNN, 11 December 2020, https://edition.cnn.com/2020/12/10/politics/read-house-republicans-texas-supreme-court/index.html

33 Barbara Sprunt, "Here are the Republicans who objected to the Electoral College count", NPR, 7 January 2021, https://www.npr.org/sections/insurrection-at-the-capitol/2021/01/07/954380156/here-are-the-republicans-who-objected-to-the-electoral-college-count; Karen Yourish, Larry Buchanan and Denise Lu, "The 147 Republicans who voted to overturn election results", *New York Times*, 7 January 2021, https://www.nytimes.com/interactive/2021/01/07/us/elections/electoral-college-biden-objectors.html

34 Max Boot, "The Republican plot to steal the 2024 election", *Washington Post*, 1 June 2021, https://www.washingtonpost.com/opinions/2021/06/01/republican-plot-steal-2024-election/; David Weigel, "The Trailer: 2020, continued: how post-Trump voting laws would have changed the last election", *Washington Post*, 11 May 2021, https://www.washingtonpost.com/politics/2021/05/11/trailer-2020-continued-how-post-trump-voting-laws-would-have-changed-last-election/

35 Sam Levine, "Republican push to recruit election deniers as poll workers causes alarm", *Guardian*, 30 June 2022, https://www.theguardian.com/us-news/2022/jun/30/republican-recruit-poll-workers-election-integrity

36 https://americafirstsos.com/

37 Hyla Winters, "Marchant is unfit for office", *The Nevada Independent*, 9 June 2022, https://thenevadaindependent.com/article/marchant-is-unfit-for-office

38 Ewan Palmer, "Full list of Trump-backed candidates who lost their

elections", *Newsweek*, 9 November 2022, https://www.newsweek.com/list-trump-candidates-lost-midterm-elections-gop-1758158

39 Caroline Downey, "'Biden team' requested Twitter scrub scandalous Hunter Biden info days before 2020 election", *National Review*, 2 December 2022, https://www.nationalreview.com/news/biden-campaign-requested-twitter-scrub-scandalous-hunter-biden-content-days-before-2020-election/

40 Garen J. Wintemute et al., "Views of American democracy and society and support for political violence: first report from a nationwide population-representative survey", medRxiv pre-print, 2022, https://www.medrxiv.org/content/10.1101/2022.07.15.22277 693v1

COMPASSIONATE CHANGE

1 Julian Borger, "Biden tells Israel not to 'repeat mistakes' made by US after 9/11", *Guardian*, 18 October 2023, https://www.theguardian.com/world/2023/oct/18/joe-biden-urges-israel-not-be-consumed-by-rage-pledges-support-netanyahu-gaza-hamas

2 Franklin D. Roosevelt, "Address at Madison Square Garden, New York City", 31 October 1936, https://www.presidency.ucsb.edu/documents/address-madison-square-garden-new-york-city-1

3 Harry S. Truman, "Rear Platform Remarks, Syracuse, New York", 10 October 1952, Truman Library (sound recording), https://www.trumanlibrary.gov/soundrecording-records/sr59-160-president-truman-rear-platform-remarks-syracuse-new-york

4 Ervin Laszlo, *The Inner Limits of Mankind: Heretical Reflections on Today's Values, Culture and Politics* (1989), p.112

5 Stephen G. Post et al., *Altruism and Altruistic Love: Science, Philosophy, and Religion in Dialogue* (2002); Ernst Fehr and Urs Fischbacher, "The nature of human altruism", *Nature*, 425 (2003); Thomas Lewis, Fari Amini and Richard Lannon, *A General Theory of Love* (2000)

6 Kailani Koenig-Muenster, "Flashback: At UN, Reagan wished for alien invasion to unite people on Earth", NBC News, 24 September 2013, https://www.nbcnews.com/id/wbna53094599

Printed in Great Britain
by Amazon